TRANSGRESSION

Martin Jay, University of California, Berkeley

Chris Jenks is Professor of Sociology at Goldsmiths College, University of London.

KEY IDEAS

SERIES EDITOR: PETER HAMILTON, THE OPEN UNIVERSITY, MILTON KEYNES

Designed to complement the successful *Key Sociologists*, this series covers the main concepts, issues, debates, and controversies in sociology and the social sciences. The series aims to provide authoritative essays on central topics of social science, such as community, power, work, sexuality, inequality, benefits and ideology, class, family, etc. Books adopt a strong individual 'line' constituting original essays rather than literary surveys, and form lively and original treatments of their subject matter. The books will be useful to students and teachers of sociology, political science, economics, psychology, philosophy and geography.

Class
STEPHEN EDGELL

Community
GERARD DELANTY

Consumption
ROBERT BOCOCK

Citizenship
KEITH FAULKS

Culture
CHRIS JENKS

Globalization – second edition
MALCOLM WATERS

Lifestyle
DAVID CHANEY

Mass Media
PIERRE SORLIN

Moral Panics
KENNETH THOMPSON

Old Age
JOHN VINCENT

Postmodernity
BARRY SMART

Racism – second edition
ROBERT MILES AND MALCOLM BROWN

Risk
DEBORAH LUPTON

Sexuality
JEFFREY WEEKS

Social Capital
JOHN FIELD

Transgression
CHRIS JENKS

The Virtual
ROB SHIELDS

TRANSGRESSION

Chris Jenks

Routledge
Taylor & Francis Group

LONDON AND NEW YORK

First published 2003
by Routledge
11 New Fetter Lane, London EC4P 4EE

Simultaneously published in the USA and Canada
by Routledge
29 West 35th Street, New York, NY 10001

Routledge is an imprint of the Taylor & Francis Group

British Library Cataloguing in Publication Data
A catalogue record for this book is available from the British Library

Library of Congress Cataloging in Publication Data
A catalog record for this book has been requested

ISBN 0–415–25757–3 (hbk)
ISBN 0–415–25758–1 (pbk)

This one is for Barbara

Contents

THE AUTHOR

Chris Jenks is Professor of Sociology at Goldsmiths College, University of London. His previous books include *Rationality, Education and the Social Organization of Knowledge* (Routledge 1976), *Worlds Apart – Readings for a Sociology of Education* [with J. Beck, N. Keddie and M. Young] (Collier-Macmillan 1977), *Toward a Sociology of Education* [with J. Beck, N. Keddie and M. Young] (Transaction 1977); *The Sociology of Childhood* (Batsford 1982); *Culture* (Routledge 1993); *Cultural Reproduction* (Routledge 1993); *Visual Culture* (Routledge 1995); *Childhood* (Routledge 1996); *Theorizing Childhood* [with A. James and A. Prout] (Polity 1998); *Core Sociological Dichotomies* (Sage 1998); *Images of Community: Durkheim, Social Systems and the Sociology of Art* [with J.A. Smith] (Ashgate 2000); *Aspects of Urban Culture* (Academia Sinica 2001); *Culture: Critical Concepts*, 4 Volumes (Routledge 2002); *Urban Culture*, 4 Volumes (Routledge 2004). He is interested in sociological theory, post-structuralism and heterology, childhood, cultural theory, visual and urban culture, and extremes of behaviour.

ACKNOWLEDGEMENTS

I would like to thank a number of people who have been touched by or who have touched me in relation to this book. To Malcolm Barnard for constant friendship, discussion, checking earlier drafts and for his perpetual and unheeded criticisms of my writing style. To John Smith also for friendship, discussion and checking drafts and for his fierce and driven intellect. Roy Boyne has been a lasting enthusiast for this work, his insights are always valued and his friendship a great pleasure. John O'Neill has been a great support and a treasure-trove of ideas and bibliographical material thanks to him for reading some of this and mostly for sustaining our friendship for so many years over such a great distance. Thanks to Mike Featherstone, editor of *Theory, Culture and Society* for his permission to reproduce the paper which is largely Chapter 4.

Special thanks to Barbara for tolerating and enjoying the peculiar biography that motivated this writing and for engendering such a nurturing environment from within which it emerged.

Justin Lorentzen my friend and erstwhile colleague deserves particular note and gratitude. It was he who jointly authored the paper forming Chapter 4, it was he that introduced me to transgression as an intellectual topic, and indeed he was the first social theorist I had encountered who was using Bataille in both an intelligent and exciting manner. He both shared but also accelerated my appreciation of the madness that passes for the social.

Finally, considerable thanks to Marcus Harvey for his kind permission to use an image of his work *Myra* for the cover of this book and to Sophie Greig at Whitecube and Nigel Hirst at the Saatchi Gallery for enabling this.

1

WHITHER TRANSGRESSION?

In olden days a glimpse of stocking
Was looked on as something shocking.
Now, heaven knows,
Anything goes.

(Cole Porter)

History has determined a cruel backdrop for this book. I began writing in the late summer of 2001 in the wake of the American outrage. Four passenger aircraft had been hijacked by persons then unknown but subsequently revealed to be members of the *al-Qaeda* international terrorist organisation. Two of the planes had suffered accurate and catastrophic collision with the twin towers of the World Trade Center in New York, one with the Pentagon building in Washington, and the fourth had crashed, upside down, presumed short of its actual target. The shock and tragedy rapidly transformed into anger and horror as the synchronicity of these events coalesced into causality. These happenings were purposive, they were deliberate and they were concerted. Thousands of people had been killed and this was an intended consequence.

Within a relatively short space of time there was a burgeoning and near global reaction. A violation had occurred, some line had been crossed. There was a growing consensus that a boundary, perhaps even a universal moral boundary, had been overstepped. Just as it was once voiced that there would be no more art or poetry after Auschwitz, September 11th began to slip into the language as a metaphor for irrevocability. Things would never be the same again. People across religions, across nations and across ideologies registered a grand transgression. Western politics now sought, strategically, to capitalise on existing alliances and to affirm new ones. The World (more or less) was to be at war with terrorism. Through this transformational cycle the social process moved to completion: the fracture gave rise to repair; the violation generated consolidation; the individual act of deviance summoned up a collective response. To transgress is to go beyond the bounds or limits set by a commandment or law or convention, it is to violate or infringe. But to transgress is also more than this, it is to announce and even laudate the commandment, the law or the convention. Transgression is a deeply reflexive act of denial and affirmation. Analytically, then, transgression serves as an extremely sensitive vector in assessing the scope, direction and compass of any social theory, as we shall see.

What then brought you to take this book down from the shelf, other than its cover or the never-to-be-repeated remaindered price? What is it about the idea of 'transgression' that captures the imagination? What resides in the word 'transgression' that reaches out, that magnetises, that touches the shadow side in us all? Is there perhaps some vicarious imaginative element involved – the supposition and fascination of sin; the desire to view through a glass darkly? It may be little more (nor less) than an interest in difference, an envy or disbelief in the excess of others, a knowledge of or desire for the niceness of naughtiness, a loathing, a prurience, a stalking mentality! Those of us cultured enough not to buy the Sunday tabloids but without the moral fibre to resist their headlines understand this zone of attraction and understand it also to be about margins and their relation to totalities.

An analysis of the concept 'transgression' will take us along a series of continua, both vertical and horizontal, such as sacred–profane; good –evil; normal–pathological; sane–mad; purity–danger; high–low; centre–periphery and so on. It is critical to realise that these continua can be understood and acted in relation to as if they were absolute, as if they were indices of stratification, and as if they were dichotomies. Indeed, for a lot of the people for a lot of the time this is exactly how they are understood. Such paradoxes contribute further to the complexity of the idea. Although always appearing to make reference to clear-cut distinctions transgressions are manifestly situation-specific and vary considerably across social space and through time. Our analysis of transgression will take us through a variety of empirical contexts such as crime, sexuality, ritual, carnival, art, culture and madness. The last is an informative metaphor:

> The psychotic, alone in his cosmos, discovers a world he does not understand and cannot control. He adopts animistic 'theories' as a measure of self-defense. The *necessity* of primitive thought becomes clearer in this context. The psychotic is identical with a world that threatens him with indescribable torments.
>
> (Ferguson 1990: 43)

Finally, this analysis will introduce a *dramatis personae* ranging from the recommended to the highly undesirable and comprising both theorists and practitioners.

It has become commonplace to regard contemporary society through the metaphor of excess. Inevitably such realisations address late capitalism in the West which is epitomised by its globalisation and its tendency to over-production – in line with our over-consumption. However, this kind of excess, excess as abundance, is not simply the topic of this book. What this work will address is conduct that goes beyond the limits; excessive behaviour or transgression. Transgression, then, is that conduct which breaks rules or exceeds boundaries. What is the character of the cultures that provide for this excessive behaviour and what are the contexts that provide for the appreciation or receptability of such behaviour? Is transgression merely a post-modern version of authentic or existential action? Is it the hyperbolic announcement of identity and difference in a society where identity and difference are paramount yet difficult to achieve?

The development of sociology confronted us with the problem of a new reality – that is, 'SOCIETY' as a thing to be studied, not just to take part in. Experientially, being in society is difficult enough, but as an object of understanding it has always presented inscrutable difficulties. What then is this thing called society?

For the greater part of the last century we were content to understand the social through conceptual vehicles like 'order', 'systems', and shared norms and values. Now, these devices served well and enabled us to sustain a feeble idea of society as being rather like the flat earth with a centre, a cohesive force and strict edges. We talked about normative conduct and deviant conduct (the latter being a weak-kneed version of the transgression that we shall address here). Increasingly it dawned on us that our simple model was unsupported by life itself. Society did not rest on an even base, there were folds and subterranean tendrils moving from part to part. The parts no longer interrelated so easily, there was no obvious harmony or agreement, but instead competition, difference and divergence.

We now had to resort to other devices like solidarity, culture and community to express pockets of agreement and to reaffirm our faith in the collective life. The discipline, having evolved in part through a competition between theoretical perspectives, shifted through a series of meta-paradigms which we regarded sequentially as the 'linguistic turn', the 'reflexive turn', the 'cultural turn' and the 'visual turn'. This macro-conceptual evolution was not just one that was driven by an individual sense of intellectual purpose. The society itself was moving more and more rapidly and the Zeitgeist was shifting (or adapting) with equal acceleration. The Thatcherism of the 1980s pronounced the death of the social and cast human relations loose onto the vagaries of market forces; at the same time the academy erupted into the era of the post-, with post-history, post-feminism, post-colonialism, post-nationalism and, overarching them all, the spectre of the 'postmodern'. Tangible metaphors of the social no longer seemed viable and our languages of order gave way to new geographies of social space, many of which appeared entirely cognitive. What remained, however, was a lingering, and real, sense of limits. Though diffuse and ill-defined, the limits, the margins, now took on a most important role in describing and defining the centre. Beyond the limits – be they classificatory, theoretical or even moral – there remained asociality or chaos, but ever more vivid and in greater proximity. Thus our new topic became the transgression that transcends the limits or forces through the boundaries.

Apart from the more obvious economic, technological and political changes that had brought our present circumstances into being there were also two grand philosophical moments that had predicted their moral consequences. First, the Enlightenment with its insistence on the ultimate perfectibility of human kind – a goal that was to be achieved by privileging calculative reason. And, second, Nietzsche's announcement that 'God is dead'.

Now, the Enlightenment ideal has meant three things: (1) that we have come to confuse change with progress; (2) that we have experimented with human excellence through various flawed political policies; and (3) that we have become intolerant if not incredulous towards excessive or transgressive behaviour. Nietzsche's obituary for the Almighty, on the other hand, has given rise to three different but contributory processes: (1) it has removed certainty; (2) it has mainstreamed the re-evaluation of values; and (3) it has released control over infinity.

A quarter of a century ago we discussed 'society' as a reality with confidence; as recently as 1990 we considered ideas like a 'common culture' without caution. Today, in the wake of a series of debates, we cannot even pronounce such holisms without fear of intellectual reprisals on the basis of epistemological imperialism. 'Identity politics' has become a new currency with different, and increasingly minority, groups claiming a right to speak and equivalence of significance. Perpetually fresh questions are raised about the relationship between the core of social life and the periphery, the centre and the margins, identity and difference, the normal and the deviant, and the possible rules that could conceivably bind us into a collectivity.

Now these kinds of questions have always been raised but in liminal zones within the culture such as the avant garde, radical political movements (anarchism and situationism), and counter cultural traditions in creative practice (Surrealism). However, such questions have now moved from the liminal zones into the centre. Berman (1985) announced 'all that which is solid melts into air'; we have all become aware that 'the centre cannot hold'. An insecurity has entered into our consciousness, an insecurity concerning our relationships with others and concerning the ownership of our own desires. We are no longer sure on what basis we belong to another being.

> Various forms of dependency – or, to put the matter less provocatively, trust – are fostered by the reconstruction of day-to-day life via abstract systems. Some such systems, in their global extensions, have created social influences which no one wholly controls and whose outcomes are in some part specifically unpredictable.
>
> (Giddens 1991: 176)

This present state of uncertainty and flux within our culture raises fundamental questions concerning the categories of the normal and the pathological when applied to action or social institutions. Such periods of instability, as we are now experiencing, tend to test and force issues of authority and tradition – truth and surety are up for question. Clearly the 1960s provide another recent example of such a febrile epoch. The difference in the experience of today with that of the 1960s is that now we cannot commit readily to change because there exists no collective faith in an alternative to the existing cultural configuration – note the almost unremarkable transition from one government to another in the UK in 1997. It is hard to be militant in a culture where there is no consolidated belief in any collective form of action or collective identity; the political right appeals to outmoded ideas of 'nation' (symbolised through currency), and the left targets minority groupings to create temporary clusterings (note single-parent families). It would seem that instability and uncertainty are experienced today in peculiarly privatised forms that rarely extend beyond ourselves or our immediate circle. Far from a fear of freedom we now appear to espouse a fear of collectivity; we have become wary of seeking out commonality with others. The vociferous politics of our time are thus 'identity politics', and the response to dominant conditions is often poetic. There is a pathos in witnessing the temporary arousal of an aimless collective consciousness, and then only in the wake of the sad and untimely death of a dilettante princess – I refer to the extended public mourning of Diana in the UK in 1997.

It is only by having a strong sense of the 'together' that we can begin to understand and account for that which is outside, at the margins, or, indeed, that which defies the consensus. The contemporary rebel is left with neither utopianism nor nihilism, but rather loneliness. Time has already outstripped Camus and his wholly cognitive rebel:

> Metaphysical rebellion is the means by which a man protests against his condition and against the whole of creation. It is metaphysical because it disputes the ends of man and creation. The slave protests against the condition of his state of slavery; the metaphysical rebel protests against the human condition in general. The rebel slave affirms that there is something in him which will not tolerate the manner in which his master treats him; the metaphysical rebel declares that he is frustrated by the universe. For both of them it is not only a problem of pure and simple negation. In fact in both cases we find an assessment of values in the name of which the rebel refuses to accept the condition in which he finds himself.
>
> (Camus 1971: 29)

And also the inspirations of the Marquis de Sade, the grand libertine, who saw God as the great criminal and whose dedicated nihilism asserted that 'vice and virtue comingle in the grave like everything else'. The possibility of breaking free from moral constraint in contemporary culture has become an intensely privatised project. As we recognise no bond we acknowledge fracture only with difficulty – how then do we become free-of or different-to? Such questioning provides the perfect moment to theorise the transgressive conduct that stems from such positionings.

Transgression is that which exceeds boundaries or exceeds limits. However, we need to affirm that human experience is the constant experience of limits, perhaps because of the absolute finitude of death; this is a point made forcefully by Bataille (1985). Constraint is a constant experience in our action, it needs to be to render us social. Interestingly enough, however, the limits to our experience and the taboos that police them are never simply imposed from the outside; rather, limits to behaviour are always personal responses to moral imperatives that stem from the inside. This means that any limit on conduct carries with it an intense relationship with the desire to transgress that limit. Simple societies expressed this clearly through mythology and more recent societies have celebrated this magnetic antipathy between order and excess through periodic 'carnival' and the idea of the 'world turned upside down', as Bakhtin demonstrates.

> Let us say a few initial words about the complex nature of carnival laughter. It is, first of all, a festive laughter. Therefore it is not an individual reaction to some isolated comic event. Carnival laughter is the laughter of all the people. Second, it is universal in scope; it is directed at all and everyone, including the carnival's participants. The entire world is seen in its droll aspect, in its gay relativity. Third, this laughter is ambivalent; it is gay, triumphant, and at the same time mocking, deriding. It asserts and denies, it buries and revives. Such is the laughter of the carnival.
>
> (Bakhtin 1968: 11–12)

Transgressive behaviour therefore does not deny limits or boundaries, rather it exceeds them and thus completes them. Every rule, limit, boundary or edge carries with it its own fracture, penetration or impulse to dis-obey. The transgression is a component of the rule. Seen in this way, excess is not an abhorration nor a luxury, it is rather a dynamic force in cultural reproduction – it prevents stagnation by breaking the rule and it ensures stability by reaffirming the rule. Transgression is not the same as disorder; it opens up chaos and reminds us of the necessity of order. But the problem remains. We need to know the collective order, to recognise the edges in order to transcend them.

This book, however, is not confined to issues of theoretical exposition and classification. The point of investigating transgression is to demonstrate its very real presence in contemporary life. The book rests on the view that a feature of modernity, accelerating into postmodernity, is the desire to transcend limits – limits that are physical, racial, aesthetic, sexual, national, legal and moral. The passage of modernity has been, as Nietzsche pointed out, a process of the oppression and compartmentalisation of the will. People have become fashioned in a restricted but, nevertheless, arbitrary way. Modernity has unintentionally generated an ungoverned desire to extend, exceed, or go beyond the margins of acceptability or normal performance. Transgression therefore becomes a primary postmodern topic and a responsible one.

This work will provide an interdisciplinary base, albeit composed by a sociologist, and an (anti)traditional approach to the concept of transgression. This will involve a history of ideas, a résumé of the major contributory theorists and a thematic discussion of significant moments and substantive concerns of these various debates. Although in large part the work will be theoretical in nature there will be whole sections that directly address and analyse substantive instances of transgressive conduct and investigate transgressive cultural productions.

PHILOSOPHICAL ORIGINS OF THE PROBLEM: ETHICAL OR LOGICAL?

Clearly a large part of our concerns in what follows will be definitional and we will address what constitutes a transgressional act. However, the meaning of an act does not reside solely within the intentionality of the actor, indeed, in most instances it resides within the context of the act's reception. Phenomenological insights or the bedrock of what we now call social constructionism advise us that meaning is located within social situations. But we need to dig deeper than this: transgression cannot be understood through some transient indexicality. Though mediated through social and cultural manifestations such as taboo, convention and law, the roots of this particular problematic are to be found in more fundamental mindsets, be they moral or logical, which inform both cultures and societies themselves. Such *Lebensfeld* bear the status of Reason.

Jervis (1999), in an eloquent and wholly convincing account of the transgressive process, locates the project largely within the realm of the moral, which is, after all, how it ultimately appears. He reveals the rich and oppressive tendency in Western society to exclude and marginalise that which it finds disagreeable and by implication to unify, consolidate and homogenise that which sustains as its core of comfortable familiarity. Thus he says:

> The transgressive is reflexive, questioning both its own role and that of the culture that has defined it in its otherness. It is not simply a reversal, a mechanical inversion of an existing order it opposes. Transgression, unlike opposition or reversal, involves hybridization, the mixing of categories and the questioning of the boundaries that separate categories. It is not, in itself, subversion; it is not an overt and deliberate challenge to the status quo. What it does do, though, is implicitly interrogate the law, pointing not just to the specific, and frequently arbitrary, mechanisms of power on which it rests – despite its universalizing pretensions – but also to its complicity, its involvement in what it prohibits.
>
> (Jervis 1999: 4)

None of this is in dispute, however there is a prior history of the transgression perspective. First there is the will to transgress, the belief in the sovereign actor that is embodied in Platonic philosophy and Christian theology (both viewed as sets of logical principles). In both views it is supposed that the actor can, and indeed should, strive to bracket the totality of what is assumed to be the case and thus to treat it as if it were contingent. For Plato the heroic quest of the philosopher (the sovereign actor) is the revelation of true meanings – this is his 'doctrine of the forms'. The perfect ideal, or form, is an essential reality of universal quality revealed only through the proper exercise of reason, it is an intellectual property. For the most part, those who are not philosopher kings are subject to a realm of 'conjecture' and 'belief' as opposed to the reality base of 'knowledge' and 'understanding'. Through a series of visual analogies ranging through 'sun', 'light', 'shadow' and 'reflection' Plato builds a rational 'seen' that is beyond and superior to the received world of appearance. Essence then lies behind appearance and exceeds appearance in purity and clarity. Plato's escapee from the parable of the cave is, having experienced the world of sunshine and vision, frightened to return to his erstwhile companions with news of the true form of things lest they tear him to pieces in disbelief. The journey from the cave into the light and into the essence behind the appearance is the inevitable saga of the seeker after truth; it is a sovereign act because it transcends the conventional categories, and it is finally transgressive because it disrupts and threatens the taken-for-granted world. Here is a paradigm.

Christian theology takes up and amplifies this narrative in as much as the power of the light on reality is generated by the Divine Creator and the epistemological quest of the Platonic soul now becomes the metaphysical search for the inner goodness of the Christian soul. Both of these doctrines privilege the imagination, that which enables us to think outside of ourselves (our cave), both privilege the subject (later to become the target of post-structuralism) and both instil a cultural commitment to overcome, transcend or transgress existing boundaries that restrict our vision. Sovereignty then is the aspiration to transcend appearance and to achieve essence.

What then of the issue of inclusion and exclusion that seems so fundamental to the transgression perspective. Here, even before we explore the moral tropes of modernity we can find roots, and logical roots, in Aristotle. Aristotle's logic, much quoted but less often read, is to be found in the dense collection of six treatise that comprise the *Organon*. Predating Kant, Aristotle argues concerning the existence of categories of thought such as substance, quality, quantity, relation and action, but sees substance as paramount. Primarily, Aristotle sediments the principles of, and the dependency upon, a formal logic current today. Originally sited as the author of the syllogism:

All men are mortal
Socrates is a man
therefore Socrates is mortal

his actual axiom runs as follows:

If all B is A, and all C is B, then all C is A

and this provides a principle to which any argument of syllogistic form can be reduced and appraised. This moment signals the instillation and implicit adoption of an Either–Or logic in Western culture. Here we see the generation of a life of binary thought and decisions. Such a principle is enforced through an emphasis on the Law of the Excluded Middle, surely another, more fundamental, version of the unacceptable other in Jervis' (1999) thesis. On/Off; Blackness/Whiteness; Male/Female become our regular currency and what becomes omitted is a key grey area, namely the idea that 'not A' is possibly a 'diminished A' rather than a B. This has serious political consequences. The grey area is the territory of the postmodern, chaos theory and more practically 'fuzzy logic'.

Let us pursue further the concept of sovereignty in action. There is a persistent theme running through both German and French philosophy (see both Marx and Baudelaire) that emphasises the ultimate plasticity and malleability of human kind. Given its time such thinking was bound up with the politics of capitalism, industrialisation and the rapidly accelerating division of labour in society. One element of this thought espouses the limitless potential of the self, but another, forward looking element massages the intense relation between man and the machine. Simply put, if we harness technology then sovereignty becomes supreme. Here we have a post-Enlightenment vision of the infinite pliability of human potential. With the advance of technological research we see mastery through Foucault's 'techniques of the body' and postmodern master beings in the form of cyborgs. Interestingly a materialist tie sustains here.

Paralleling this supremacy is an ambivalence and a suspicion. In the late nineteenth and early twentieth centuries (before the First World War demonstrated the dystopian nemesis burgeoning within the relation between man and machine) there was a growing intellectual concern with the human limitations on the mobilisation of technology and the potentially ungovernable politics that would stem from it. We could build 'Titanic' ships but we should not build titanic men or states. Instead of enhancing human potential, technology could be viewed as an incursion into human sovereignty, a kind of imperialism (stalked by hubris). Perhaps in response, Bataille began to blur expressive notions of political economy with symbolic ideas of the gift and exchange derived from anthropology. Similarly we witness both Adorno's and Benjamin's seemingly elitist vacillation between applauding the benefits of mass culture and yet bemoaning the manifest loss of originality and 'aura'.

Pefanis (1991) sets out from the view, which he describes as 'now conventional', that the heretical interpretations of Hegel proffered by Alexandre Kojève in his 1930s Sorbonne lectures were axial in establishing much of the subsequent French intellectual 'addresses and transgressions' of social theory. The concepts of 'the end of history' and the 'disappearance of man' are clearly identifiable post-structuralist themes and their conduit into intellectual debate were Bataille and Lacan, both staunch followers of Kojève's theorising. Whereas Hegel's system recommends a sovereignty in fulfilling some version of Reason (a notion that resonates with the coalescence of a Christian deity and the German *Geist*), the new, post-Kojève reading emphasises and elects the unspoken element of desire, and reforms the Master–Slave dialectic into a new form of struggle for recognition.

Hegel's megalomaniacal system completes with the triumph of the Sage and an absolute knowledge becomes instilled in human discourse. Neither Bataille nor Lacan believed that this supposed utopian moment would satisfy individual desire. Thus the project diverts towards a redefinition of the subject and the progress of post-structuralism becomes marked by the gradual exorcism of Hegelian dialectics from contemporary thought. So Foucault says:

> Our age, whether through logic or epistemology, whether through Marx or through Neitzsche, is attempting to flee Hegel.
>
> (Foucault 1971: 28)

Hegel's great historical vehicle, his *Phenomenology of Spirit*, wends not towards its *telos* but towards dispersion, fragmentation and new forms of transgression. So Pefanis (1991) delights us with:

> The great historical machine lurches, groans, and grinds to a halt in the sands of time. Powerless to conquer this final frontier, to fulfil its mission of delivering *society* to the colonized regions, the beached behemoth is a disquieting spectacle. It is a scandal: unable to progress against the force of its own inertia or to stem the flow of the irritant medium this or that fantastic mechanism, the great machine responds by reprogramming the coordinates of its own destination – henceforth nowhere – and recommending its subjects to the project of reproduction and system maintenance: damage control. At the end of history we are all mechanics tending the autoteleological machine.
>
> Was the great machine ever what it was cranked up to be? The precondition of historical society was the suppression of the archaic, the very possibility of its existence the suppression of the nonhistorical. Lyotard's idea of fantastic archeology reveals the nonhistorical in Bataille's transgressive, Foucault's silence, Deleuze's schizo and Baudrillard's dead (and much else besides). At the end of history the transgressive laughs, the mad walk free, the silent speak and the dead live. . . .
>
> (Pefanis 1992: 9)

We will revisit and unpack many of these themes and issues later in the book.

So the assumed, the mythic, the discursive space that is sovereignty is unbounded, we have come to understand it and anticipate it as an imperative, indeed as a drive. This is both the ancient (i.e. Plato) and postmodern view. Sovereignty is a force but is not wedded to power, except perhaps in Foucault. The postmodern view has largely broken its ties with the materialism of Marx but it still carries a similar set of assumptions. In its most extreme contemporary form the sovereign act is bound to utterance, thus many modern theorists, following Derrida and Heidegger, speak of 'bringing things into being'. In Renaissance terms Grace provided the possibility of harnessing the power of talent, not technology, which was not as we know it today. Fantasy provided the *techne*, it was the ability to envision the good, the better and the perfect. Fantasy, however, was always compromised by 'sin'. If fantasy meant that 'I speak myself', if fantasy implied that 'I bring things into being' then clearly this challenged the deity and was to be held in check as hubris, the sin that summoned up nemesis. This sin and sanction dyad prefigures the fracture and repair of transgression.

I trust that I am sedimenting here a taste of the gathering, snowballing, accumulating effects of a commitment to freedom, to self, to sovereignty, through the historical process. The irreversible pressure is to more and more extreme action. If the key to human competence is freedom or plasticity then the essence of human performance is that it must demonstrate lack of limit. The rationale of the serial killer need be no more coherent than Sir John Hunt's response when asked why he sought to conquer Everest – 'Because it's there' he replied.

Before we leave our introduction and move to the body of the text it is important to note that aside from the ancient, systems driven and esoteric philosophical roots of our transgressional problematic (accompanied by the forceful Messianic input), there are powerful secular and scientific paradigms that defy yet not depose the issue in our thinking. In opposition to the well-established Aristotelian canon of binary logic, Darwin, writing in the nineteenth century, gave thesis to the possibility that the distinction between A and not-A is not an absolute categorical differentiation but an evolution of difference. Therefore all difference becomes fluid. Fluidity is an important metaphor here. Through the evolutionary process a distinction arises between A and B. B occurs where the interruption (of evolution) is so great that we can no longer sustain the undifferentiated category A. What governs the content and interaction in and between categories A and B is the environment in which they sit, not intentionality. Crudely, the 'survival of the fittest' is not about competition but rather the adaptation of dispositions. This provides an early model of *autopoesis*. Darwin draws on theories of reason and consciousness, not derived from a characteristic set of ideal guarantees but from a rootedness in the organism and its environment. This begins from and espouses the idea of limited plasticity. Indeed the evolutionary hierarchy is articulated through levels of plasticity with the lower species demonstrating low levels, while the human species is envisioned as having a high, but by no means unlimited, level of post-natal plasticity. Instead of speaking of infinite plasticity we now consider a range of dispositions, which are nevertheless negotiable. These appear to provide structures in what might otherwise appear as a chaotic framework of phenomena. Transgression now becomes less easy to conceive of.

So as we step off into the unknown and investigate if, indeed, the centre can hold, let us formulate our position so far. We have set the topic of transgression, offered a nominal definition, hinted at its genealogy, introduced its purposes, processes and margins, and met, at a distance, some of the leading contributors to the debate. Concepts such as power, will, desire, market and violence will recur in the text, they can all mark transgression and all have a suddenness, a magnitude and an over-the-topness that demands conventional understandings (never forget Hitler or the World Trade Center). If transgression produces an alteration then without an identifiable positivity it does not produce an alterity. This has been the problem of the Western avant-garde throughout the twentieth century. If transgression produces an alterity it does not necessarily compromise the past, as we shall see.

2

THE CENTRE CANNOT HOLD

In this chapter we will investigate the notion of boundary in social thought. We do this because the concept of transgression proceeds from an assumption and a recognition of 'that' which can be transgressed. So the story which always precedes the commission or acknowledgement of a transgressive act is the constitution of a centre, a centre that provides for a social structure, and a structure of meaning that is delimited or marked out by boundaries. Quite simply, until the fencing is erected around the recognised and recognisable territory then it is not possible to cross that line and enter, invade or trespass into another place. This all sounds extremely straightforward, very concrete and merely geographical but, of course, these boundaries are entirely analytic, multi-dimensional and virtual, and yet known to members of a society within a spectrum of interpretation. The real problem then lies in a conceptualisation of the centre and the structure that it maintains and the processes by which the centre becomes known. In many senses the elucidation of this 'reality' has been the mission of sociology since its inception. What is it that holds people together in the whole range of social relationships that they inhabit from family, through institution, to community and society?

A further complexity here is that much of the social thought within which the concept of transgression would have currency denies the necessity of sociology's inauguration and, as part of the 'post-'s' rejection of grand narratives, has little truck with such monolithic and totalising concepts as 'society'. However, my obligation is to provide an informed history of ideas and within a sociological and anthropological framework and, as I said at the end of the last chapter, transgressions even theoretical transgressions, do not necessarily compromise the past. Here then are some sociological grounds for the social, for the establishment of boundaries and for the maintenance of those boundaries. What also follows, in negation, is the very possibility, if not necessity, of transgression.

DURKHEIM'S SOCIETY *SUI GENERIS* AND FORMS OF SOLIDARITY

At around the turn of the nineteenth century Durkheim opened up a new landscape for our attention. Philosophical, political and economic paradigms extending back to the pre-Socratics had addressed the ordered relations between people, but Durkheim originally maps, through his science of ethics, the social 'world'. This is an ontological space, a source of causality, and the primary context for the functioning of all previously considered theories of human conduct. What Durkheim achieved at a more analytical level than merely founding a discipline (though this is achievement enough) was an awakening of vision and a cognitive commitment to a new perceptual territory. Many previous nineteenth-century explorers revealed whimsical sights fit for the new tourist, be it traveller or taxonomer, but Durkheim's 'social' was hard, factual, contested and ripe with the propensities to both change and explode. This was no space for the tourist, but rather a battleground for the social scientist *qua* moral scientist. So compelling were the images in interlocking constellations he laid before us that their existence, though not their interpretation, went without challenge until the end of the twentieth century. This latter-day assault on the social world emerged as part of a Western manifestation of egoism in the form of 'retro' eighteenth-century economic theory, and also as a dimension of de-traditionalisation in Baudrillard's conception of the post-. Both of these challenges were, incidently, anticipated in Durkheim's corpus of work through his concepts of 'forced' and 'anomic' divisions of labour:

> . . . the potential to reopen modernist closure is not found in the lax pluralities of many 'posterities' but in the rather more awkward constraints of Durkheim's notions of solidarity and the normative. The impulses of much postmodern theory are too ironic, to ready, like Baudrillard to keep 'simulacra' within the index of negativity and

alienation, too ready like Lyotard to define the sublime in terms of an act of continued negation.

(Smith 1995: 253)

Durkheim's vision was both complex and truly 'visionary'. The irony is, however, that his thought has become ideologically passé. Crude appropriations of Durkheim manage his ideas as simply positivist, functionalist and essentially conservative. Rather more sophisticated, yet still conventional, views of Durkheim treat his work diachronically and at three different levels. First, *substantively* his concerns are understood as demonstrating a shift from institutions to beliefs. Second, his work is gathered *theoretically* within an evolutionary thesis, that is, his manifest preoccupation with the transition from simple societies into the form of complex societies. It is suggested through constructing a rigid framework of morphologies that he attempted to establish the functional conditions for the moral bond along an historical continuum. Finally, his *methodological* commitment is witnessed as a development from an early positivism, and indeed empiricism, through a series of analytic encounters which lead ultimately to the inappropriate character of this method and the emergence of a new, yet not entirely articulated, style of address. This chronology is well expressed by Parsons (1968) as Durkheim's movement from 'positivism' to 'idealism' – so we are presented with a version of an 'epistemological break'.

I suggest that Durkheim's programme may be viewed as occasioned by real social change – the experience of modernity and the threatening spectre of postmodernity – and perhaps, at one level, as attending concretely to that experience of change.

Over and over again, Durkheim comments on the uneasiness, anxiety, malaise, disenchantment, pessimism, and other negative characteristics of his age. His comments on the leading proponents of the *fin de siècle* spirit – among them, Bergson, James, Nietzsche, and Guyau – are mixed with sympathy as well as outrage. But his remarks on the Enlightenment philosophers, Hobbes, Montesquieu, Rousseau, Comte, Kant, Saint-Simon, and others, are unequivocally critical with regard to their naivete, optimism, and simplicity.

(Mestrovic 1991: 75)

However, at an analytic level, Durkheim's corpus generates different and predicted methods for different sets of problems which are, in turn, echoes of the two different manners through which people might realise their world. In this way Durkheim's insights are not linked specifically to the moment of their occurrence but have applicability to the rapidly transforming conditions of modernity into late-modernity. He enables us to find stability in the face of pending chaos, which in turn provides the grounds for both consensus and transgression.

The methodological programme is provided with its models through Durkheim's thesis in *The Division of Labour*. This work may be regarded as grounding all of Durkheim's theorising. The two forms of solidarity revealed in Durkheim's text, the Mechanical and the Organic, can be treated as metaphors for different ways of being in the world, different ways of seeing and understanding the world and thus for different sociological approaches to the world. Indeed, they are paradigmatic, they reveal different models of boundary maintenance and thus different and original possibilities to transgress.

Mechanical solidarity is a mode of both cognition and accounting that is preoccupied with description. This betrays an habitual realism with no distinction at work between objects-in-reality and objects-in-thought. It renders all understanding obedient to the criteria of literalism. This way of being is clearly primary to and celebrated through the twin traditions of positivism and empiricism that have engaged and stalked sociological reasoning, and subsequently mediated its relation to the wider culture, from its inception at the close of the nineteenth century up until its threatened fragmentation in the present day. Beyond these metatheoretical considerations, the mechanical epistemology bestows a particular, practical status upon the theorist, a status that enables such continuous literal description by and through the privileged difference of the sociologist. The sociologist is thus realised through expertise; the sociologist is as a high priest. High priests lay down the law with power, by diktat, with visibility and with universal recognition.

In the latter mode – the second yet simultaneous vision, that of the organic solidarity – we are offered understanding not through description but through espousal. Within organicism difference becomes accepted, it becomes conventional. The taken-for-grantedness of difference emerges as the grounds on which we begin to understand the other, thus difference itself must be regarded as a form of equivalence. In this context, the understanding of difference requires not the privileged description of that which is sundered from self, but an espousal in the dual sense of an analytic wedding to or sameness with the other and an adoption or indeed advocacy of that other's position. The theorist now experiences a dramatic change in status; the reification of expert and high priest as describer of the mundane becomes itself secularised and a part of that realm of the mundane. The theorist becomes like Garfinkel, an espouser of and equivalent to the lay member. Similarly, the lay member is enjoined in the ethno-methodology of the sociologist to both artfully see, on a shared plane, and apprehend. Boundaries become less clear, categories become less well insulated – 'what do you have to do around here to get a reaction?'

Let us then work with the two forms of solidarity. They enabled Durkheim to account for real social change along an historical continuum; the inspiration for this change being the degree of moral density, and the key to decoding its form being the manner of aggregation.

REPRESSIVE SANCTIONS AND RESTITUTIVE SANCTIONS

Within Durkheim's major thesis on solidarity, the *Divison of Labour*, he is at pains, simultaneously, to stress both the real and compelling nature of the forms he is elucidating and yet also to show that these forms are intangible. We cannot see, touch or feel solidarity but we all experience its compulsion, its force and its action-orientation all of the time. So Durkheim seeks out a tangible marker of solidarity which is, at the same time, apparent to all members of a society. Here he speaks, as he so often does, of types of law, and here we can see the singularly significant impact of this thesis for an understanding and contexting of the very idea of transgression. He says:

> But social solidarity is a completely moral phenomenon which, taken by itself, does not lend itself to exact observation nor indeed to measurement. To proceed to this classification and this comparison, we must substitute for this internal fact which escapes us an external index which symbolizes it and study the former in the light of the latter.
> This visible symbol is law.
>
> (Durkheim 1964a: 64)

And he goes on to inform us that the form of law and sanction that marks out mechanical solidarity is *repressive* whereas the form of law and sanction that marks out organic solidarity is *restitutive*. Thus in mechanical solidarity,

> The link of social solidarity to which repressive law corresponds is the one whose break constitutes a crime. By this name we call every act which,

> in any degree whatever, invokes punishment . . . Surely there are crimes of different kinds; but among all these kinds, there is, no less surely, a common element. The proof of this is that the reaction which crimes call forth from society, in respect of punishment, is, save for differences of degree, always and ever the same.
>
> (Durkheim 1964a: 70)

whereas in organic solidarity,

> The very nature of restitutive sanction suffices to show that the social solidarity to which this type of law corresponds is of a totally different kind.
>   What distinguishes this sanction is that it is not expiatory, but consists of a simple *return in state*. Sufferance proportionate to the misdeed is not inflicted on the one who has violated the law or who disregards it; he is simply sentenced to comply with it. If certain things were done, the judge reinstates them as they would have been. He speaks of law; he says nothing of punishment.
>
> (Durkheim 1964a: 111)

So, in essence, Durkheim is telling us that in a simple or tightly bound society, in a society where the normative standards are clear and apparent and shared, the law is exercised in a passionate and expiatory fashion. A crime (or transgression) offends against the shared collective consciousness, it is therefore a crime (or transgression) against society itself. The punishment that is always invoked is a symbolic reformation of the collective against the offending individual. The nature of the social reaction reveals the common symbols and shared taboos; the reaction to their fracture buttresses, restores and reaffirms their shared character and constraint. However, in a society where the form of solidarity has become more diffuse and less recognisable, in a collective form the symbolic response to transgression has to be an attempt at the restoration of the status quo and a declaration of difference because there cannot be a surge of shared sentimental reaction where no common values, standards and normative constraints apply.

In the mechanical situation it is difficult to know how an actor could generate sufficient sense of individuality to commit the transgressive act and in the organic model it is difficult for the potential transgressor to know at what possible level and in what possible way an act might evoke a reaction.

Let us return, with these legal indicators in mind, to our two models of solidarity. Within mechanical solidarity, our first model, we have a primary ontological commitment to the inherent order in the social world. This order is an essential metaphysic which is mobilised, in human terms, through the pre-social yet gregarious urges of the 'primitive horde'. Humankind is disposed to sociality by virtue of its species being, and a person's experience of him/herself and of others within that sociality is through and by virtue of the social bond. The social bond, which is based on resemblance (a pragmatic ordering principle), is maintained by a strong collective consciousness. The collective consciousness is, in turn, transcendent – it is projected out as God (an unquestioning ordering principle). The a priori status of the deity is not contentious in mechanical solidarity; people and their understandings are held in check by faith – the world is experienced as inherently ordered, humankind itself is contingent upon that order. Such conservation of order also legislates for the finite. The world is comprised of a fixed and limited number of segments and their possible relation – the model is, in Durkheim's own formulation, 'mechanical'. Society, then, is intrinsically ordered, transcendently regulated and mechanistically maintained.

Such ruthless and unerring finitude has two epistemological consequences. First, the reduction of social phenomena to things, at hand, but not wilful nor independent. Such 'thing-like' status as derives from this shared, condensed symbolic order itself leads to the experience of phenomena in the constant, particularistic here-and-now of an unchanging cosmos. The convenient methodological tools of such experience are the senses, sight and touch and sound; they are concrete. The second consequence is the reduction of the person as a potential theorist. People within this form of life operate only on the surface, they are essentially irrelevant, except as a messengers; indeed, they too are relegated to the status of being one more 'thing' located mechanically within the order of things; they have no 'intentional' relation with phenomena other than themselves.

The singular and absolute authority of the God that symbolises mechanical solidarity ensures a unitary and necessarily shared epistemology. The strict rule system is worked out by taboo relating to the infringement of good conduct. The firm correspondence deriving from a restricted and condensed symbolic repertoire ensures only limited room for dissent – the same correspondential unequivocal symbols make for solidaristic and consensual group membership. The individual member, if indeed he is distinguishable as such, has only a positional responsibility to the rules of community; this emphasises the reliance on one methodological way and further contributes to the weak sense of self – 'self as anyman' as McHugh (1971) puts it. In fact, such is the antipathy towards egoism within such a community that in methodological terms, 'self' becomes the source of all bias and corruption, as the *Rules of Sociological Method* (Durkheim 1964b) instructs us we must 'eliminate all preconceptions'. Clearly, imagination can lead us astray; we may break the rules waywardly!

In the *Rules* the tone is prescriptive, it is as if Durkheim were legislating for the conduct of a scientific community. To suggest that such legislation were accompanied by repressive sanction would be to press the metaphor through analogy into simile; but the work is clearly 'laying down the laws' for the recognition (ontology) and recovery (epistemology) of sociological phenomena and the rules are hardly stated in an equivocal or flexible fashion.

The *Rules* has been variously described as a manifesto (Lukes 1985; Thompson 1982) in as much as it seeks to establish the rule system for a social science, but also in as much as it seeks to describe the nature of sociological phenomena. Hirst (1975) captures this element well with his sense of Durkheim as pioneer, staking out the vacant territory for sociology and thus ring-fencing the particular facticity of sociology from all other facticities. Of course the character of this facticity is crucial. In what sense is it present, perhaps as a 'sign', and for Durkheim as a sign of different forms of relation both in-reality and in-thought? This, in turn, releases social phenomena from the epistemological imperialism of psychology, biology, individualist metaphysics and, indeed, commonsense. So in this way, sociology's object is located, provided with a special identity and offered up for observation and understanding through a finite set of explicit transformational rules.

The primary entities that comprise a social world are social facts, they are the 'absolute simples', the irreducible elements that, in unique combinations, constitute different societal forms. Social facts are also the primary units of analysis. Durkheim seems at this stage to draw no distinction between objects of reality and objects of science, yet it is social science which releases such facts from their obscurity. The language of sociology brings this form of facticity into focus. The social facts are:

> every way of acting, fixed or not, capable of exercising on the individual
> an external constraint or again, every way of acting which is general

throughout while at the same time existing in its own right independent of its individual manifestation.

(Durkheim 1964b: 13)

and we are further instructed to

consider social facts as things.   ·

(Durkheim 1964b: 14)

The social facts, then, are typified through three major characteristics: externality, constraint and generality. They are *external* in the sense that they have an existence independent of our thought about them, they are not simply realised or materialised by the individual member and further they predate that member, and as such constitute any world that he enters. They *constrain* in as much as they are coercive when infringed; normal social conduct falls within their conventions and manifests their reality, attempts to act otherwise than normatively transgresses the implicit and explicit rule structure and invokes constraint. Their *generality* derives from their being typical, normal, average, sustaining and not transitory, and morally good in the sense that they maintain the collective life – they are the very fabric of social 'nature', their generality enables them to speak for themselves, but through the auspices of sociological patronage; that is, they have a sociological facticity (and they enable transgression).

This last characteristic is further mobilised in Durkheim's method through the invocation that 'The voluntary character of a practice or an institution should never be assumed beforehand' (Durkheim 1964b: 28), which provides for the possibility that even the most arbitrary, isolated or seemingly random occurrence of a social phenomenon may, on further observation, be revealed to be yet a further necessary component within a systematic and stable social structure – indeed, the inherent order of things predicted in mechanical solidarity.

Durkheim continues to inform us that social things are 'givens' and that they are subject to the practice of observation; this then becomes a central analytic problem, namely to discover the rules that govern the visual existence of social things. We are given rules of recognition and assembly and we are to combine these rules with the social fact's proportions of thing-like-ness that we have already considered. So social facts are resistant to our individual will, our attempts to alter or amend them; they are objectively available, that is, free of possible interpretation or value judgement, and they are irreducible to other phenomena. They are, in terms of the social world, all that is the case. More than this, all manifestations of a social fact are linked by causality – the mechanical whole seems complete.

Recognition of the social facts remains, however, a problem. Although their existence is *sui generic* they do not have form. Their reality does not consist in a material or physical presence, they are more experienced than tangible. Their manifestation is as constraint; they are invisible prison walls. Clearly they can be witnessed but only in as much as they inhabit or are realities – so Durkheim instances the legal system, the use of French currency, and the French language, all extant structural features embodying social facts. Ultimately, then, they are representations which arise from and are indicators of the collective consciousness – the methodological rules of the scientific community. It is interesting that within mechanical solidarity the social facts constrain the individual and yet the social member remains largely untheorised as an alternative causality.

THE NORMAL AND THE PATHOLOGICAL

An important methodological distinction in the *Rules* is that made by Durkheim between the concepts of the *normal* and the *pathological*. This distinction is entirely relevant to our growing understanding of the idea of transgression. He says that

> for societies as for individuals, health is good and desirable; disease, on the contrary, is bad and to be avoided.
>
> (Durkheim 1964b: 49)

and also, in more general terms, that

> One cannot, without contradiction, even conceive of a species which would be incurably diseased in itself and by virtue of its fundamental constitution. The healthy constitutes the norm par excellence and can consequently be in no way abnormal.
>
> (Durkheim 1964b: 58)

This crucial distinction, then, refers to social facts that are typical and general (the normal) as opposed to those that are irregular, particular or transitory. It is a useful distinction to exercise but we need to ask also why the concepts should have been employed, as they would seem to operate at two levels. First and most obviously, at the concrete level of actual social members, the *normal* facts are those which constitute solidarity and continuity and the *pathological* are those which manifest individualisation, fragmentation and interruption. In their different ways the two orders of social fact are markers of good and concerted conduct within the collective life. Second, at the analytic level, and this is their main thrust, it might be suggested that the normal/pathological distinction is a moral distinction or election mode by the theorist in advance of his commitment to a programme of methodology. It is the theorist's projection of notions of choice and arbitration into the particular form of social structure that emanates from a mechanical form of life. The binary opposition contained within the normal/pathological distinction resembles the binary cognitive code necessary for the articulation of the individual and collective interests within a mechanical solidarity. Issues have to be resolved in absolutes of Yes and No, Collective and Individual, the lack of a developed division of labour disenables the proliferation of views of justifiable positions. Thus as the dialectic between normal and pathological facts can be seen to have a remedial and beneficial function at the concrete level of the social member, so also it has a function in the methodological social engineering of the theorist who seems to construct these facts as mechanically coherent.

Durkheim defines the normal in terms of the average, a definition which must continue to re-affirm itself – a sure feature of mechanical reproduction. The pathological are structurally transitory and thus inappropriate for our study; thus instead of using the concept 'pathological' to refer to inherent threats within a social structure Durkheim uses it to establish the a-social character of individual manifestations and through this to sanctify the altar of collective purity. Pathological behaviour serves as a negative reinforcement for the collective sentiments; crime creates outrage, punishment gives rise to expiation, the normal has its boundaries once more confirmed.

The average equates with the healthy which in turn equates with the good. Durkheim's method is clearly monotheistic in this particular model, which is wholly appropriate for the structure of institutions and consciousness that it is, at one level, seeking to illuminate – namely primitive, simple, religiously based, coherent societies.

Whereas Durkheim's earlier works revealed a mechanically explicit concern with the specification of the natural unequivocal moral order of society in terms of generalities, their constraining influence and thus their causal significance – the *sui generic* mechanistic reality – in his later work, particularly *Elementary Forms of the Religious Life* (1971), he shifts to explain the non-observable, the non-material, the realms of mind, knowledge and symbolic representations; what Alexander (1988) has seen as the appropriate grounds for an analysis of culture. Substantively we move from institutions to beliefs, from laws and contracts to epistemologies and cosmologies. When Durkheim begins to write his implicit epistemology, it reveals how a natural moral order is equivocally intelligible from within a complex interpretive network of diffuse symbols.

Durkheim is quite clear in his Introduction to *Elementary Forms* that he is involved in an analysis of totemism, in the first instance, as a critical illumination of his general theory of religion; this however, is in turn only one facet of his wider theory of knowledge, the culmination of all his studies. It is, then, the epistemology that is his principal, underlying concern throughout the study, and religion may be conceptualised relating to the symbolic system through which man addresses his world and through which his world and his consciousness are constructed. The importance of religious theory goes far beyond an examination of the social character of ceremony or ritual – it indicates the very nature of human knowledge. So, for Durkheim, religion sheds light not only on what people believe but more fundamentally on what and on how they think.

The substantive truth value of elements comprising a mechanical order is attested to by Durkheim in the Introduction to the *Elementary Forms* when he states that there exist in society no institutions that are based upon a lie. Thus all religious practice, whatever form it takes, translates some human need. Religions embody a specific social function which is their recognisable constraint, their governance of human conduct.

Durkheim's concern with the origins of symbolism is made paramount in his discussion of the 'categories of understanding' – that is, the ultimate principles which underlie all our knowledge and which give order and arrangement to our perceptions and sensations, thus enabling us 'to know' at all. He wishes to establish the social derivation of these basic categories like, for example, concepts of space, time, class, substance, force, efficacy, causality, etc. – all concepts which were taken to be universally valid fundamentals of all human thought.

> Instead of Durkheim's saying 'the unconscious is history', one could write 'the a priori is history'. Only if one were to mobilize all the resources of the social sciences would one be able to accomplish this kind of historicist actualization of the transcendental project which

consists of reappropriating, through historical anamnesis, the product of the entire historical operation of which consciousness too is (at every moment) the product. In the individual case this would include reappropriating the dispositions and classificatory schemes which are a necessary part of the aesthetic experience as it is described, naively, by the analysis of essence.

(Bourdieu 1993: 256)

Reviewing the dominant epistemological explanations Durkheim dismisses the types of idealism which depict the ultimate reality behind the world as being spiritual, informed by an Absolute, or those which account for the categories as being inherent in the nature of human consciousness. Such an 'a priorist' position, he says, is refuted by the incessant variability of the categories of human thought from society to society; and, furthermore, it lacks experimental control, it is not empirically verifiable. Indeed, such a position 'does not satisfy the conditions demanded of a scientific hypothesis' (p. 15). In this section he can be read as addressing the Kantian edifice which has a theory of mind as that being informed by divine reason. For Kant the categories exist somehow beyond the individual consciousness as prior conditions of experience and without which experience would be meaningless and chaotic – the divine reason is thus made manifest through individual consciousness.

Durkheim also criticises the varieties of subjectivism, in particular the theory stating that individuals construct the categories from the raw materials of their own particular empirical experience or perception; that is, we each infer and create our own unique set of categories from the peculiar orderings of our own sensations. This is the extreme logical position of the tradition of empiricism, and in this context Durkheim is addressing the anthropology of Tylor and Frazer. Durkheim suggests that although the categories of thought vary from society to society, within any one society they are characterised by universality and necessity. Thus for the subjectivists, since all sensations are private, individual and different, it is difficult in terms of their theory to account for how people generally come to possess and operate with the same categories within particular societies.

Durkheim also, at this stage of his work, dissociates himself from any materialist standpoint. In order to avoid deriving mind from matter, or invoking any supra-experiential reality, Durkheim says that it 'is no longer necessary to go beyond experience' – and the specific experience to which he is referring is the 'super-individual reality that we experience in society'. He considers that men do not make the world in their own conscious image any more than that the world has imposed itself upon them, indeed 'they have done both at the same time' (pp. 16–18). Although within the *Elementary Forms* he makes occasional reference to 'objectivities' and to 'the nature of things' he continues to speak throughout to a 'super-individual reality' which is not the material world – it is society as a symbolic universe.

For Durkheim, society is the fundamental and primary reality; without it there is no humankind – but this is a reciprocal dependency. Society can only become realised, can only become conscious of itself and thus make its influence felt through the collective behaviour of its members – that is, through their capacity to communicate symbolically. Out of this concerted conduct springs the collective representations and sentiments of society and, further, the fundamental categories of thought, for they too are collective representations. So humankind finds expression only in and through the social bond; and, of course, this bond is itself an expression of sociology's epistemology.

> Anthropology and in particular Durkheim in the *Année Sociologique* group developed a tradition that is continued in the structuralism of Levi-Strauss. And while Bourdieu takes issue with the Durkheimian model, the social determinism that works via the formation of individual habitus indicates a continued fascination with what might be called Kantian subjectivity, and with the social bases of cultural classification. Certainly, the generation of schemes of classification and of social distinction in the practice of social relations is an essential ingredient in the formation of social and individual identity.
>
> (Lash and Friedman 1992: 4)

The movement from the early to the late Durkheim depicts a move from form to content. The *Rules* instances a firm positing of society as a concrete reality and implies an abstract and implicit concept of the person within this model; man as consciousness emerges as an epiphenomenon of society. In the place of a member's consciousness the *Rules* substitutes collective responses to constraint. Such positivism sets a strict limit to human understanding and creativity – the limit being not merely the isolated individual's sense impression, but the sense impressions of the individual as a compelled member of a unified collective consciousness. The collective consciousness is thus the teleological representation of the ultimate and finite reality structure.

THE SACRED AND THE PROFANE

In the later Durkheim symbolism is produced as fundamental to cultural formation, it can give rise to the self as potentially analogous to society but also as potentially different from that society. Thus symbolism is consciously creative, its occurrence and its interpretation, both by lay members of particular forms of society and by Durkheim as the methodological architect of these different forms of understanding, distances the sign from the signified. The capacity to symbolise opens up the distinction between objects-in-thought and objects-in-reality which were conflated in Durkheim's early realist epistemology. The content of the person is now imbued with potential and choice. Durkheim articulates this sense of diffusion between the collective and the individual representations through his concepts of the 'sacred' and 'profane'. Initially, the presence of sacred things provides a substantive criterion for the existence of religion. Sacredness, then, denotes religiosity.

At another level, this common characteristic of all religious belief, namely the recognition of the sacred and the profane, presupposes a classification of all things, actual and imaginary, into two opposing domains. The two realms are not alternatives, they are profoundly distinct, ranked in terms of power and dignity, and insulated by antagonism and hostility. This is the essentialism at the root of transgressive conduct: 'The sacred is par excellence that which the profane should not touch, and cannot touch with impunity' (Durkheim 1971: 40). The two orders jealously patrol their own boundaries to prevent the contamination of one by the other and thus the perpetually revivified structure of interdictions or taboos serves to keep things apart. Transition from one realm to the other is not wholly precluded, and it requires not movement but metamorphosis.

At yet a further level Durkheim's notions of the sacred and the profane reflect the experiential tension between the social interest and the personal interest. The sacred may be seen to represent public knowledge and social institutions, and the profane to represent the potential of individual consciousness – it is that which is always threatening to bring down the sacred; it is that which, in Douglas's (1966) terms, promises 'danger', as we shall soon see. The bifurcation of human interests provided for by these deep structural binaries reveals the grounds of the epistemological differences between the mechanical positivism of the early Durkheim and the organic hermeneutic of the late Durkheim, and these grounds are moral.

> Douglas selected for inclusion a part of Hertz's book on the hand . . . in which he argues that the distinction between right- and left-handedness concerns the sacred and the profane. He saw this as a widespread distinction that could not be explained in terms of 'nature'. He did not deny that there were physical differences between the two sides of the body, he only denied that such differences explained the consistency with which diverse cultures affirm the priority of the right hand. Hertz's interest in the hand derived from the fact that it stood for an abstract principle – the sacred and the profane must be kept separate and their relationship strictly controlled for the sake of (a sense of) order.
>
> (Jordanova 1994: 253)

The early work proceeds from compact, continuous symbols. Such symbols occur as social facts which are contingent upon mechanical perception; we feel their constraint, we observe their presence. Their sacredness derives from their reification (or substantively their deification) into constant components of a consensus world view. This characterises the method, it emanates from close, shared, uncritical communities of thinkers, and its moral imperative is a demand for obligation, a membership of unquestioning allegiance.

The later Durkheim takes up a concern with the potency of diffused, fragmented symbols. This is a symbolic universe potentially populated by varieties of egoism. Within such a model all shifts towards the ascendance of the individual over the collective threaten to produce a crisis in our classificatory systems – a deregulation, a condition already predicted in *Division of Labour* as 'anomie'. With reference to primitive religion Durkheim shows us in the *Elementary Forms* that a 'totem' is identified with an object of nature and thus produces it as different and knowable, that is, as having boundaries. The totem is in itself symbolic of the social group that produced it as a totem. Thus proliferating groups within any social structure 'objectify themselves' in material objects as totems; the totem then acts as an emblem which the member identifies with and thus, through identification, remains part of his group. Elementary methodic practices, like ritual, can now be seen to involve the periodic celebration and renewal of collective sentiments by way of the symbolic totem.

The impact of the study of totemic religion on Durkheim's later epistemology, then, is that totems seem to demonstrate the beginnings of understanding. Totems are not the things themselves, they stand for or in the place of things and forms of relationship – in this sense they are metaphoric. Thus they instance a break from the continuity provided by compact symbols between material reality and consciousness, they act as a mediating order whose status derives from the work of interpretation. Totems, then, belong to difference, in that they require the individual to relate to them as something other than they manifestly are; totems also are derived from difference in that they are brought into being through an elementary affective division of labour. In both these ways totems are potentially profane, that is, they most forcefully give rise to the tension between consensus understanding and belief, and individual interpretation. To live in a world of diffused symbols but to share that world requires an organic epistemology, it requires self-conscious discipline and commitment, not a sense of obligation of allegiance.

The organic epistemology rests on the distinction between the sign and the referent; things are not as they appear. Their appearance is contingent upon intentionality which is saved from animalism through a theoretical commitment to a principled way of formulating the world. This is the community experience of the shared totem of an elected tradition. The constraint inherent in the positivistic mechanical model, comprised of *sui generic* and the spatialised consciousness, now requires individual representation. The organic form of life is ordered, as it is social, but its order derives not from determinism but from interpretation and reflexivity. It presents itself reflexively as a formulation which is open to and available for reflexive formulations. The disciplined character of this new way of realising the world depends not on obedience to external methodological rules but on a thoughtful explication of grounds – its availability. This subtle normative order may be likened to the experiential constraint of taboo, but the sacred writ is no longer clear to us, as Durkheim has told us:

> the old gods are growing old or already dead, and others are not yet born it is life itself, and not a dead past which can produce a living cult.
>
> (Durkheim 1971: 427)

There is an early resonance here with the direction in which Nietzsche will develop our problematic, as explored in Chapter 3, and then Bataille (following Nietzsche), as explored in Chapter 4. Pefanis (1991) expresses the latter development in a penetrating synoptic passage:

> . . . the death of God. With this death so disappears the transcendental

> guarantee of individual sovereignty, and what also disappears is that limit condition in thought that God represented; there is no exteriority of being. This lack of an existential guarantee, though hardly regretted, is associated with the demise of the 'sacred' (a theme of the Durkheimian school), and leads in Bataille's thought to a strategy and a method (as opposed to a project) of going to the limits, of thought, notions, beliefs and morals – and then transgressing those very limits in order to delimit their operation. . . .

(Pefanis 1991: 45)

The rules are no longer clear and we are freer because of this. Our responsibility, however, is to constitute the social world and to believe in those constitutions, for, as Durkheim says, we can no longer receive the world with a fixed stare, that is, from closed systems of knowledge:

> for faith is before all else an impetus to action, while science, no matter how far it may be pushed, always remains at a distance from this. Science is fragmentary and incomplete; it advances but slowly and is never finished; but life cannot wait.

(Durkheim 1971: 431)

That 'life cannot wait' is sufficient as grounds and manifesto for the emergent and proactive visionary. Durkheim's double vision was no absolutist triumph over the will; his dual ways of being/seeing provided inspiration and fortitude in the face of modern and late modern tendencies to blur and distort both the boundary and the category contained. Though images became unclear and indecisive with the progress of the century, some certainty, through moral and altruistic purpose, was provided by Durkheim's view. His purpose must remain, however, for the active theorist qua social member to peer onwards and yet beyond. The postmodern visionary is no longer bound to concerns with the dimension of 'heaven to earth' in ensuring pure sight, but rather with a concentration on horizons for the combined human and political purposes of providing fixity in the face of nausea and future in the face of time's end.

MARY DOUGLAS AND THE CONCEPTS OF PURITY AND DANGER

All cultures, it would seem, have mechanisms through which they either resolve or come to terms with anomolies which would otherwise disrupt or indeed defy their basic assumptions. The sense of order within society is, then, hedged around with notions of risk. The risk is not a real entity but its perception provides for a way of sustaining the fragility of the bonds that hold us together. As Douglas herself has said:

> The very word 'risk' could be dropped from politics. 'Danger' would do the work just as well. When 'risk' enters as a concept in political debate, it becomes a menacing thing, like a flood, an earthquake, or a thrown brick. But it is not a thing, it is a way of thinking, and a highly artificial contrivance at that.
>
> (Douglas 1994: 46)

The nature of the risk, the threat, and the ways in which that risk is handled are most instructive concerning the moral bond and the social structure of the society in question. Herein lies the artistry of transgression, the diagnostic role of transgression, and the value of transgression as a touch-stone of social relations.

Douglas works from primitive religion to demonstrate the impact and centrality of rituals of purity and impurity within society in general. She tells us that the movement or transformation from one realm to another is an act of pollution and that all societies have public symbolic displays that are meant to restrict or indeed prevent such pollution. And so Douglas says:

> Pollution ideas work in the life of society at two levels, one largely instrumental, one expressive. At the first level, the more obvious one, we find people trying to influence each others behaviour. Beliefs reinforce social pressures . . . Political power is usually held precariously and primitive rulers are no exception. So we find their legitimate pretensions backed by beliefs in extraordinary powers emanating from their persons . . . Similarly the ideal order of society is guarded by dangers which threaten transgressors . . . The whole universe is harnessed to men's attempts to force one another into good citizenship. Thus we find that certain moral codes are upheld and certain social rules defined by beliefs in dangerous contagion . . .
>
> [A]s we examine pollution beliefs we find that the kind of contacts which are thought dangerous also carry a symbolic load. This is a more interesting level at which pollution ideas relate to social life. I believe that some pollutions are used as analogies for expressing a general view of the social order.
>
> (Douglas 1966: 13–14)

Society is, then, a complicated classificatory system. It is a system that is simultaneously cognitive, political and moral. The cognitive element stems from a tradition that Douglas shares with Durkheim, Mauss and Evans-Pritchard, namely that the basic categories of things are categories of people. Even though our contemporary scientific taxonomies seems light-years away from primitive cosmologies they are nevertheless connected without a break in continuity. The interlocking and hierarchical forms of relationship that the primitive enjoys are projected out onto the natural world through the symbolic mode of totems, and each sector of the natural becomes transformed into the cultural through understanding and incorporation. Different animals exist within a branching classificatory system which is a reflection of the pattern of kinship groups, clans and moieties that constituted the matrix of social belonging in a simple society. So the cognitive structure reflects the patterning of social relationships and the political strategies that people develop to preserve the status quo and also, necessarily, to keep the existing pattern of relationships intact. Politics enforces those taken-for-granted assumptions. The moral bond, then, assures that the expressive element of a society is maintained through collective sentiments. To attempt to alter the classificatory system is to strike at the heart of the social. Transgressor beware; you may test the boundaries but you may also bring down the full weight of Durkheim's retribution on your head and this is not something that you can talk your way out of. Galileo, for example, paid the ultimate price for challenging the dominant system of classification; Darwin had the good fortune to espouse his form of heresy in slightly more enlightened times. The experience of social life is as the experience of a series of compartments, each pure on the inside and insulated around the margins. The space between these compartments is dangerous and threatens not just the marginalised individual but the whole system. The journey through these spaces and its successful management (or not) will be explored soon through the work of both Van Gennep (1902) and Turner (1974). And Douglas summarises the transgressor thus:

> The polluting person is always in the wrong. He has developed some wrong condition or simply crossed some line which should not have been crossed and this displacement unleashes danger for someone . . . Pollution can be committed intentionally, but intention is irrelevant to the effect – it is more likely to happen inadvertently.
>
> This is as near as I can get to defining a particular class of dangers which are not powers vested in humans, but which can be released by

human action. The power which presents a danger for careless humans is very evidently a power inherent in the structure of ideas, a power by which the structure is expected to protect itself.

(Douglas 1966: 136)

And she continues:

The idea of society is a powerful image. It is potent in its own right to control or to stir men to action. This image has a form: it has external boundaries, margins, internal structure. Its outlines contain power to reward conformity and repulse attack. There is energy in its margins and unstructured areas. For symbols of society any human experience of structures, margins or boundaries is ready to hand.

(Douglas 1966: 137)

Now Douglas's arguments are no arcane dissertation applying solely to the distant, exotic and primitive peoples hidden around the globe and accessible only to the subtle reach of the anthropologist. This anthropology is practical and applied, and speaks (through its self-acclaimed structuralism) of universal and deep-structural dispositions that are common to all of our humanity, albeit in a variety of surface-structural forms. Take, as we all mostly do, sexuality. Douglas provides a rich treasure-house of exemplars concerning its regulation across humankind; however, we do not require a saturation of ethnographic data to grasp the point, we need only look to ourselves and the contemporary context of our own sexual conduct. We are all fully aware, both implicitly and explicitly, of the variety of permissable combinations of relationship that are available to us – the purity resides in adult, heterosexual, monogamous union, preferably further qualified by ethnicity, religion and even social class. Variations on this configuration are clearly available and equally clearly the outcome of political process, in many cases still unresolved. Gay relationships are recognised in contemporary society, but are all the surrounding issues concerning property and legality and parenthood as yet equivalent? Monogamy is still at a high premium in permanent relationships, perhaps not so in pre-permanent relationships but certainly not on the basis of gender equality. Age differences in partners seems less of a contentious issue until one of the couple emerges from the category 'child' at which point the senior partner, by dint of the corruption, defilement and pollution wrought through the exchange of their bodily fluids, becomes a contemporary danger *nonpareil*. Sex with a child qualifies the miscreant (transgressor) for occupancy of a category far beyond most people's imaginings, a monster circus that pales the 'slags', 'philanderers', 'whores', 'adulterers', 'queers', 'dykes', 'trannies', 'S and Ms', 'dog-botherers' and even 'mother-fuckers' into insignificance. Paedophilia is surely the hyperbole of pollution, an act or lifestyle that induces not just displeasure but flesh-creeping loathing in a society that simultaneously feeds on a diet of fast-food entertainment sexuality, and one that is not even two centuries away from such manifestations of behaviour being accepted as routine.

Sex marks the spot! Clearly we experience social life, in this instance through our sexuality, as consisting of people joined or separated by a series of lines which have to be honoured and preserved. Some of these lines are guarded by moral codes, others by sharp physical sanctions. Beyond the approbation of the collective other we also know that sexual practice is further organised in relation to the issues of chastity, virginity, menstruation, potency, sexually transmitted disease, HIV and guilt. It is a local playground for transgression and its repression provides for a sumptuous libidinal swamp of both waking and unconscious fantasy and reversal. To this degree the internal transgression is a categorical journey, unshared and perhaps unsharable, but testimony to the power of the outside, its constraint and regulation through taboo. Those dark places further compel us to watch others either for liberation or relief, or perhaps for salvation.

Even in an age of reason we are all still stalked by narratives of blindness caused by masturbation, mutants engendered by consanguinity and so on, the instrumental fables that protect an expressive order. In effect, then, the pollution is neither high nor low, it resides in the space of transition but is inherent in both orders. 'Therefore we find corruption enshrined in sacred places and times' (Douglas 1966: 210).

The centre of things is gradually and eventually delineated but, as Douglas asserts:

> . . . wherever the lines are precarious we find pollution ideas come to their support. Physical crossing of the social barrier is treated as a dangerous pollution, with any of the consequences we have just examined. The polluter becomes a doubly wicked object of reprobation, first because he crosses the line and second because he endangers others.
>
> (Douglas 1966: 165)

And so the transgressor's solitary journey becomes a collective bandwagon as the cycle of fracture and repair repeats:

When the community is attacked from outside at least the external danger fosters solidarity within. When it is attacked from within by wanton individuals, they can be punished and the structure publicly reaffirmed.
(Douglas 1966: 166)

TALCOTT PARSONS AND BOUNDARY-MAINTAINING SYSTEMS

There can be no work in the sociological tradition that is more complex, more comprehensive and more single-minded than Talcott Parsons's *Social System*. Parsons's work establishes a magnificent structure of social organisation integrating the dimensions of action and constraint. This edifice operates at the levels of the economic, the political, the cultural, the interactional and the personal – it is thus intended to both permeate and saturate all expressions of collective human experience. The work constitutes the oneness of the social world through two guiding metaphors: first, that of 'organicism', which speaks of the unspecific, the living and is concerned with content; second that of a 'system', which makes reference to the explicit, the inanimate and is concerned with form. A perhaps prophetic and yet somewhat dystopian vision emerges of a stable and integrated society functioning with a cybernetic efficiency. This social system seeks to transform or merge difference into communality. The boundaries within and around the system are extremely firm; they are apparent, and they are consensual. Change and deviancy present major conceptual difficulties here and any transgression would require special explanation. The expectation of the system is that its mechanisms for social and cultural reproduction are so invasive, in relation to the individual, and pervasive, in relation to the society as a whole, that 'transgression' should not present a problem at all. Now, remember, this is no empirical description of a society, it is a sophisticated model that enables the analysis of real societies in their functioning – albeit from a particular value position. Parsons's value position is that which preserves order and stability above all else. He is unashamedly 'right' in his view and you are either with him (and middle America) or, for some unintelligible reason, against him. These latter observations are not meant to trivialise the power and delicacy of Parsons's thinking but to provide a sense that here transgression could never be an heroic concept.

. . . the fact remains that all social action is normatively oriented, and that the value-orientations embodied in these norms must to a degree be common to the actors in an institutionally integrated interactive system. It is this circumstance which makes the problem of conformity and deviance a major axis of the analysis of social systems . . . The crucial significance of this problem focus derives as we have seen from two fundamental considerations; first that the frame of reference of action makes the concept of orientation a primary focus of analysis and second, the fact that we are dealing with the 'boundary-maintaining' type of system, which defines what we must mean by the concept of integration of the system.

(Parsons 1951: 251)

Parsons's concerns are grounded in the Hobbesian problem of order. However, within the sociological tradition, Hobbes's *Leviathan*, the monstrous form of the political state which provides for and simultaneously symbolises the unity of the people, is supplanted by the concept of 'society'. Society becomes the monitor for all order and it further inculcates a set of rules of conduct which are enforced less by individual will and political sovereignty than by society's own pre-existence. This supra-individual monolith remains the unquestioned origin of all causality and all explanation within an order-based sociological tradition. O'Neill has formulated the problem thus:

. . . we will uncover the archaeology of docility that runs from Plato's *Republic* through to Parsons' *Social System*. Such an inquiry does not discover a single strategy for the production of the docile citizen. Rather, what appears is a plurality of discursive strategies . . . The two registers of docility reflect two sides of the same problem of social control, namely, how is it that individuals can be induced to commit themselves *morally* to a social order that seeks to bind them to itself *physically*, i.e., in virtue of its discovery of certain laws of association. The conventional wisdom holds that Parsons' structural functionalism sublimates the moral question in favour of its analytic resolution, overriding critical consciousness with the normative claims of social consensus. Whether from a Hobbesian or Freudian perspective, sociology has always flirted with the discovery of a social physics . . . The dream of the social sciences lies in the search for control strategies that would overlap the micro and macro orders of behaviour in a single order of administration . . . In other words, despite the analytic power of the Parsonian vision, the discipline of sociology is not only a cognitive science but a moral science whose object is the social production of a docile citizenry.

(O'Neill 1995: 26–7)

To grasp the extent of the constraint that Parsons has institution-alised we require a brief rehearsal of the main features of the social system. Simply stated, the edifice is evolved from the top down. That is, it begins from a presumption of binding central consensus values and trickles down to an anticipated conformity at the level of the individual personality. When Parsons speaks of the production of a general theory of action within the system, he is addressing the persistent translation of universal cultural values into particular social norms and orientations for specific acts. Put another way, he is asking how is it that social actors routinely develop the social norms that inform their day-to-day conduct from the deeply embedded cultural sentiments at the very heart of the social system. How does the collective consciousness become real in the minds of individual people? It is the social norms that provide the constraints by which the interaction between the basic dyad of Self and Other is governed (and we should note that 'self' and 'other' are referred to as Ego and Alter in the Parsonian lexicon). Thus the persistent and necessary translation of cultural values into social norms provides the dynamic within the System. Within the context of Parsons's first metaphor, it is as if the organism pulsates and its life-blood circulates from the universalistic centre to the particularistic individual cells that constitute the mass. Social action conceived of in these terms is what Parsons refers to as 'instrumental activism'.

The social norms become axial to the total apparatus; they are realised as both the means and the ends of all action within the system. Beyond this the social norms also provide the source of 'identity' between the individual actor and the complete system, and the overall social order itself resides in the identity between the actor and the system. The concept of 'identification' is an important one to Parsons and one that he developed from a reworking of Freud. In Freud's theory of psychosexual development the narcissistic infant was thought capable of a primitive form of object-choice, called 'identification', in which it sought an object conceived of in its own image which it therefore desired with an intensity matched only by its love for itself. In Parsons's social system the social norms are the source of this identity because they diminish the potential distinction between the self and the collectivity by engendering a coinciding set of interests for both the self and the collectivity. It is through this basic identification that individuals become committed to the social system, that they become claimed as members and, significantly, that their behaviours cohere. The social norms therefore establish the ground rules of social life and any social system achieves stability when the norms are effective in governing and maintaining interaction.

We should now look, in broader terms, at how the social system is constructed and how its multiple segments articulate. At another level this will involve a moral tale of how the living body, the 'organism', is generated, and how, through its functioning, it transmogrifies into a machine. From the outset the system is confronted by the problem of order; however, it is simultaneously defined by Parsons in terms of that very order. At the analytic level, the social order is maintained by two pervasive system tendencies which are shared by all systems whether they are social, biological, linguistic, mathematical or whatever. These tendencies Parsons calls 'functional prerequisites' and they signify, first, the drive towards self maintenance and, second, the drive towards boundary maintenance. These functional prerequisites refer to the inside and the outside respectively: the former to the system's capacity to sustain itself, to maintain its own equilibrium and to regulate its internal homeostatic balance; and the latter to the system's continuous capacity to pronounce its difference from other systems, to demarcate its boundaries and thus to stand in a positive and delineated relationship to its environment. We should note that these two systems do emerge primarily from bio-systems theory and they constitute the point at which the metaphors of the systemic and the organic merge.

> We are here concerned with what has been called the 'boundary-maintaining' type of system. For this type of system . . . the concept of integration has a double reference: (a) to the compatibility of the components of the system with each other so that change is not necessitated before equilibrium can be reached, and (b) to the maintenance of the conditions of the distinctiveness of the system within its boundaries over against its environment.
>
> (Parsons 1951: 36, footnote)

If we examine the actual framework of the social system more closely we find that it is further comprised of three distinct sub-systems. It is the functional interchange between the sub-systems which provides for both the evolution of the overall system and its emergent qualities. The purposes of the sub-systems are to ensure the survival, the maintenance and the growth of the wider system. They are: the 'physical' sub-system, the 'cultural' sub-system and the 'personality' sub-system.

As alluded to earlier, there is a significant psycho-analytic dimension in Parsons's theorising about the child which appears not simply through his application of certain Freudian categories but more insistently through the urgency with which he emphasises the need to penetrate inner selves. Essentially the social system is finally dependent upon the successful capture of total personalities. This capture eclipses the possibility of individual divergence, dissolution, dissent or difference. Clearly this directly addresses our topic of transgression.

Despite the compulsive Freudian drive in Parsons's constitution of the child there is a paradox here, namely that in a strong sense personality theory and the consequent specification of identity emergence are not very important in his work. Parsons parades his primary commitment throughout and this is a commitment to addressing the problems relating to the stability of complex social formations. Personalities are, of course, significant here, but their embodiment, namely social actors, come to be constructed in terms of the features they display that are pertinent to their functioning in the wider context, not those relevant to their difference and individuality. It is their qualities as cogs in the machine that are to be stressed. The system seeks to undermine the autonomy of the self and any subsequent expression of difference. Following from such an aspiration Parsons's theory is characterised by a stable unitary isomorphism. This entails that all structural aspects of the social world – from total social systems, through sub-systems and particular institutions down to the constitution of individual personalities – are to be viewed as formally analogous to one another. Thus personalities are microcosmically analogous to total social systems; they share the same form, content and repertoire of responses and they are similarly oriented in relation to the same universal set of choices or 'pattern variables'.

With this isomorphism in mind we can proceed to the fundamental elements of the Parsonian personality theory, which he calls 'need dispositions'. The need dispositions display two features: first, a kind of performance or activity; and second a kind of sanction or satisfaction. Here then are the perfect ingredients for a homeostatic balance between desire and satiation. At a different level, as it is the case that all 'need dispositions' have built-in regulators, we also witness Parsonian governance at work, namely the iron hand of coercion concealed within the velvet glove of normative constraint. The essential conceptual model remains that of a naturalistic personality comprised of a battery of 'need dispositions', the gratification of which is neither wholly compatible with nor entirely possible within the personal and material limitations imposed by the social structure. Desire and constraint clash head-on and the outcome is the greater good of the collectivity.

> The definition of a system as boundary-maintaining is a way of saying that, relative to its environment, that is to the fluctuations in the factors of the environment, it maintains certain constancies of pattern, whether this constancy be static or moving. These elements of the constancy of pattern must constitute a fundamental point of reference for the analysis of process in that system. From a certain point of view these processes are to be defined as the processes of maintenance of the constant patterns.
>
> (Parsons 1951: 482)

As with Freud's theory before, in Parsons the social bond is seen to reside in repression. The threat of infantile sexuality and the difference presented by childhood must be treated as pathological. Based on this commitment and given the integrity of a system contingent upon isomorphism the socialisation process serves effectively to maintain both the inside and the outside within the requirements of order. That is to say that the socialisation process maintains the personality system and by implication the whole social system through the very process of optimising gratification within the limits placed by the social structure. It is a perfect regulatory mechanism; it both incorporates and contains. The boundaries are maintained such that the centre should always hold.

VAN GENNEP AND *RITES DE PASSAGE*

Van Gennep was writing at the same time and on the edge of Durkheim's *l'Année* group. His contribution to anthropological thought is both singular and formative. Having assimilated the concept of boundary as central to human and social experience he went on to explore the symbolism, the emotionality and the practical difficulties presented in the transition through or across boundaries. These were the rites of passage from one category or status to another. In a lighthearted sense one might see his work as a transgressive's workshop manual. Of course, this is not the case. The transitions to which he refers are frightening, dangerous and damaging but also predictable, expected and routine. Transgression is always a step into the unknown and a step that is without precedent. He is interested in movements at the periphery, crossings of the threshold, entries and exits to social categories and statuses and the symbolic apparatus that both accompany and enable them. As Mary Douglas put it:

> . . . Van Gennep had more sociological insight. He saw society as a house with rooms and corridors in which passage from one to another is dangerous. Danger lies in transitional states; simply because transition is neither one state or the next, it is undefinable. The person who must pass from one to another is himself in danger and emanates danger to others. The danger is controlled by ritual which precisely separates him from his old status, segregates him for a time and then publicly declares his entry into a new status. Not only is transition itself dangerous, but also the rituals of segregation are the most dangerous phase of the rites. So often do we read that boys die in initiation ceremonies . . . [the] dangers express something important about marginality.
>
> (Douglas 1966: 116)

These transitions are all, always at some level, about death and rebirth. The demise of boyhood and the beginning of manhood; girl to woman; single to married; working to retired; child to citizen and so on. An interesting danger of the transitional zone is the category adolescent created quite recently in the West which describes the twilight arena of crypto-adulthood and quasi-childhood, a lack of status that is defined by ungovernable mayhem. Van Gennep is always concerned with both the dynamism and also the generality of such process.

> . . . we encounter a wide degree of general similarity among ceremonies of birth, childhood, social puberty, betrothal, marriage, pregnancy, fatherhood, initiation into religious societies, and funerals. In this respect, man's life resembles nature, from which neither the individual nor the society stands as independent. The universe itself is governed by a periodicity which has repercussions on human life, with stages and transitions, movements forward and periods of relative inactivity.
>
> (Van Gennep 1960: 3)

Van Gennep delineated a three-part transmutation within *rites de passage* both across social space and through social time. The symbolic narrative runs inexorably from ordered world to ordered world, involving a release (separation) and an acceptance (reaggregation). However, these two symbolic footprints are punctuated by a site of value-less, nihilistic freefall (margin or limen) where almost anything can happen. This is seen in the example of adolescence. This 'in-between' stage is also the space that has been picked up by Turner (1974) and developed as his theory of 'liminality'.

VICTOR TURNER AND LIMINALITY

Turner makes no disguise of his debt to Van Gennep, he speaks of 'borrowing' the concept of liminality. His insight, however, is into the intricacies of the transitional, non-ordered, space/time outside of conventional space/time. In a delightful passage he tells us:

> Liminality is a term borrowed from Arnold van Gennep's formulation of *rites de passage*, 'transition rites' – which accompany every change of state or social position, or certain points in age. These are marked by three phases: separation, margin (or *limen* – the Latin for threshold, signifying the great importance of real or symbolic thresholds at this middle period of the rites, though *cunicular*, 'being in a tunnel', would better describe the quality of this phase in many cases, its hidden nature, its sometimes mysterious darkness), and reaggregation.
>
> (Turner 1974: 232)

And it is this mysterious darkness that he seeks to illuminate but not depotentiate. The status (or rather lack of status) location that he theorises is, in many senses, culturally imperceptible. The individual liminar, who Turner accounts for as a traveller or a passenger, is marked out by ambiguity – that is, they are not marked out at all. Their image is hazy, they occupy a cultural miasma rather than any identifiable class or fixed position. They are, in the well worn phrase, 'neither one thing nor t'other'. We must conceive of a domain that is, of course, in time yet timeless. Its atemporality derives from the fact that it is a domain without any of the recognisable (and thus measurable) attributes of the individual's past status or his status yet to come. The liminar's outsiderhood derives then from his lack of structural referents within a particular symbolic system, unlike marginals who simply fall short. The transgressor may aspire to a permanent state of liminality but his purpose is in the power of his expulsion and his elan resides in the disruption to the status quo.

Man truly does not live by bread alone; he is 'turned on' by legend, literature, and art, and his life is made glowingly meaningful by these and similar modalities of culture.

(Turner 1974: 165)

To step wilfully outside of these modalities is to elude meaning.

FREUD AND TABOO

I want to end this chapter with Freud. His work is not truly nor simply about margins in social life but I do not know where else to put him and he will not go away. Freud addresses our topic primarily in his consideration of *Totem and Taboo*, where from the outset he acknowledges the difficulty in providing an adequate definition, a difficulty shared by anthropologists and social theorists more generally.

> The meaning of 'taboo', as we see it, diverges in two contrary directions. To us it means, on the one hand, 'sacred', 'consecrated', and on the other 'uncanny', 'dangerous', 'forbidden', 'unclean' . . . Thus 'taboo' has about it a sense of something unapproachable, and it is principally expressed in prohibitions and restrictions. Our collocation 'holy dread' would often coincide in meaning with 'taboo'.

(Freud 1950: 18)

He takes as a working hypothesis the idea that taboos are prohibitions, boundaries in the broadest sense, that cultures place around a whole range of possible phenomena from specific things, through places, to people and, most significantly, to courses of action: 'Taboos are mainly expressed in prohibitions . . . ' (Freud 1950: 69). There is a creeping evolutionism inherent in the thesis which exercises the notion that the savage mind, which has its categorical system enforced and buttressed by the constraints of taboo, is comparable with childhood learning mentality and the intellectual disposition of adult obsessional neurotics. The child, through socialisation, is forbidden to do some things or relate to some objects or places. These prohibitions become very deep-seated but are also experienced by the individual in an emotionally ambiguous fashion. The forbidden engenders the fruit of desire itself, thus another stream in the understanding of transgression emerges. What is forbidden, what is beyond the boundary, what is potentially unclean carries with it a propulsion to desire in equal measure. The banned fuels and magnetises the lust, and the condemned object, place, person or course of action takes on a mesmeric eroticism. This, for Freud, illuminates our civilised concepts of conscience:

> If I am not mistaken, the explanation of taboo also throws light on the nature and origins of conscience. It is possible, without stretching the sense of the terms, to speak of taboo conscience or, after a taboo has been violated, of a taboo sense of guilt. Taboo conscience is probably the earliest form in which the phenomenon of conscience is met with . . . Indeed, in some languages the words for 'conscience' and 'consciousness' can scarcely be distinguished.
>
> (Freud 1950: 67–8)

It also establishes the binary grounds for our assumption of 'good' and 'evil':

> According to him [Wundt], the distinction between 'scared' and 'unclean' did not exist in the primitive beginnings of taboo. For that very reason those concepts were at this stage without the peculiar significance which they could acquire when they became opposed to each other.
>
> (Freud 1950: 24–5)

Although, inevitably taken from a psycho-analytic perspective, Freud spends much of the work considering the personality, practice and isolation of the contemporary neurotic and the appropriate treatment regime, his broader cultural explorations enhance our growing view of the transgressive act standing within a socio-cultural context and also serving a twofold social function of death and renewal.

> It is feared among primitive peoples that the violation of a taboo will be followed by a punishment, as a rule by some serious illness or by death. The punishment threatens to fall on whoever was responsible for violating the taboo. In obsessional neurosis the case is different. What the patient fears if he performs some forbidden act is that a punishment will fall not on himself but on someone else . . . Here then the neurotic seems to be behaving altruistically and primitive man egoistically. Only if the violation of the taboo is not automatically avenged upon the wrong-doer does a collective feeling arise among savages that they are threatened by the outrage and thereupon hasten to carry out the

omitted punishment themselves. There is no difficulty in explaining the mechanism of this solidarity. What is in question is fear of an infectious example, of the temptation to imitate – that is, of the contagious character of taboo. If one person succeeds in gratifying a repressed desire, the same desire is bound to be kindled in all the other members of the community. In order to keep the temptation down, the envied transgressor must be deprived of the fruit of his enterprise; and the punishment will not infrequently give those who carry it out the same outrage under colour of an act of expiation. This is indeed one of the foundations of the human penal system and it is based, no doubt correctly, on the assumption that the prohibited impulses are present alike in the criminal and in the avenging community. In this, psycho-analysis is more than confirming the habitual pronouncement or the pious, we are all miserable sinners.

(Freud 1950: 71–2)

This passage is worth quoting at length as it resonates with so many of the juxtapositional pairs that have acted as markers throughout this chapter, including Durkheim's forms of solidarity and retributive as opposed to restitutive justice.

In a much later work, *Civilization and Its Discontents* (1930), Freud once again addresses the boundaries between the self and the collectivity and focuses on what he referred to as 'the irremediable antagonism between the demands of instinct and the restrictions of civilization'. What he establishes here is the spatial sense of a social world, a civilisation, held intact by the dams and constraints built into individual psyches through the work of successful psycho-sexual development. The social world is constituted as a kind of 'organic repression' and clearly the self emerges, as if enabled, through this process of constraint. The social bond, then, resides in repression. Transgression continues to build as an issue of morality, civilisation, asociality and eroticism. The introduction of the notion of civilisation to the equation is interesting. What this allows for is the possibility of transgression as an issue of lifestyle or social stratification. We may look to the metaphors of 'squalor', 'coarseness', 'baseness' and even 'barbarism' through which the West has viewed the Third World or, indeed, the Victorian middle classes routinely understood the great lumpen outcast working populations in their own cities. Although Freud was also concerned with the discontents that were inherent within the social condition as it systematically transported humankind further and yet further out of touch with its nature, others, such as Norbert Elias, have seen the gathering of manners and, shall we say, mannerisms, through modernity as part of an historical progress, a *Civilising Process* which serves to equate transgression with deviance.

3

TO HAVE DONE WITH THE
JUDGEMENT OF GOD

This chapter seeks to introduce the philosophical foundations of many
of the arguments to follow. The German tradition, in the form of Hegel
and Nietzsche, both established and challenged a whole range of beliefs
fundamental to Western society. In so doing they began a heated conversation in post-structural and postmodern thinking that remains unresolved
today but within which transgression of the sacred becomes a pivotal
conceptual vehicle.

> . . . whether it is through logic or epistemology, whether through
> Marx or Nietzsche our entire epoche struggles to disengage itself from
> Hegel.
>
> (Foucault 1971: 28)

Apart from the overshadowing influence of Kantian epistemology,
British philosophy in the second half of the twentieth century had an
ambivalent relationship with German philosophy. It all appeared preoccupied by grand visions of power, overwhelming systems linking thought
and citizenship, and an ethical dimension that could be construed as
extreme. More specifically the work had become associated with the politics
of its national boundaries and, rightly or wrongly, the monumentally

anti-human movements that had emerged within that span. Hegel, one way or another, had inspired Marx and thus, by implication, the bloody revolutions that had stirred and slaughtered in the distortions of his wake; he was also seen to have a continuity with Hitler. Popper described Hegel, at considerable and vituperative length, as an enemy of the open society:

> Hegel's influence, and especially that of his cant, is still very powerful in moral and social philosophy and in the social and political sciences . . . Especially the philosophers of history, and of education are still to a very large extent under its sway. In politics this is shown most drastically by the fact that the Marxist extreme left wing, as well as the conservative centre, and the fascist extreme right, all base their political philosophies on Hegel; the left wing replaces the war of nations which appears in Hegel's historicist scheme by the war of classes, the extreme right replaces it by the war of races; but both of them follow him more or less consciously.
>
> (Popper 1947: 29–30)

Nietzsche, the poor demented poet of infinite human possibility, was seen to be the direct inspiration for National Socialism and for the vile taint of holocaust transgression from which the designation, humanity, will never rightly recover. So, regarding them both, Bertrand Russell in his overambitious precis of Western philosophy, and when at his most complimentary, says of Hegel that he is extremely difficult to understand and that he is extremely influential (both points it would be hard to disagree with). And of Nietzsche he opines:

> . . . I think the ultimate argument against his philosophy, as against any unpleasant but internally self-consistent ethic, lies not in an appeal to facts but in an appeal to the emotions. Nietzsche despises universal love, I feel it is the motive power to all that I desire as regards the world. His followers have had their innings, but we may hope that it is rapidly coming to an end.
>
> (Russell 1946: 739)

French philosophy, political theory and social thought has, however, shared a much closer association with both Hegel and Nietzsche. Indeed, both thinkers could properly be described as formative and certainly as setting the agenda for post-structuralism and much of postmodernism, particularly through the conduits of Bataille, Lacan, Derrida, Foucault,

Deleuze and Guattari. This, of course, is the context within which we approach their ideas in pursuit of our topic, transgression. Both Hegel and Nietzsche provide and instil the energy, the drive, the ontology and, actually, the epistemology to transgress.

Both thinkers provide a view, though not a common view, on history, on morals, on human achievement and on the deity. They have paved the way to post-Enlightenment uncertainty, nihilism, violation and desecration. A battery of concepts emerges, as a set of themes in their work, which have a continuous impact on our modern theorising. Hegel celebrates the Ideal Spirit (*Geist*) and thus establishes a theodicy:

> . . . the transformation of Christian eschatology into the philosophy of history, culminating in the teaching of Hegel that the human mind is essentially identical with the rational order of history, and so with God.
>
> (Rosen 1969: 64–5)

Hegel develops the dialectic not as a theory of knowledge but as a theory of being; he historicises the Master–Slave relation and he vaunts the Rational and the Absolute. Nietzsche has done with the judgement of God; he commits to the re-evaluation of values; and he recommends and aspires to the will to power. Let us begin our exposition with a look at Hegel. We will then pass to an additional contribution from the ideas of Alexandre Kojève (teacher of Rosen quoted above), whose original reading and subsequent lectures on Hegel's *Phenomenology of Spirit* were most directly influential on the young Bataille and Lacan, and then conclude this chapter with a reading of Nietzsche. All of this will, I trust, provide the grand philosophical framework within which transgression becomes a meaningful move.

HEGEL ON HISTORY AND LOGIC

> No one today who seriously seeks to understand the shape of the modern world can avoid coming to terms with Hegel.
>
> (Smith 1989: 14)

Despite the urgency of his presence in modern thought Hegel is older than we might imagine. Hegel lived between 1770 and 1831; he grappled with and in many senses completed Kant's project; he certainly influenced Marx but also inflamed Kierkegaard's existential irony. His philosophy, beyond being impenetrable in places, combines a rich amalgam of elements. It contains a powerful mysticism that drives a vivid and compelling universe which is, at the same time, self-confirming. The universe it builds is both coherent and cohesive, such that it has come to be described as a 'systems philosophy' – and that system contains its own method of validation. And the method of validation, though presented as an epistemology, is in fact an ontological affirmation, as it is about 'spirit', individuals and human action – the moving force of history. The elision of epistemology and ontology is, perhaps, the grand confusion that ignites the post-structuralist challenge, critique, and what we have referred to earlier as Foucault's flight.

Hegel manifests a deep-seated scepticism towards both the necessity and the possibility of difference. It is not so much that things or people are not different but rather that their meaning does not reside in the fact that they have a separate existence. There is an unreality inherent in the idea of separateness. The world is not 'made up of'; it does not 'comprise'; it is not a 'collection' of isolated and individual entities be they human or natural. The only reality for Hegel, the dominant and overwhelmingly pressing reality, is that belonging to the totality and the whole. The totality is a complex, interrelated system and the parts which are intelligible as parts gain their meaning from the meaning that is provided by the spiritual form of the totality. Now what we know of systems is that they are self-maintaining and boundary-maintaining (though Hegel's system cannot have boundaries for they would exclude the somethingness or nothingness which is other than the system and for Hegel the system is all that is the case). So we have a system that is self-maintaining and also everything. The other feature of systems is that although they contain the elements of a *physics* (to change, evolve, move – Hegel's sense of history) they are also dominated by a *statics* (the process of reproduction, replication, continuity – Hegel's sense of logic). It is for this reason that Hegel's system eschews the primacy of Kant's two fundamental categories of thought 'time' and 'space'. For Kant these two forms of experience inevitably locate all things; for Hegel these two dimensions divide phenomena, they proliferate multiplicity and they allow separateness. Time and space cannot be believed from within Hegel's system. Our eyes and minds return, of necessity, to the totality. So Hegel tells us:

> Spirit is herewith self-supporting, absolute, real being. All previous forms of consciousness are abstractions of it. They are so because spirit

analyzed itself, distinguished its own moments, and dwelt a while on each of them. This isolating of these moments presupposes spirit itself and subsists therein; in other words, the isolation of moments exists only in spirit, which is existence itself. Thus isolated, the moments have the appearance of reality existing as such; but that they are only moments or vanishing quantities is shown by their advance and retreat into their ground and essence; and this essence is just this moment and resolution of these moments.

(Hegel, *Phenomenology of Spirit*, 1807)

The much-quoted Hegelian dictum 'The real is rational and the rational is real' comes into play here. The philosopher in making such a pronouncement is not concluding some hard-nosed empiricist debate about the status of facts and reality. Rather, what we are getting in this summation is a primary commitment to the nature of being, an assumption that precedes a whole paradigm of thinking. Hegel is not concerned to measure, capture or even apprehend some sense of finitude as specified in things. This is no answer to a 'what is a table?' kind of question. Hegel is stating, from within his vision, his system, that being constitutes the whole of reality, and that being is rational. There is a persistent slide between the concepts of mind, being, reason, reality, spirit and God. This is not a logical statement (though he speaks and writes of logics) as we know it. This is a metaphysical and, indeed, spiritual belief in an 'Absolute', a totality that defines and knows all things within a common universe. Whatever is, is meant to be and here we begin to grasp the relentless determinism that Marx's view of history elicited from his partial mentor. History evolves from inevitability to entelechy by virtue of potentiality – human potentiality. Think here of a complex of: transgression as an historical quest; revolution as a form of transgression; Marx's alienation being a statement concerning being in a state of self-estrangement demanding transgression . . . more of this later.

Hegel's logic, which we now recognise to be a sophisticated exercise in metaphysics, contains two central elements which have subsequently been regarded as major contributions to philosophical thought. First we have a law of non-contradiction. That is to say that truth cannot contain propositions that are opposed, e.g. 'all swans are white but some swans are black'. However, the systems import of this law is that reality; the totality, spirit, cannot be self-contradictory. We cannot conceive of anything which exists other than reality, the absolute cannot be juxtaposed with the non-absolute. This is the area of questioning that exercises contemporary astrophysics in terms of 'what is at the edge of the universe?' or 'where does space end?' And second, the reason for the sustainability of non-contradiction within reality and the historical process is what we now all refer to as the dialectic. The dialectic is a dynamic and perpetual process (both at the level of individual argument and also at the level of historical change). The dialectic is an energy, a force. We have come to know it, though not in Hegel's own terms, as a three-part sequence of *thesis*, *antithesis* and the emergent *synthesis*. At an interactional level this may comprise 'point', 'counterpoint' and 'resolution'; and at a grandiose, macro, Marxist level 'bourgeoisie', 'proletariat' and 'revolution'. The antithesis always abrogates the thesis and the fecund combination provides for a purer and emergent form in synthesis. An example from Hegel would be the Absolute as Pure Being set against the Absolute as Not Being with the synthetic form emerging as the Absolute as Becoming.

> The dialectical principle, for Hegel, is the principle whereby apparently stable thoughts reveal their inherent instability by turning into their opposites and then into new, more complex thoughts, as the thought of being turns into the thought of nothing and then into the thought of becoming. This principle, Hegel tells us, is 'the soul of all truly scientific knowledge', and it is what gives his thinking its distinctive character by breathing life and freedom into the concepts which he thinks through, and by making his thought *move* in a way that ordinary thinking is simply not used to.
>
> (Houlgate 1991: 61)

This triadic advance is fundamental to mind, to knowledge as a whole and to the complete historical process according to Hegel. And he, like Marx to follow him, charts the stages of historical development, the stages of human knowing, the stages of citizenship and the stages of Being. So as we move from ancient China to the Prussian State we also move from sense perception to self-knowledge (Hegel's examples). The resolution and the becoming are always a finer state (no pun intended), self-knowledge and pure citizenship are the finest forms of knowing and being and constitute a oneness of subject and object. That final distinction and difference is dispensed with. Our vigorous and dynamic participation in Reality as a whole, both through history and through knowledge, renders us more real and thus more rational. To repeat, the dialectic is not a method.

The concept's moving principle, which alike engenders and dissolves the particularizations of the universal, I call 'dialectic' . . . [The] dialectic of the concept consists not simply in producing the determination as a contrary and a restriction, but in producing and seizing upon the positive content and outcome of the determination, because it is this which makes it solely a development and an immanent progress. Moreover, this dialectic is not an activity of subjective thinking applied to some matter externally, but is rather the matter's very soul putting forth its branches and fruit organically . . . To consider a thing rationally means not to bring reason to bear on the object from the outside and so to tamper with it, but to find that the object is rational on its own account; here it is mind in its freedom, the culmination of self-conscious reason, which gives actuality and engenders itself actuality and engenders itself as an existing world.

(Hegel, *The Philosophy of Right*, 1820)

We are led then to contemplate an advanced form of history/being/ thinking where thought is conscious of itself. Ideas, not objects, become the source and goal of conscious intentionality. This is the outcome of the dialectical motion of the historical process. All human actions, all changes, forces, revolutions and manifestations through history become part of a coherent and intelligible pattern that is inherent in mind. This is an appealing thesis but it is difficult at times to decide whether Hegel's view of history describes or whether it actually informs the passage of events. What, of course, we are being presented with is a thesis on transformation, its grounds, its mechanism, its process and its energy. History is the struggle of humankind overcoming and transforming various configurations of relations, relations of power, relations of property, social relations in general. Existing relations, in their different ways, oppress and inhibit the human potential for pure being and absolute knowledge. Human achievement transcends the restrictive binaries that are set in the dialectic of the historical ontological process.

Hegel's philosophy has no social import if the absolute cannot be thought. If we cannot think the absolute this means that it is therefore not our thought in the sense of not realized. The absolute is the comprehensive thinking which transcends the dichotomies between concept and intuition, theoretical and practical reason. It cannot be thought (realized) because these dichotomies and their determinants are not transcended.

(Rose 1981: 204)

The European progressive, revolutionary and Marxist tradition has nurtured a volatile relationship with the corpus of Hegel's work, with the serene side being most carefully developed by Georg Lukács, the Hungarian cultural philosopher. Lukács, who was once rather crudely referred to as 'the Marx of aesthetics', regarded Hegel as a fount of all knowledge and he developed his critique and resistance to both neo-Kantian idealism and what he saw as Nietzsche's irrationalism in the light of this. As his work developed into a fully sculpted critique of bourgeois modernism because of its individualism and decadence, he revealed a typically Hegelian commitment to metaphysics, a resistance to positivism and a strong vision of his theorising as being essentially social and political. This mosaic of elements provided the source of his concept of a 'totality' (continuous with that of Hegel) which he applied to art and literature.

> The goal of great art is to provide a picture of reality in which the contradiction between appearance and reality, the particular and the general, the immediate and the conceptual, etc., is so resolved that the two converge into a spontaneous integrity . . . The Universal appears as the quality of the individual and the particular, reality becomes manifest and can be experienced within appearance.
>
> (Lukács 1970: 34)

The philosopher Jacques Derrida is more equivocal in his relation to Hegel. On the one hand, he experiences a compelling fascination with the great system and espouses the view that inevitably intellectuals will be perpetually drawn and re-drawn to an engagement with this totalising body of work that binds thought and history inexorably. On the other hand, Derrida's deconstruction is anything but in tune with the Hegelian dialectic, quite the contrary. Where Hegel finds solution, flow and emergence through synthesis, Derrida stands against such resolve. Deconstruction is intolerant of the fusion and depotentiation of dichotomies that occurs in Hegel's metaphysics. Deconstruction needs displacement, reversal and upheaval. For Derrida, all cognitive, literary and philosophical oppositions are based on an imbalance of power (the dyad predicted by Hegel's Master–Slave dichotomy which will shall investigate shortly). Textual transgressions are required to overthrow the conventional and oppressive hierarchy. What Derrida does, in contradistinction to Hegel's coming together through the dialectic, has been described as follows:

> . . . to locate the promising marginal text, to discover the undecidable

moment, to pry it loose with the positive lever of the signifier, to reverse the resident hierarchy, only to displace it; to dismantle in order to reconstitute what is always already inscribed.

(Spivak's Preface to Derrida 1976: lxxvii)

Other contemporary French thinkers such as Jean-François Lyotard, Gilles Deleuze, Felix Guattari and primarily Michel Foucault have all been more livid in their criticisms of Hegel, in parallel with their opposition to and rejection of much of structuralism (wherein their arguments were also seeded). Simply stated, and we shall revisit this block-vote objection, they regard Hegel as an authoritarian and as a megalomaniac. They see his system as 'totalising', that is a philosophy of 'everything at all times' which runs counter to the post-structuralist urge to interrogate identity and difference. They see his philosophy of history as inevitable, relentless, deterministic and fateful in ways that stifle their postmodern desires to interrupt and fracture 'grand narratives' of time and culture. And they see his dialectic as setting oppositions within philosophy and society, which embody violence, hierarchy and oppression (e.g. man/woman, black/white, straight/gay, sane/mad, normal/pathological, true/false, appearance/essence) and treating them as benign and resolvable as opposed to the political incentive of deconstruction.

Let us look again at Hegel and return to his legacy and his beneficiaries further on in the text. A seriously important feature of Hegel's ideas is the non-separability of history and truth. For most philosophers, and implicitly for most social theorists, there is a realm of ideas that are essential and absolute and there is a realm of ideas that are historically specific. Sociology classically addresses the way that social and cultural formations are understood through an attempt to reconstruct the mindset of an epoch. Durkheim's solidarities that we visited in the previous chapter are descriptions of the ways in which societies have organised themselves through different historical periods according to the way that people understood their relationship to each other. Liberal anthropology has moved from a position of understanding non-Western cognition as if it were stupid or 'primitive' and now sees it as different and context-specific. All of this begs the question, however, as to whether 'anything' therefore 'goes', that is, a relativism leading to a nihilism because it is impossible to provide grounds for producing a hierarchy of judgement. And there is also the problem of justifying the mode of thought one employs to make sense of other and different modes of thought. We might just be brave enough to say that the routine sexism displayed in the division of labour in pre-industrial societies is intelligible given the mode of thinking employed by those people, but where do we stand on issues like female circumcision, child abuse, mass extermination and ethnic cleansing? We would surely find great difficulty in relativising such barbarities. So the idea of an absolute truth stalks our understandings. For Hegel any divergence or antagonism between history and absolute truth is misleading and unfounded. Similarly the abandonment of an idea of absolute truth in the form of science, philosophy or theology is mistaken. Hegel tells us that the absolute truth of being is found in human self-determinacy through history. Humankind is no one thing but comes in to being, constantly, through the historical process. That there is no formalism in the specification of human being means that we can be, and are, many things and many forms because of places and times, but that we are historical is the absolute truth of humankind. History and truth are coterminus. This is a startling moment, a moment of great illumination, a moment when the philosophical juggernaut flattens the intervention of subject difference. East or west, ancient or modern, all are real and all are rational. Human being finds itself in history, is found through history and finds history.

> The present world and the present form and self-consciousness of spirit contained within them all the stages that appear to have occurred earlier in history . . . What spirit is now, it has always been; the only difference is that it now possesses a richer consciousness and a more fully elaborated concept of its own nature . . . Those moments that spirit appears to have outgrown still belong to it in the depths of its present.
>
> (Hegel, *Lectures on the Philosophy of World History*, 1830)

Let us reformulate Hegel's sense of phenomenology. Within the work itself the metaphors proliferate, there is an enormous sense of power and dynamism driven by a vision which is both deeply religious and yet in touch with human achievement. The work is also scholarly yet highly poetic. Hegel conveys a strong sense of an upward journey during which knowledge becomes less finite and of greater quality. This metaphoric journey is richly textured and layers reveal a transition from the at hand to the universal; the individual to the collective; the laity to the deity; object to subject; and the commonsense to the philosophic – this is the transition of history too. Humankind, thought and being all pass through stages, not plateaus but 'whirling circles'.

The particular individual, so far as content is concerned, has also to go through the stages through which the general mind has passed, but as shapes once assumed by mind and now laid aside, as stages of a road which has been worked over and levelled out. Hence it is that, in the case of various kinds of knowledge, we find that what in former days occupied the energies of men of mature mental ability sinks to the level of information, exercises, and even pastimes, for children; and in this educational progress we can see the history of the world's culture (delineated) in faint outline.

(Hegel, *Introduction to Phenomenology of Spirit*, 1809)

These stages of thought, like the stages of civilisation culminating in the Germanic State, are punctuated with historical and philosophical achievements of great merit (Hegel being much taken by both the French Revolution and Napoleon's heroic triumphs on the battlefield) which provide markers for humankind's struggle towards self-realisation. The completion of the historical process sees the unification of human reason with the Absolute, and this is another sense of the totality. Through this staged process consciousness, as we have already stated, becomes conscious of itself, again a unification, a totality.

Because history is distinct from and more important than mere temporality, and because the notion of history is equivalent to the notion of development into form, it follows that critical theory, and in particular its real historical preconditions, can of necessity never be grasped in the present . . . For the Hegelian dialectic this problem does not arise; because its position is that of attained wisdom, the terminus of Spirit's odyssey of self-realisation.

(Heywood 1997: 52)

Self-consciousness is therefore consciousness in touch with its own integrity and necessity. Self-consciousness however, is also alone, that is in isolation. Hegel must now reveal a unifying principle, which Marx crudely appropriated in terms of class-consciousness and the transition from 'in-itself' to 'for-itself'. He does this through an invocation of the deeply metaphoric, yet often concretised, dialectical coupling of the Master and the Slave. These are forms of consciousness, types of being, ways of being in the world. They are concerned with what Heywood (1997) refers to as 'self-realisation' and the announcement of that realisation as a form of recognition – it is here that we move to a sense of commonality, a dialectic involving a shared reality, though not one involving equivalence. Self-realisation is potentially and actually combatorial. Hegel's conceptualisation of the meeting of individuals in thought, in discourse or in action, is one that is constituted around the notion of struggle, indeed mortal struggle. The resolution of such struggle divides humanity through triumph and submission, but this is not a fallen or permanent positioning. What remains is a dependency and a reciprocity. The triumphal Master has gained a recognition but only in relation to the sublimation of the Slave side – a radical contingency. There is a tension of separation (but not division) between the self-realised subject condition and the non-recognised, failed object condition. Herewith we find the space for Hegel's/ Marx's concept of alienation: it is spirit, self-realisation, work, labour in a state of self-estrangement. So when we find Hegel telling us about how a Slave may become resigned to his destiny we are hearing a theory of false consciousness, a failure to self-realise. All rationalisations (ideologies) of unfreedom represent failures to become and a passive resolve on the part of the Slave to avoid the confrontation with the Master and take refuge in a belief in a transcendental God. The Master now needs the Slave in order to persist and the Slave uses the conditions of his oppressive relation to the Master as the grounds for change, growth, becoming – historical 'self-realisation'. So the disruptive, revolutionary potential is built into Hegel's system as a fateful element in the historical process. Overcoming the binary oppression has become an inspiration for Marxist movements, Black power movements, feminist movements, existentialism, Surrealism, deconstructionism and postmodern dissatisfaction with the truths and planetary policies of late-modernity. The Master–Slave dyad is a central metaphor in Hegel's work, which has been developed, with the most profound influence, in the lectures of Kojève, as we shall soon see.

In the conclusion of this section of the book we must now address Hegel's relation to Christianity, which we have alluded to throughout this brief exposition but which is also most critical to the meaning of this chapter in the context of transgression – to have done with the judgement of God! The final atheism of the German tradition can be regarded as understanding religion in two ways. First, religion demonstrates the gulf between human potential and human reality, and second (its appeal to the Slave), it extends hope in the face of human unhappiness. It is arguable that Hegel was both a Christian philosopher and a philosopher writing in relation to the powerful influence of Christianity. Either way, the *Phenomenology of Spirit* moves through a series of narrative moments (finding homologies in the 'stages', the 'assent' and the 'circles' previously referred to) which lead us to Calvary and the Cross. The whole work can be read as a denial and ultimate abolition of exteriority. We begin engulfed in the quagmire of nature, objects, utter thing-like-ness and by 'reaching for the stars' we achieve the Absolute Spirit. The penultimate moment we explore is a flawed representation of the Absolute in the form of Christianity and we conclude with the dissolution of the dualism between subject and object at the symbolic stroke of the Crucifixion. This is also the end of history and the beginning of post-history (Fukuyama 1992). The phenomenology completes; the Master, the philosopher, man (but not alone in reason) steps outside history and the possible judgement of anything beyond himself. Powerful yet threatening stuff, it engenders a dread, a fear of freedom, an ontological insecurity, all sensations which inhibit the sovereign action of the transgressor.

KOJÈVE'S INTERVENTION

Alexandre Kojève (1902–68), a philosopher of Russian origin but educated in Berlin, emerges as an axial figure in our search for transgression. It was Kojève's philosophical destiny to bring the ideas of Hegel forward on the platform of contemporary French Marxism but in a form that both addressed the mounting fear of Hegel's overwhelming totality and also provided a range of grounded, earthly, embodied and desire-laden concepts that would enable postmodernism and post-structuralism to speak. Kojève is one of those strange, low profile figures in the history of ideas, only published in collections assembled by others, conveying most of his thoughts by private communication or in pedagogic form, and yet surrounded by an aura of power and admiration. His readings of Hegel's *Phenomenology of Spirit* have been variously described as 'anthropological' (Rose 1981), 'existential' (Houlgate 1991; Bloom in Kojève 1969) and a 'secularization' (Rosen 1969), and they thus clearly involve some descent from heaven to earth while addressing issues of self-reflexivity missed by Marx.

> Kojève is the unknown Superior whose dogma is revered, often unawares, by that important subdivision of the 'animal kingdom of the spirit' in the contemporary world – the progressivist intellectuals. In the years preceding the second world war in France, the transmission was effected by means of oral initiation to a group of persons who in turn

> took the responsibility of instructing others, and so on. . . . This
> teaching was prior to the philosophico-political speculations of J.P.
> Sartre and M. Merleau-Ponty, to the publication of *les Temps modernes*
> and the new orientation of *Esprit*, reviews which were the most
> important vehicles for the dissemination of progressivist ideology in
> France after the liberation. From that time on we have breathed Kojève's
> teaching with the air of the times.
>
> (Patri 1961: 234)

Kojève delivered a series of highly influential lectures on Hegel's
Phenomenology of Spirit at the *École Pratique des Hautes Études* in Paris during
the six years preceding the Second World War. The theme of these lectures
was a Marxist, existentialist reading of Hegel that was much influenced by
Heidegger, quite an explosive cocktail! After the war Kojève continued
with his philosophical concerns while working in the French Ministry of
Economic Affairs as a leading architect in the development of the Common
Market. More recently there has been conjecture as to whether he was in
fact a KGB agent. The 1933–9 lectures were remarkable not just for their
content but for the audience they attracted, which included such rising
stars as Georges Bataille and Jacques Lacan, but also Raymond Aron, Jean-
Paul Sartre, Maurice Merleau-Ponty, André Breton, Pierre Klossowski and
Raymond Queneau (later Kojève's editor).

One of the primary thematic strengths of Kojève's reasoning is the
constant affirmation, both explicitly and implicitly, of the significance
and import of the philosopher and the philosopher's task. This is not simply
a restatement of the long-held view that a philosophical consciousness
is in some sense a superior form of being and knowing but rather a sense
that the elevated nature of philosophical knowledge derives from its self-
reflection, primarily then, its knowledge of self. Although philosophical
endeavour has always been concerned with knowing about that which is
other than self, the Hegelian project, here recharged, is concerned with
knowing oneself and explaining the practice of one's own understandings.
This fillip for the autonomy of the philosopher provided a launch pad for
the contemporary French intelligentsia scattering from self-confirming
orthodoxy into self-asserting heterodoxy. The project (if it can be described
in the singular) of post-structuralism, or heterology, is to confront the long-
standing philosophical narrative of legitimation and to subvert it through
deconstruction. Reality is rational and this is discovered through self-
exploration.

Kojève was also a fierce and ironic exponent of the 'end of history' thesis first stated by Hegel. For Hegel this would amount to a human unification with the Absolute and a citizenry marked by the satiation of their desires – a peace and a secular heaven where spirit has no more to reveal and the past can be contemplated without the fear of a historicity of the present. For Marx this would have been the late, and yet to be revealed, stages of communism. Neither Marx nor Kojève was privileged to see the collapse of the Berlin Wall. Indeed, Marx had never seen the construction of the Berlin Wall nor the concretisation of communism into a practical form of state in the Soviet bloc, China or Cuba. Kojève had: he knew of the corrosions that had been occurring to the ideal absolute set out in the *Communist Manifesto*. Thus Kojève came to suggest, slightly tongue in cheek, that the end of history might be found in contemporary American society – the land of *haute* capitalism populated by the red-neck, pulp-consuming, couch potatoes that Adorno encountered a few years later when he moved the Frankfurt Institute to the US to avoid the Nazis! Kojève is, in fact, announcing that the completion of the task of modernity may be accompanied not by Utopia but rather by a decay and re-animalisation of humankind. In the often quoted footnote to the second edition of his published lectures he states:

> If one accepts 'the disappearance of Man at the end of History,' if one asserts that 'Man remains alive as animal' with the specification that 'what disappears is Man properly so-called' one cannot say that all the rest can be preserved indefinitely: art, love, play, etc.' . . . 'The definitive annihilation of Man properly so-called' also means the definitive disappearance of human Discourse (Logos) in the strict sense . . . What would disappear, then, is not only Philosophy or the search for discursive Wisdom, but also that Wisdom itself. For in these post-historical animals, there would no longer be any '[discursive] understanding of the World and of self.'
>
> (Kojève 1969: 160–1)

However, he then reveals that in 1959 he has found, in Japan:

> . . . a Society that is one of a kind, because it alone has for almost three centuries experienced life at the 'end of History.'
>
> (Kojève 1969: 161)

and that:

> 'Post-historical' Japanese civilization undertook ways diametrically
> opposed to the 'American way.'
>
> (Kojève 1969: 161)

With such inspiration we might begin to see why the young French intelligentsia scattered wilfully into their heterodoxies.

Kojève opened up the concept of desire in Hegel as an urgent existential issue. He sought to explore a dimension through which real, practical individuals could aspire to self-realisation and thus unite in reason. This, in part, lead to a search for a more sociological/anthropological critique of the idea of totality in Bataille's work (as we shall see in the next chapter), but neither Bataille nor Lacan find the Hegel/Kojève explanation of the satiation of desire in the citizenship of post-historical society satisfactory. The Master–Slave pattern of relationships progresses through history in a life and death battle for recognition over an idea or principle, the recurrent issue of honour. It is as if the willingness of an individual to risk his life indexes an historical shift from mere survival to living for a purpose – an elevation from animal to species being. The victor in the struggle can, however, never truly vanquish the other because of the necessary dialectic of oppositions. Thus:

> The Hegelian 'stand-off' constitutes human value as the imaginary
> effect of a desire for recognition that, though having a dialectical
> structure, can never be achieved. The value of the master is dependent
> upon the recognition and desire of the other who has, in refusing to
> go beyond the stand-off, become a slave and is therefore rendered
> unworthy of recognising the master's humanity, thereby precluding its
> completion. While the latter is ironically abandoned to an inhuman
> solitude, the former has the opportunity to work to overcome abjection.
>
> (Botting and Wilson 2001: 106–7)

It is the double negation that so troubled and exercised Kojève's followers, the 'stand-off' always represses the desire, the contingency of the Master and Slave denies the possibility of absolute fulfilment and complete recognition. The desire is always restrained by and expressed through the other and here we move to the principle of sovereignty previously explored by the Marquis de Sade and Camus and later reformed by Bataille.

> In the Kojèvian schema, transgression operates as an inverted figure
> of the dialectic, its end in the sense of an outcome. In Bataille's texts

interpretation of transgression has to be linked to the loss of philosophical and authorial sovereignty, and hence the loss of the place
which is accorded the human in the human sciences.

(Pefanis 1991: 3–4)

Beyond this, the actors in the metaphorical struggle evade any confrontation with death, which for many existentialisms and heterologies
is the singular most powerful driver of conduct, desire, moral choice and
transgression. So for Bataille and the 'transgressive' thinkers to follow,
desire must be expressed more fully and elsewhere.

Kojève's appeal to the growing band of young French intellectual
Marxists derived less from its proximity to the outbreak of the Second
World War than to the bland orthodoxies that had become distilled
in communist thought. Largely because of the literal, descriptive, correspondential version of Marx that was then concretised into the form of
Stalinism, and because of the authoritarian brutalism that was becoming
the trademark of such a regime and its thought style, the European Zeitgeist
was shifting towards a welcome for any reading of Marx that re-opened
discourses of democracy, justice, personal choice and anti-elitism. In the
1970s, after Althusser had declared an 'epistemological break' in Marx's
thought and directed attention to the 'scientific' later Marx, this alternative,
non-positivistic Marx was to be found in the early 'ideological' work such
as *The German Ideology*, but in the late 1930s the idealist revival was to be
found in a return to Hegel and specifically *The Phenomenology of Spirit*. As
Matthews (1996) puts it:

Kojève's Hegel historicized reason, and so made possible a rational
view of history. The *Phenomenology of Spirit* was taken as the key
Hegelian text for this purpose, since it offered a vision of reason as
gradually emerging from human experience, and (as Kojève saw it at
least) of human beings progressively achieving their own humanity. On
this view, to be human was not a mere biological or otherwise natural
fact about the members of our species, but rather an achievement, to
be progressively realized; and the way in which it was realized according
to Hegel pointed forward, on Kojève's reading, to the Marxist account
of human history as the history of class conflict.

(Matthews 1996: 112–13)

The shift from a positivistic to an idealist reading of Marx was part of a
search for the centrality of consciousness. Humankind has more, and is

more, than a simply cognitive relation to the world. Merely 'knowing' subjects float, without intention, around the compulsion of external and objective forms. But humankind exceeds these limitations, humankind transcends such animal passivity. Humankind is both a process towards and an achievement of self-consciousness, that is, the knowing of the self as a self and in relation to other objects that are not self. The momentum of this achievement is history itself and it is the philosopher's task to understand and articulate the necessary conditions for the realisation of self-consciousness. Classical philosophy, philosophy before Descartes, made no efforts to liberate the self-conscious human being from the status of merely knowing and this established a precedent for the dominance of epistemology over ontology. The history of post-Cartesian philosophy has been the increasingly radical liberation of the self in relation to the world. What Kojève (after Hegel) demonstrated as the secret ingredient in this liberation was 'desire', an element (and a concept) that post-structuralism would later canonise through a spectrum of interpretations. To want, to need, to love, to hate, to desire is to engage an utterly subjective self-consciousness to the thing-like-ness that comprises objects other than the self; and also to put them in their place in relation to the self. The very idea of desire, of course, opens the door to the very possibility of transgression through the primacy of self.

> The (conscious) Desire of being is what constitutes that being as I and reveals it as such by moving it to say 'I . . . ' Desire is what transforms Being, revealing to itself by itself in (true) knowledge, into an 'object' revealed to a 'subject' by a subject different from the object and 'opposed' to it. It is in and by – or better still, as – 'his' Desire that man is formed and is revealed – to himself and to others – as an I, as the I that is essentially different from, and radically opposed to, the non-I. The (human) I is the I of a Desire or of Desire.
>
> (Kojève 1969: 3–4)

Desire, it would seem, forms the bridge between subject and object and although it brings them together in a manner not previously established it also leaves them both intact. Both are what they are but desire heightens the contingency and the absolute resistance that they each proffer. Desire never makes the other object simply malleable to the subject's wishes. Animals, however, also 'want' things but there is a distinguishing dimension to human desire that coalesces with the true state of self-consciousness. The ultimate signature of human desire is that it desires human desire . . .

this convoluted statement means that self-conscious human beings want/ need/desire the recognition of other human beings with whom they both share the world and share an understanding of the world. This is not so complex, in modern parlance we all 'love to be loved', 'want to be wanted', 'like to be recognised' and enjoy gaining the respect of others. The serpentine path of reason we are now treading brings us back to the centrality of the Master–Slave metaphor.

What distinguishes humankind from animals is a form of desire that seeks the desire (recognition) of others. As this is a moving force in the historical process people are moved to compete with one another to gain 'mastery', that is the recognition of the other. The loser in this competition takes on the mantle of 'slavery'. However, this does not terminate the historical process because the Master now requires the Slave's labour to transform the world. The Master's experience of the world is thus mediated through the practice of the Slave. The Slave, on the other hand, through transforming nature becomes the driving force in history and the struggle for supremacy renews. For Kojève, though, the final struggle to achieve the end of history is not a terminal battle from which only one group will emerge victorious (as had become Marxist orthodoxy) but rather a plateau at which all will struggle to overcome the Master–Slave dichotomy; all will struggle to overcome either authority or oppression, all will struggle to reach the world in a non-mediated form and seek to transform it by and through their creative labour. This is the truly egalitarian ethic adopted by the new European left-wing which sought to dispose of the necessity of seeing conflict as an essential part of human nature when human nature is aspiring to its finest form. But the struggle remains, the struggle is perpetual, hence Kojève was said to have produced Hegel as a terrorist. The overriding concept of negation emerged as central both in theory and practice. Negation is both the force that moves the dialectic but also a force, paradoxically, without resistance. Negativity without use moves us towards an idea of revolt in an absolute form.

Whether this was actually Hegel's view, or Kojève's view, or an adaptation of Marx's view is less important than that it set a new agenda for critical French thought in the second half of the twentieth century. Such was the impact of Kojève's intervention.

NIETZSCHE ON MORALITY AND POLITICS

There can be no further dispute concerning the pivotal role played by Nietzsche's work in the reconfiguration of twentieth-century philosophy and social thought. Nietzsche himself died at the inception of that epoch after a decade of silence. Though his brilliance goes unchallenged many have sought to place him outside of the mainstream of disciplined Western thought, perhaps because his assault on the accepted canons of reason, argument, self-presentation and ethics seemingly derives from a place as yet unexplored. The damage that he inflicts on the intellectual taken-for-granted gains much of its power from its foreign and unaccountable origins. Nietzsche's mind is both literary and deeply troubled, and his ideas, often expressed in poetic and aphoristic form, at least disrupt but, more significantly in our terms, systematically transgress the paradigms of philosophical speech.

In aphorism 125 of Nietzsche's *The Joyful Science* a madman declaims the 'death of God'. Insanity was an oft-recurring motif in his work witnessing the margin separating genius from tolerance, the normative from the unknown, and even the taken-for-granted from the glaringly obvious. Madness most often spoke of the visionary principle of reality within his writing as within his life. And madness has been taken up as a margin/marginalising zone for exploration in the lives and work of subsequent French theorists including Bataille, Foucault, Lacan, Althusser, Deleuze, Guattari and Artaud, to name a few. Following the revelation of the death of God, Nietzsche raged through a highly productive period of about five years during which time he wrote *Thus Spake Zarathustra*, *Beyond Good and Evil* and *On the Genealogy of Morality* (all of which will figure in the following exposition), followed by five more theses in the remaining two years before 1889 when he fell into incomprehension and terminal paralysis.

That 'God is dead' has become a kind of simple mantra that people repeat when questioned over Nietzsche's work. It is repeated so often that it can appear if not silly then at least mildly presumptuous. For sure, the significance of such an utterance as the grounds for a new age of understanding can lose their significance through overexposure. The actual import of the utterance ranges from the concrete to the most alarmingly analytic. In one sense Nietzsche can be seen as heralding the dawn of a secular society, manifestly not a dream come true. That much of the globe is still at war precisely because of different interpretations of the deity testifies to the falsity of this proposition. However, we need to read Nietzsche from the other direction. If we see him in the context of the end of history thesis, the point at which humankind reaches a true and self-conscious appreciation of the world, then he is not making an empirical description of a real state of affairs. Rather he is laughing ironically at the old conceits through which humankind still mediate, distort and spoil their world. If God is indeed dead then all that proceeds in the name of religion is a lie, an absurdity or at best a distortion. If this were not challenge enough Nietzsche's secularisation thesis does not stop at religion, it depotentiates the rules for truth and the conventions of authority. There is no final arbiter in the sky, there is no life after death nor resurrection, there is no ultimate truth. If we lose this backdrop of certainty, the ideal forms and the universal grammars that compose the universe, then we are thrown back on a new realisation: humankind is responsible and humankind is centre stage. The new historical focus falls upon the action of the person, the conduct of the self – *mea culpa* – the world is now built in my image. Beyond this, the alarmingly analytic, if God is dead then infinity is released upon the universe, upon humankind and upon the individual consciousness. The nausea that this induces stems from the lack of containment, nothing is held in check, fragility and volatility become the tenuous principles through which any version of the world is structured. Nietzsche would probably say 'look to thyself!' His writing heralded the rise of European nihilism but his political response was not a call to anyman and certainly not everyman. Nietzsche invokes a new order of being, a self-seeking messenger of history, a warrior unencumbered by centuries of Christianity, liberalism and socialism; a stranger to the shackles of equality, fraternity, pity and care. This is the new dawn of epistemology and ontology, there is an existentialism here, a seismic sociological message and the seeds of the postmodern. In many senses transgression of the foundations of Western social life has become a necessity.

> When I came to men I found them sitting on an old conceit: the conceit that they have long known what is good and evil for man. All talk of virtue seemed an old and weary matter to man; and whoever wanted to sleep well still talked of good and evil before going to sleep.
>   I disturbed this sleepiness when I taught: what is good and evil no one knows yet, unless it be he who creates. He, however, creates man's goals and gives the earth its meaning and its future. That anything at all is good and evil – that is his creation.

> And I bade them overthrow their old academic chairs and wherever
> that old conceit had sat; I bade them laugh at their great masters of
> virtue and saints and poets and world-redeemers, I bade them laugh
> at their gloomy sages and at whoever had at any time sat on the tree of
> life like a black scarecrow. I sat down by their great tomb road among
> cadavers and vultures, and I laughed at their past and its rotting,
> decaying glory.
>
> (Nietzsche, Thus Spake Zarathustra, 1885)

Here, then, is the message of the master. Nietzsche, the newly (re)discov-
ered philosopher of the postmodern, had, it is argued, predicted and
applauded the advent of this age of negative alchemy (see Vattimo 1988;
Jenks 1993). His philosophical stylistics were certainly concerned with
the redundancy and disassembly of morality. Nietzsche made a series of
sonorous philosophical pronouncements concerning both the topic and
purpose of philosophy and the weaknesses and degenerations that its
conventional form had wrought. Among the most serious and lasting is
that uttered in the allegorical guise of *Zarathustra*, a figure devised to
represent the 'self-overcoming of morality'. This primarily transgressive
pilgrim of the postmodern has spent ten years contemplating on a mountain
top, accompanied only by pride (in the form of an eagle) and wisdom
(symbolised by a snake). It is time for Zarathustra to descend and as he does
so he witnesses, through a series of encounters, the wastelands of humanity
around him. He rebuffs a saint who directs him to help man through prayer.
'God is dead' he replies, there can be no help outside of man himself, there
is no salvation (this echoes the Hegelian criticism of the Slave mentality).
What the philosopher is announcing is the collapse of the centre and the
consequent decentralisation of values. In contradistinction to all of those
turn-of-the-century metaphors from social theory stressing 'integration',
'solidarity', 'community', 'structure', 'instrumentality' and 'culture', in
sum, the language of *unification* and *consensus*, Nietzsche is recommending
dispersion and *fragmentation*. The survival of the human spirit no longer rests
in the hands of the collective but in the affirmation of the new triumphal-
ist, the individual in the incarnation of the *Übermensch* (the overman).
Humankind must escape from the protective and pacifying politics of order
into a celebration of life as 'the will to power'. This is not a route for all,
but for some. We cannot all transgress.

> *I teach you the overman.* Man is something that shall be overcome. What
> have you done to overcome him? All beings so far have created

something beyond themselves; and do you want to be the ebb of this great flood and even go back to the beasts rather than overcome man? What is the ape to man? A laughingstock or at least and embarrassment. And man shall be just that for the overman: a laughing-stock or a painful embarrassment. You have made your way from worm to man, and much in you is still worm. . . .

Behold, I teach you the overman. The overman is the meaning of the earth. Let your will say: the overman *shall be* the meaning of the earth! I beseech you, my brothers, *remain faithful to the earth*, and do not believe those who speak to you of otherworldly hopes! Poison-mixers are they, whether they know it or not. Despisers of life are they, decaying and poisoned themselves, of whom the world is weary: so let them go.

(Nietzsche, *Thus Spake Zarathustra*, 1885)

Nietzsche is a didactic rather than a persuasive philosopher; he is forthright in telling people how best to live their lives and the key lies not in some collective ethic, either religious or secular, but in the overthrow and abandonment of the beliefs and conventions of the common person. *Zarathustra* espouses three significant doctrines: the will to power, the suspicion and revaluation of values, and the eternal return. For Nietzsche life is primarily a will to power. This implies the belief in self-control, self-affirmation and self-determination – the seizing and forging of one's present and one's destiny almost always at the expense of other. To manage one's destiny is to refute, overcome and cast aside the values of others, they become barriers to true purpose. However, neither an alternative set of values nor the consequences of exercise of power are in themselves desirable. If they conclude they establish a new set of conventions, a new set of barriers. Only power and the constant revaluation of values are worthwhile. There is no end of history, no golden age but an eternal recurrence of constraints on the exercise of the will to power.

Life is not a rehearsal and does not benefit from modesty, obedience or claiming second place. The will to power is the existential self-affirmation of destiny through authentic and reflexive choice. The values of others are obstacles to the realisation of the will, they are inhibiting and, particularly in the soporific form of collective beliefs like Christianity, are constraining and worthy of violent opposition. Values, ideologically designated as 'virtues', such as altruism, pity and meekness, are corrupting and depotentiating of the will to power. It must be the *Übermensch* who will inherit the earth, but not in a finite state. This is no millennial philosophy searching for the 'good' society in a stable recognisable form – such is the 'conventional' sociological discourse of Marx, Weber and Durkheim – there is no *entelechy* for Nietzsche: his telos is the instability of process. The power of the will and the constant revaluation of values are the 'good', in themselves. No 'end' point can, or should, be envisaged, no new or improved set of values is the purpose of being, but only the challenge to convention. Here we have no 'end of history' but the doctrine of eternal returns. If there can be no end then the process built on the 'grand narratives', 'myths' or 'values' of history are nothing more than the eternal returns of circumstances, ideas, people and things.

Nietzsche's work most often imparts its message in a mocking and ironic tone – this is a carefully managed device and not a sign of weakness.

> The importance of *Zarathustra* is that, at least on one level, it is a book which dramatises and ironises the felt need for a politics of redemption in an age of nihilism. If this is the case, then it becomes impossible to construe the overman as an ideal will bring mankind salvation. Nietzsche's yearning for a new humanity can itself be seen as an expression of the nihilistic condition he wishes us to overcome. It reveals a dissatisfaction with the present, with 'man', expressing the same kind of negative attitudes, such as revenge and resentment towards life as it is, which characterises the ascetic ideal.
>
> Nihilism chiefly signals a crisis of authority. In the wake of the death of God, humanity seeks new idols who will command and provide a new metaphysical foundation for morals. In *Zarathustra* Nietzsche dramatises the predicament in which modern human beings find themselves, and shows both the necessity and the impossibility of instigating a new legislation. How can new values be fashioned and legislated when the transcendental basis which would support them has been undermined? In the age of nihilism, not only is it imperative to rethink the value of truth, but equally the value of morality, of justice, and of law.
>
> (Ansell Pearson 1994: 102)

And, just so, at the conclusion of *Thus Spake Zarathustra* the people elect a new God, a donkey! The ass provides all of the qualities required from a deity: (1) it is ultimately the servant of man' (2) it is silent and is therefore never mistaken; (3) it is stupid and thus the world is built in its image.

Nietzsche's philosophical position is well summarised in the title of his next work, *Beyond Good and Evil*, an amoral and apolitical locus from which to 'deconstruct' the thought and practice of other, more embodied and contexted, epistemologies and codes. His intuitive, anti-deductionist, anti-rationalist ideas challenge the classical tradition of philosophy and fly in the face of the metaphysical project, a knowledge of being. All metaphysical systems and ethical paradigms disguise assumptions and interests that are committed to the preservation of a weak stasis, the stagnation of the will and the triumph of mediocrity over the strength of creative being.

In a letter to the historian Burckhart, dated 22 September 1986, Nietzsche describes the central theme of *Beyond Good and Evil* as 'the contradiction between every conception of morality and every scientific [i.e. biological and physical] conception of life'. The work extends and aggravates the damage started by *Zarathustra*. It is Nietzsche's function to take us to the dark side of the moon, to pull the curtain away while the philosopher speaks and to reveal that he still has a whip in his hands while he is mouthing platitudes about 'freedom' and 'equality'. He sees no philosophical system as interest free. He wishes to expose the hidden or implicit assumptions upon which ethical traditions and metaphysical empires are constructed. The first chapter of the book is entitled 'About Philosophers' Prejudices' and so he continues. Essentially ideas which maintain the life force, which propel the will to power are far more significant than homilies approved by logicians, foundationalists or seekers after ultimate truths.

> It seems to me more and more that the philosopher, as a necessary man of tomorrow and the day after tomorrow, has always found himself, and always had to find himself, in opposition to his today: the ideal of the day was always his enemy. Hitherto all these extraordinary promoters of man, who are called philosophers, and who rarely have felt themselves to be friends of wisdom, but rather disagreeable fools and dangerous question marks, have found their task, their hard, unwanted, inescapable task, but finally also the greatness of their task, in being the bad conscience of their time. By applying the knife vivisectionally to the very virtues of the time they betrayed their own secret: to know of a new greatness of man, a new untrodden way to his enhancement. Each time they have uncovered how much hypocrisy, comfortableness, letting oneself go and letting oneself drop, how many lies were concealed under the honoured type of their contemporary morality, how much virtue was outlived.
>
> (Nietzsche, *Beyond Good and Evil*, 1886)

Stated simplistically the message seems to be that all moral systems are interested and thus pragmatic, they move from a chosen starting point and they aim at a specific and predicted end. They are never universal in the sense that in the beginning there were non-contradictable truths, or, when there was mankind there was only one possible way that it could organise its affairs and its relations between people, or, when civilisation reaches a certain level of development certain moral principles necessarily apply. Truth is not an issue here. For Nietzsche the value of an idea, what it does, is more important than claims about its veracity which may always be disputed. This resonates with the notion that political philosophies, ethical codes and even scientific ideas do not become powerful because they are true, on the contrary, they become true because they are powerful – such is the will to power. There is no position to which one can remove that is not established by value judgements. Nietzsche is critical of Kant's a priori truths and of Hegel's dialectical antitheses. Indeed the whole space of representation between the subject and object or essence and appearance is challenged. This directs us more and more towards Lyotard's critique of 'grand narratives', to Baudrillard's 'simulacra' and to Derrida's 'deconstruction'. Values obscure the will to power and the will to power is all that is the case, indeed it is so basic as a life force that for Nietzsche it proceeds the elementary desire for self-preservation. Philosophical concerns with 'free will' are absurd, there is no such binary as free and non-free will, there is only strong will and weak will. Strong will always transcends the herd, as was predicted by *Zarathustra*. Strong will and thus the *Übermensch* will find its way despite the masses. 'A people is nature's detour to arrive at six or seven great men – and then to get around them' (Nietzsche, *Beyond Good and Evil*, 1886).

Following in the wake of this violent assault on the collective ethic is the clamouring Babel that postmodernism designates 'polysemy', the many voices within a culture waiting to be heard all with an equivalence and a right, ranging from the oppressed to, simply, the previously unspoken. Note Ansell Pearson here:

> There are two main problems with Nietzsche's radically subversive views on truth and knowledge. Firstly, if we have no access to a reality independent of our categories, and if we can never know what is 'true' and what is 'false' in any real . . . sense, how is it possible for Nietzsche to claim that reality is 'will to power'? Secondly, how can he avoid the problem of relativism? One of the problems facing Nietsche's doctrine

of perspectivism is that the interpretative pluralism it seems to be promoting – the view which holds that there is no single truth about the world, but only different interpretations which serve the need of ascending and descending forms of life – can easily degenerate into a theoretical anarchism in which all claims to truth are taken to be nothing more than expressions of an assertive will to power possessing equal validity.

(Ansell Pearson 1994: 18)

In *Beyond Good and Evil*, sub-titled 'Prelude to a Philosophy of the Future', Nietzsche targets the past masters of his trade from Plato, through the Stoics, to Kant, Spinoza, Leibniz, Hegel and Schopenhauer. None of these system-bearers speaks of anything but the past and a desire to cling onto its stability. The philosophy of the future must presumably emanate the will to power and it must dispense with the necessary binary of true and false and look to the fuzzy ground within that opposition where not-true does not mean false. Unlike the narrative form of *Zarathustra* with its vignettes and fables related by a fictional character, in this work Nietzsche is firmly present, he is the 'untimely man', he is the will to power that dares to challenge the citadel of reason upon which (arguably) our civilisation is built. Not only are philosophical systems in the firing line but religious systems also, and primarily Christianity, which he regards as a degenerate force and a thinly disguised metaphysics. In philosophy there is not (and he is recommending there should not be) mystifications and lies about objectivity and impersonality. The will is not in place to offer a mirror to reality. The philosopher of the future must guard against assimilation within the project of science. Science is not without importance but it, too, precludes the exercise of the will to power.

In the philosopher . . . there is nothing whatever impersonal; and above all, his morality bears decided and decisive testimony to who he is – that is to say, to the order of rank the innermost drives of his nature stand in relative to one another.

(Nietzsche, *Beyond Good and Evil*, 1886)

Nietzsche's perspectivism, which is also seen as a version of subjectivism, resists the idea that there are values inherent in the world, in things, or in states of affairs. But neither is he saying that individuals per se generate their own values. He is making a more sociological point about values being socially constructed but then becoming conventions and thus fact-like. Tanner explains this well:

Nietzsche is the first philosopher to exult the fact (yes, there are facts, and this is one of the most important, since it is a fact about values) that value is not something we discover, but something we invent. At the same time, he is acutely aware of the extent to which values are heavily dependent on one kind of fact – the nature of those doing the valuing. And he is just as aware of the extent to which the individual valuers are liable to derive their values from the culture of which each of them is a member, and to think that because they feel the values imposed on them, it is the world in general that is doing the imposing, and not the group of which they are members.

Hence Nietzsche's overriding concern . . . with the typology of cultures.

(Tanner 1990: 20–1)

It would appear that a core imperative in Nietzsche's work at this stage is a commitment to the transvaluation of values that must follow from an unfettered development of the will to power. This is surely the work of the warrior previously introduced, the *Übermensch*. However, this figure makes no appearance in *Beyond Good and Evil*. For whatever reasons his quest is taken up in the discussion of 'nobility' at the end of the work. This is, in effect, a discussion of the conditions of greatness and is, at one point, reconstituted through the Master–Slave dichotomy that we previously considered in Hegel and Kojève. For Nietzsche the Master's morality forges the future; that of the Slave resists, erodes and stands in the way.

A morality of the rulers is, however, most alien and painful to contemporary taste in the severity of its principle that one has duties only towards one's equals; that towards beings of a lower rank, towards anything alien, one may act as one wishes or 'as the heart dictates' and in any case 'beyond good and evil' . . .

(Nietzsche, *Beyond Good and Evil*, 1886)

Think now of the necessity of transgression to the historical process!

In his next book, *On the Genealogy of Morality* (the last work we shall look at in this section), Nietzsche conducts an historical search for the origins of certain moral concepts, and in some sense the thesis mobilises the project set out in *Beyond Good and Evil*. This is an important contribution to ethical and political theory that both evaluates and traces the evolution of fundamental concepts such as justice, law, guilt, conscience and responsibility. Nietzsche repeats that morality is always an historical construct and that any investigation of the past will reveal the evolution of moral concepts. Far from seeing modernity as the pinnacle of moral development he diagnoses a moral desert, a nihilism, which requires arresting, overthrowal by a radical new version of morality. This new morality has an aristocratic route and elements are to be found in antiquity – hence our genealogy, a search for lineage and ancestorial intimations. Nietzsche sees axial moments at which decisions were made concerning the nature of humankind which engendered a kind of enfeeblement in the human spirit and disguised weakness and its corrosive, degenerative tendencies with a series of ideological motifs of altruism and egalitarianism. This is a very difficult message to stomach for a twenty-first-century liberal but then our soft tolerance is precisely part of his challenge. Equal rights, pity, self-sacrifice, forgiveness, all now regarded as superior human qualities, are in place to justify a certain disposition and a failure to grasp the will to power. The very essence of what we know to be 'good' is, paradoxically, what Nietzsche sees as 'bad', thus what the contemporary morality regards as 'evil' may hold the key to the future. We are forced to accept that the 'evil' person has potentially a greater significance that the 'good' person. This needs some unpacking.

On the Genealogy of Morality consists of three essays. The first is titled '"Good and Evil", "Good and Bad"' and in effect picks up the discussion of the Master and Slave moralities engendered in *Beyond Good and Evil*; Nietzsche has not exhausted this topic yet. What he describes for us is the genesis of Christianity where all men are equal before God (thus any subsequent political critique equally applies to modern egalitarian socialism). Ancient Judaism, in common with what Nietzsche has elsewhere referred to as the 'pre-moral period of man', contained certain noble moral features. Primarily moral action was seen to be that which conformed with custom or the dominant authority of the time. The advent of Christ the Redeemer changed all of that. Christianity and the philosophies in its wake have elected a strong and central concept of the individual, the self, the subject, but not strong in a Nietzschean sense of willful. The Christian strength resides in the centrality of the human self in accountablity, responsibility and thus morality and politics. Instead of moral action being that which equates with tradition we now look backwards to motive and intention – the individual subject is the source of both the act and the meaning of the act. The Christian ethic then introduces individual psychological causality, and all of this is enshrined in a 'right' – the freedom to act! What this, in turn, brings about is a transformation of the dichotomy good/bad (as in fitting or not fitting) to an evaluative one of good/evil. So 'evil' can only be a possible designation of conduct and person if it is preceeded by a belief in responsibility, free will and eventually the totality in the form of the 'soul'. Great men may commit great deeds but have bad motives, they may be naughty great men, evil great men – they are dragged down by the mentality/morality of the slave which mobilises evil as a force to defame. Thus for Nietzsche, if Christ was the redeemer of the sick, the poor and the weak then he began the corruption of noble values, he began the slaves' revolt. Contemporary nihilism is part of this politics of revenge against the master.

> This Jesus of Nazareth, as the embodiment of the gospel of love, this 'redeemer' bringing salvation and victory to the poor, the sick, to sinners – was he not seduction in its most sinister and irresistible form . . . Did Israel not reach the pinnacle of her sublime vengefulness via this very 'redeemer' . . . Is it not part of a secret black art of a truly great politics of revenge, a far-sighted, subterranean revenge, slow to grip and calculating . . . could anyone . . . think up a more dangerous bait? Something to equal the enticing, intoxicating, benumbing, corrupting power of that symbol of the 'holy cross' . . . to equal that mystery of an unthinkable final act of extreme cruelty and self-crucifixion of God for the salvation of mankind?
>
> (Nietzsche, *On the Genealogy of Morality*, 1887)

Modernity, for Nietzsche, is marked out by this politics of revenge. The slave morality is not strong, it is not life enhancing, it does not announce and affirm itself, it limpets onto that which it seeks to oppose and brings it down. Evil, which is the strength of the master, is the enemy of the people. In the vast shadow cast by greatness lurks revenge and resentment, what Nietzsche refers to as *ressentiment*.

> The beginning of the slaves' revolt in morality occurs when *ressentiment* itself turns creative and gives birth to values: the *ressentiment* of those who, being denied the proper response of action, compensate for it with imaginary revenge. Whereas all noble morality grows out of a triumphant saying 'yes' to itself, slave morality says 'no' on principle to everything that is 'outside', 'other', 'non-self': and this 'no' is a creative deed. This reversal of the evaluating glance – this inevitable orientation to the outside instead of back onto itself – is a feature of *ressentiment*.
>
> (Nietzsche, *On the Genealogy of Morality*, 1887)

The second essay in the *Genealogy* is called "'Guilt", "Bad Conscience" and Related Matters' and it is a psychology of man's inner sense. As we might have predicted, Nietzsche here takes a further index of contemporary senses of civilisation, namely the human conscience, and reveals its dark and oppressive underbelly. The growth of conscience in the human species is no flowering of an internal seed, rather it represents constraint, control, imposition and the violence of social structures. Conscience is enforced and impressed upon the person. It is the mechanism of social control taken to its most acute, to the inside. Just as Freud would later reveal (see our discussion in Chapter 2), while the *id* requires external policing, the *super-ego* provides its own through self-maintaining mechanisms of surveillance such as 'guilt' and 'shame'. The expression of such sentiments shows a human, delicate, moral dimension to being, for we know that to be guilt-free and shame-free is the province of the psychopath, the ultimately evil person (though interestingly such embodiment is an increasingly sited icon of the postmodern condition; see Seltzer [1998] on the serial killer). However, if we approach this formulation from the other direction, as Nietzsche always invites us to, we see that the moral bond that happily binds us together resides in repression, that repression in turn diverts, distorts and disfigures true human purpose and self-affirmation. In sum, that the social has become formed at the cost of the will to power. The anger and aggression that the individual should vent upon the collectivity for forcing his socialisation into a particular mould is, ironically, inverted onto the self. We feel guilty for not living down to the standards of the collective life, our pain is our badge of good citizenship. This is truly the territory of slave morality. Now hear this correctly, Nietzsche is not applauding the ideological bully-boys and child-murdering inadequates who have misappropriated his views as justifications for their sad dance. Neither Hitler nor Ian Brady represent the embodiment of the *Übermensch*. Here we are being invited to look at other ways, to give consideration to the elan of transgression, to investigate the complex of mechanisms by which humankind, the greatest of all beings, finds itself in its current, and perpetual, circumstances.

> The heavens darken over man in direct proportion to the increase in his feeling shame at being man. The tired, pessimistic outlook, mistrust of life's riddle, the icy 'no' of nausea at life – these are not signs of the wickedest epoch of the human race: on the contrary, they come to light as the bog-plants they are only in their natural habitat, the bog, – I mean

> the sickly mollycoddling and sermonizing, by means of which the animal 'man' is finally taught to be ashamed of his instincts. On the way to becoming an angel . . . man has upset his stomach and developed a furry tongue so that he finds not only that the joy and innocence of animals is disgusting, but that life itself is distasteful.
>
> (Nietzsche, *On the Genealogy of Morality*, 1887)

The third major essay of the *Genealogy* is 'What Do Ascetic Ideals Mean' and here Nietzsche looks at self-denial and human suffering.

> For an ascetic life is a self-contradiction: here an unparalleled *ressentiment* rules, that of an unfulfilled instinct and power-will which wants to be master, not over something in life, but over life itself and its deepest, strongest, most profound conditions; here, an attempt is made to use power to block the sources of the power; here, the green eye of spite turns on physiological growth itself, in particular the manifestation of this in beauty and joy; while satisfaction is looked for and found in failure, decay, pain, misfortune, ugliness, voluntary deprivation, destruction of selfhood, self-flagellation and self-sacrifice.
>
> (Nietzsche, *On the Genealogy of Morality*, 1887)

Nietzsche dispenses with the Christian view that pain is ennobling, that self-sacrifice is good for the soul. The ascetic ideal always diminishes humankind, not because it lacks a will to power but because it defames embodied being.

The campaign is complete, Nietzsche has disassembled morality from the Godhead to the level of individual conduct. He has transported his readers from 'what is the best way to act?' to the proposition 'why judge an action at all, and on what criteria?' He reaches for the unthinkable question, 'what is the value of morality?' Nietzsche remains, in Bataille's words, 'the fiercest of solvents'.

How, then, did I get you here? What, in summary, has been the point of this diversion into German philosophy? Though complex, the point is, I hope, clear. Transgression, in whatever form it might take, is as old as the nature and reinforcement of rules – which it breaks. However, the relation between rule and transgression can appear random, capricious, individualistic, pathological, accidental or even silly. What philosophy reveals is purpose. Hegel's dialectics of negativity engaged us in the historical process by which progress was achieved through opposition, conflict and defeat. Kojève translated Hegel's vision into a more egalitarian prospect for the end of history. Nietzsche showed primarily the absolute necessity of humankind not succumbing to the accidents of history. This whole tradition (including its considerable internal divergencies) specifies humanity as the maker of history, the maker of worlds and not merely the species being that experiences worlds, however self-consciously or sensitively. Transgression and its capacity to challenge, fracture, overthrow, spoil or question the unquestionable can no longer be contained as naughtiness or occasional abhorration. Transgression is part of the purpose of being and is the unstable principle by which any stasis either sustains or transforms. This does not make all transgressions either 'good' or 'bad', it renders them purposive. In the same way, all rules are neither 'good' nor 'bad' and their sanctity no longer resides in the judgement of God!

4

EXCESS

... at the root of this discourse on God which Western culture has maintained for so long . . . a singular experience is shaped: that of transgression. Perhaps one day it will seem decisive for our culture, as much a part of its soil, as the experience of contradiction was at an earlier time for dialectical thought.

(Foucault 1977a: 33)

Standing upon the philosophical platform established in the last chapter here we go on to investigate some of the more contemporary thinkers who have worked with, or around, the theme of transgression in the promulgation of their various post-structuralisms or heterologies. To begin with, however, let us take a further informative diversion into yet another element in the socio-cultural-historical context within which these ideas become meaningful.

Nisbet (1976) develops a stimulating thesis on the aesthetic parallels between the emergence of sociology and the figurative, metaphoric and critical character of nineteenth-century *fin de siècle* literature, painting, Romantic history and philosophy. Within this thesis he describes 'modernism' as the 'rust of progress'. Nisbet speaks of an intellectual malaise that seemed to gain ground hand in hand with the very spirit of progress. This malaise, it would seem, critically addressed the grounds on which progress was supposed to have been accomplished. And, we are informed, the malaise flourished after Hegel, as if the principle of negation clearly impacted upon the collective consciousness.

> What gives this malaise its distinctive character is that it is founded upon a reaction to precisely the same elements of modernity which figured so prominently in the major expressions of the vision of Western progress: industrialism, technology, mass democracy, egalitarianism, science, secularism, and individual liberation from traditional values.
>
> (Nisbet 1976: 115)

Modernism was a dominant movement in the arts and the emergent social sciences. As a movement it carried with it an acute response to the developments that focused our attention upon the conflicts, meaninglessness, upheaval and ultimately the damage to the human condition that were wrought by the structural condition of modernity and the concrete processes of modernisation. Modernism has come to signify the powerful clustering of intellectual trends, most particularly artistic initiatives, that emerged around the mid-nineteenth century. It is also apparent why the deeply rooted association of Marxism with critical tendencies in European thought can be seen in modernist terms – Marx was, after all, offering the disassembly and disposal of capitalism, industrialisation and alienation. Indeed, Berman has described Marx as 'the first and greatest of modernists' (Berman 1982: 129).

BAUDELAIRE AND MODERNISM

The French poet and essayist Charles Baudelaire (1821–67) was foundational in asserting a wide-ranging and challenging manifesto for modernism, and in many senses his anger, his darkness and his corruption have remained associated with the elan of such thinking. His famous statement on the topic of modernity runs as follows:

> . . . it is much easier to decide outright that everything about the garb of an age is absolutely ugly than to devote oneself to the task of distilling from it the mysterious element of beauty that it may contain, however slight or minimal that element may be. By 'modernity' I mean the ephemeral, the fugitive, the contingent, the half of art whose other half is the eternal and the immutable.
>
> (Baudelaire 1964: 12)

What Baudelaire proposed with his concept of 'modernity' was both ontological and epistemological. That is, he saw it as a new object for artistic address but also a new quality, experience and understanding of modern being. So, modern art becomes preoccupied with newness, with breaking rules, with stepping outside of constraint and convention. Such art inevitably moves towards the conceptual as it is dedicated to critically considering its own position in relation to the past. However, the artist of 'newness' is beset by an original set of problems, both intellectual and technical, concerning how possibly, let alone best, to record that which is ephemeral?

> . . . in trivial life, in the daily metamorphosis of external things, there is a rapidity of movement which calls for an equal speed of execution from the artist . . . Observer, philosopher, *flâneur* – call him what you will; but whatever words you use in trying to define this kind of artist, you will certainly be led to bestow upon him some adjective which you could not apply to the painter of the eternal, or at least more lasting things, of heroic or religious subjects.
>
> (Baudelaire 1964: 4)

Central to Baudelaire's conception of the modern and his intellectual reaction to modernity was that he negated and transgressed conventional morality in thought, word and deed. He was a waster, a dandy, an addict, a drunk, a dilettante, a depressive, in many instances a malign influence, indeed a character with ' . . . an unerring flair for the decadent' (Spengler 1926). This is also the man that Walter Benjamin described as 'the lyric poet in the era of high capitalism'. Baudelaire's mastery and his leading role in the modernist movement is captured between the two, seemingly irreconcilable stereotypes expressed by Eluard as follows:

> How could such a man, made like none other to reflect doubt, hatred, contempt, disgust, melancholy, how could he display his passions so plainly and drain the world of its contents in order to emphasize its disordered beauties, its sullied truths, sullied but so pliable and convenient?
>
> (Eluard quoted in Poulet and Kopp 1969: 9)

Baudelaire propounds 'the metaphysics of the provocateur' (Benjamin 1969). Within this he intellectually liberates his city from the governance of Haussmann and his architectural constraint; he denies the significance of any political action based on rational considerations; and he relentlessly reveals that rationalism in any form is a falsehood – all propositions that have gained greater support and popularity in our time than in his own. Baudelaire in the guise of the *bohème* or the *flâneur* walks rings around the prevailing orthodoxies in art, politics, literature and social policy. Baudelaire's short life preceded Nietzsche's with an overlap of some twenty-three years. There is little or no evidence of any cross-fertilisation between the two thinkers but it is intriguing that they both sought to undermine and cast into doubt the moral standards that were paradigmatic for their generation, and the condition of what had come to be seen as European civilisation at its most imperially dominant. Both thinkers were deeply melancholic in contemplation of their historical epoch, but whereas Nietzsche's transgressive urges were avowedly intellectual, Baudelaire extended this into the realm of the corporeal also – he may well have dyed his hair green, and there were rumours of him eating babies' brains! Sartre defined Baudelaire's ethical position as follows:

> To do Evil for the sake of Evil is to do the exact opposite of what we continue to affirm is Good. It is to want what we do not want – since we continue to abhor the powers of Evil – and not to want what we want, for Good is always defined as the object and end of the deepest will. This was Baudelaire's attitude. Between his acts and those of the normal sinner there lay the same difference as between black magic and atheism. The atheist does not care about God because he has decided once and for all that He does not exist. But the priest of the black mass hates God because He is loveable; he scorns Him because He is respectable; he sets himself to denying the established order, but at the same time, preserves this order and asserts it more than ever.
>
> (Sartre 1946: 16)

So Baudelaire seems to be telling us that as a foundation for our modern understandings we have to concede that social experience lacks the predictability, fixity and reproducibility of traditional structures. Taken-for-granted forms of understanding such as temporality, spatiality and even causality could no longer frame our relation to the real or its representations. Out of such a paradigmatic shift in world view the sociologies of Marx, Weber and Durkheim emerged bearing the pathology clauses of modernity in the shape of 'alienation', 'the iron cage' and 'anomie' respectively. Beyond this the new sociologies had to describe new forms of phenomena and establish new forms of explanation. Perhaps most ahead of the game in both respects was Simmel in his pursuit of the contingent (see Frisby 1985); he was ultimately the sociologist of modernity.

How then does the rise and formation of modernity fit into our account of transgression? In the wake of Hegel's negation, Nietzsche's revaluation of value, and Baudelaire's affirmation of the instability of 'modern' experience and reality, we are provided with a set of conditions that engender at least a questioning attitude, but more robustly a challenging, demanding and disobedient attitude in the affairs of humankind, particularly in Europe. Featherstone formulates it eloquently as follows:

> The basic features of modernism can be summarized as: an aesthetic self-consciousness and reflexiveness; a rejection of narrative structure in favour of simultaneity and montage; an exploration of the para-doxical, ambiguous and uncertain open-ended nature of reality; and a rejection of the notion of an integrated personality in favour of an emphasis upon the destructured, dehumanized subject.
>
> (Featherstone 1988: 202)

Now many of the characteristics cited in this quote, and others gathered from the description of modernism above, appear to be, if not identical to, at least in continuity with the defining features (in as much as they can be gathered) of postmodernism. Much has been written on the modernism/postmodernism continuity/discontinuity debate with some heavy theoretical guns being assembled on each side (see a good summary in Smart 1993). The resolution of this debate is not significant here. Suffice it to say that it is inconceivable that postmodernism could have emerged without its precursor modernism. We can also assume that the urge and necessity to transgress has provided a lubricant, if not a vehicle, for the challenge to established authority inherent in both modernism and postmodernism. Certainly many of the leading figures in postmodern and post-structuralist writing have had the designation placed upon them after the event of the influence of their work. Just so with the main protagonist of this chapter, Georges Bataille. Pefanis arrests the needless indecision of this debate well:

> That it is possible to simultaneously call Bataille a modernist, pre-modernist, and postmodernist says as much about our own theoretical tendency towards closure as it does about Bataille. The first thing to say about the discourse on Bataille is that it exhibits a certain tendentious-ness; no less evident in Habermas's claim that French postmodernism

embarked on the path of self-destruction when it followed Bataille, than in Foucault's claim that Bataille's thought is a guiding light in the darkness of a new era of the *unthought*.

(Pefanis 1991: 40)

BATAILLE AND EXCESS, AND FOUCAULT

Georges Bataille (1897–1962) presents an extraordinary figure whose ideas have been most instrumental in the project of this book. Although he could claim no monopoly over the term, his work, perhaps beyond all others, is closely associated with the concept of transgression. Paradoxically, Bataille spent twenty years of his adult life as a librarian at the *Bibliothèque Nationale* in Paris; I say paradoxically because his work, as his lifestyle, stand in opposition to the quiet, retiring, rather introverted stereotype that a librarian brings to mind. He was subject to violent interludes, which subsequent treatment subdued, but as Stoekl (1985) tells us, no force ever staunched his intellectual violence, which saw him through life. Bataille seemed obsessed by and wrote erratically on topics such as 'death', 'excess', 'transgression', 'eroticism', 'evil', 'sacrifice', 'Fascism', 'prostitution', 'de Sade', 'desire' and other more conventional topics, but always in an unconventional manner. Now this selection of tabloid headlines and the dark hint of unpredictability are not intended to either sensationalise the man nor simply reduce his work to an aspect of creative malady. There was, however, an intense energy, wildness and vandalism about Bataille, which he manifested to the full, that make his medieval scholarship, Marxist studies, association with Surrealism, involvement in secret societies, rumours of human sacrifice, pornographic writing, and drunkenness and fornication, all coherent parts of his total persona. Hussey summarises this clearly when he tells us that:

> . . . Bataille was a distinguished and influential figure, editor of the respected journal *Critique*, whose long rivalry with André Breton had established him and his circle as a rallying point for dissident Surrealists. Bataille, who combined a diligent career as a librarian at the Bibliothèque nationale with a thirst for excess and violence in philosophy and politics, also had a reputation as an eroticist. Bataille's fictional writings were notorious for their blasphemy and sadistic content; Bataille's own personal life was alleged to match anything found in his fictions.

(Hussey 2002: 86)

So, larger than life, decadent, depraved, and fêted in his own time by a small but highly influential group of friends including Jacques Lacan, Michel Leiris, Maurice Blanchot, Pierre Klossowski and Roger Caillois. Nevertheless, Bataille remained a minor figure on the European intellectual landscape. Ironically, after his death and in the later part of the twentieth century, Bataille has been resurrected as the new intellectual avatar, the unspoken father of heterology and the post-, the 'prophet of transgression' (Noys 2000). The literature by, on or about Bataille has proliferated and he is now seen, increasingly, to be a central and seminal figure – a fame that he would have resented for mainstreaming his maverick thoughts. However, despite the modern preoccupation with his capture, Bataille's ideas remain labyrinthine, obscure, multiply-fuelled, fierce, neglectful of tradition and simultaneously poetic and repulsive. He does not warm, welcome or seek either agreement or consensus. Bataille appears often to be working through the obligations of a Sadean 'sovereign man', the reader can 'take it or leave it' and the pursuit of inspiration is clearly more important than that we should join hands and applaud his achievements. His topics are dictated by no agenda other than his own libidinal force and his desire will be heard. Leiris, his friend for many years, described him as 'the impossible one, fascinated by everything he could discover about what was really unacceptable' (Leiris quoted in Habermas 1984: 79). However, this does not mean that he is without a trajectory; his work is coherent but the narrative is very much internal. He is intensely engaged in the Hegelian struggle for recognition and yet stands somewhere on the cusp of such political action, sliding from an address of the community, the collective, to the decentred manifestation of difference that inhabits contemporary 'identity politics'. His rage is with the economics of capitalism and the economics that this mode of production inserts in the relationships between people, yet his fear stems from the loss of God and the subsequent threat to individual sovereignty. He has exhausted the limitations of Marxism. He wants to counter the negation of Hegel with the revaluation of values recommended by Nietzsche. He seeks to replace dialectics with genealogies. And he wants a focus on the unconscious. The pornographer, that he is sometimes formulated as, 'goes to the limit', exposes his interiority, ironises the pornographic tendencies of capitalist social structures, plays with metaphors that reveal the patterns of exclusion, expulsion and dehumanisation that are rife within the twentieth century (including both fascism and Stalinism). He writes so as not to be followed, which truly the transgressive never can be. So, for example, when Bataille writes about bodily excrement and the politics of excrement he is talking about shit because it is rude, because it figures in some advanced sexual fetishism, because it was a preoccupation of de Sade's, but he is also talking about the body of collective social life and those excreted, excluded, expunged, like the bad, the insane, the deviant, the poor, the marginal, the dispossessed. The transgressor or the transgressive act can take us to these places without obeying the niceties of manner, politeness or style.

> For Bataille, transgression was an 'inner experience' in which an individual – or, in the case of certain ritualized transgressions such as sacrifice or collective celebration (*la fête*), a community – exceeds the bounds of rational, everyday behaviour, which is constrained by the considerations of profit, productivity or self-preservation. The experience of transgression is indissociable from the consciousness of the constraint or prohibition it violates; indeed, it is precisely by and through its transgression that the force of a prohibition becomes fully realized.
>
> (Suleiman 1990: 75)

Foucault (1977a) provides a brilliant prolegomenon to Bataille's concept of transgression even though it was written a year after Bataille's death. It was part of an homage to Bataille and contributed to his newly collected works. It is a piece of writing one suspects would achieve the grudging approval of its subject. Foucault begins with modern sexuality, the new age delimited by de Sade and Freud and freed from the grasp of Christianity. And yet the old vocabulary of sexuality provided depth and texture beyond the acts immediacy. With the absence of God, with morality no longer obeisant to a spiritual form, we achieve profanation without object. The Godless vocabulary of modern sexuality achieves limits and prescribes ends in the place previously held by the infinite. 'Sexuality achieves nothing beyond itself, no prolongation, except in the frenzy which disrupts it' (Foucault 1977: 30). Freud further prescribes our limits through sexuality by employing it as the conduit to the unconscious. Our vocabulary of sexuality today shows no continuity with nature but rather a splitting enshrined in law and taboo. As God is dead then there is no limit to infinity, there is nothing exterior to being, and consequently we are forced to a constant recognition of the interiority of being, to what Bataille calls sovereignty – the supremacy, the rule, the responsibility, and the mono-causality of the self. This experience is what Foucault describes as the limitless reign of limit and the emptiness of excess. So there are wonderful possibilities bestowed on humankind and on human thought through the death of God but there are also difficulties posed that appear insurmountable. The only way that a limitless world is provided with any structure or coherence is through the excesses that transgress that world and thus construct it – the completion that follows and accompanies transgression. Transgression has become a modern, post-God initiative, a searching for limits to break, an eroticism that goes beyond the limits of sexuality. God becomes the overcoming of God, limit becomes the transgression of limit. The nothingness of infinity is held in check through the singular experience of transgression.

> Transgression is an action which involves the limit, that narrow zone of a line where it displays the flash of its passage, but perhaps also its entire trajectory, even its origin; it is likely that transgression has its entire space in the line it crosses. The play of limits and transgression seems to be regulated by a simple obstinacy: transgression incessantly crosses and recrosses a line which closes up behind it in a wave of extremely short duration and thus it is made to return once more right to the horizon of the uncrossable. But this relationship is considerably more complex: these elements are situated in an uncertain context, in certainties which are immediately upset so that thought is ineffectual as soon as it attempts to seize them.
>
> (Foucault 1977a: 33–4)

There exists, then, an absolute contingency between a limit and a transgression, they are unthinkable, futile, and meaningless in isolation. The meaning derives from the moment of intersection between these two elements and from all that follows in the wake of this intersection. There is an inevitable violence in the collision and a celebration in the instantaneous moment at which both limit and transgression find meaning. Limit finds meaning through the utter fragility of its being having been exposed, and transgression finds meaning through the revelation of its imminent exhaustion. This is an orgasmic juxtaposition. But equally clearly the power and energy of both elements derives from the perpetual threat of constraint or destruction presented by the other.

> Transgression, then, is not related to the limit as black to white, the prohibited to the lawful, the outside to the inside, or as the open area of a building to its enclosed spaces. Rather, their relationship takes the form of a spiral which no simple infraction can exhaust. Perhaps it is

like a flash of lightning in the night which, from the beginning of time, gives a dense and black intensity to the night it denies, which lights up the night from the inside, from top to bottom, and yet owes to the dark the stark clarity of its manifestation, its harrowing and poised singularity; the flash loses itself in this space it marks with its sovereignty and becomes silent now that it has given a name to obscurity.

(Foucault 1977a: 35)

This startling visual image throws light on our earlier considerations of limits in Chapter 3, where the rule, that which it contained and its occasional penetration all appeared much more clearly drawn. The comforting certainty of structuralist binaries has been painfully relativised and exposed in the Foucauldian exposition above. We find other sustained examples of such critique in post-structuralist work, Deleuze, for example, invokes the metaphor of a 'rhizome' (*mille plateaux*) in relation to social process, indicating that it is possible for phenomena to be both surface structural and deep structural in an undulating fashion, their grammar does not have to remain captured in one register. He also employs the notion of 'the pleat' (*le pli*), a fold in a map that enables new conjunctions, crossings, juxtapositions and coincidences of contours, places and features in much the same way that contemporary consciousness both disaggregates and re-orders the social according to different structures of relevance. In many senses such theoretical tropes serve to crystallise the central characteristics of the post-structuralist 'differance' which have been summarised by Mouzelis (1995) as threefold: (1) it is anti-foundationalist, it defies origin accounts and mono-causality, it resists fixed, orienting binaries and explodes them at least into continua if not randomness, it broadens the gap between the signifier and the signified; (2) it de-centres the subject, if not the 'death of man' thesis then certainly the sense that self, subjectivity and personhood are not the causal initiations of social action, process or event; and (3) it disposes of the idea of representation or empirical referent.

To return to Foucault's account of transgression: the relationship between transgression and limit is both blindingly simple, like the lightning flash, but also overwhelmingly complex, like the spiral which relates the two. The event of their intersection cannot therefore stand within a code, it is essentially outside, it is amoral. Foucault insists that the relationship must therefore remain free on notions of scandal or the subversive, anything negative; and in abstraction this is so. As Bataille himself tells us:

'evil is not transgression, it is transgression condemned' (Bataille 2001: 127). In practice, of course, all contemporary transgressions relate to the mad, bad and dangerous because pre-post-structuralist life, that is, everyday life, is riven with code, binary, law, opposition and negation, and indeed anything but genealogy as its method. The Moors murderers, the Kray Twins, the James Bulger killers, Osama bin Laden cannot be seen as either outside of or ahead of their time, they are oppositional manifestations, they are significations of evil and darkness, we claim their limits as our consensus and we actually fight for the right of such recognition (in a way that Hegel would have understood). Nevertheless, Foucault persists; his role is not as apologist for everyday life. For him (and Bataille), transgression is not oppositional, disruptive or transformational: 'Transgression is neither violence in a divided world (in an ethical world) nor a victory over limits (in a dialectical or revolutionary world)' (Foucault 1977: 35). Transgression announces limitation and its obverse. This is the beginning of what Foucault calls the 'nonpositive affirmation' of contemporary philosophy; one can detect here the early traces of a post-modern manifesto. This is also heralding what Bataille had called the 'inner' or 'interior experience', that is, an experience free of disciplinary, professional, moral constraints, which, like his own work, can relentlessly question, aggravate and unsettle all things certain. Bataille has become Nietzsche and the questioning of limit in the face of certain limitlessness can be seen as a kind of secular rediscovery of the sacred, the arbiter of the end of experience.

Foucault continues to vaunt the transgressive turn in contemporary thought. He sees Bataille's writing as confronting the issue of language and language use in philosophy in a way that resonates with the important idea about Wittgenstein's *Philosophical Investigations* being actual investigations in progress. Bataille, then, is invoked as a transgressive method, a transgressive challenge, a messenger of transgression, and the new post-Hegel, post-Kant, post-limit, way forward.

> 'the philosophy of eroticism' . . . the experience of finitude and being, of the limit and transgression? What natural space can this form of thought possess and what language can it adopt? Undoubtedly, no form of reflection yet developed, no established discourse can supply its model, its foundation, or even the riches of its vocabulary. Would it be of help, in any case, to argue by analogy that we must find a language for the transgressive which would be what dialectics was, in an earlier time, for contradiction? Our efforts are undoubtedly better spent in trying to speak of this experience and in making it speak from the

depths where its language fails, from precisely the place where words
escape it, where the subject who speaks has just vanished, where the
spectacle topples over before an upturned eye – from where Bataille's
death has recently placed his language.

(Foucault 1977a: 40)

This is quite a claim and a hard one to affirm, even in nonpositive ways!

BATAILLE AND EROTICISM

Although Bataille produced several pornographic novels, including *Madame
Edwarda* and *The Story of the Eye*, and although his works are steeped in
eroticism, his one monograph singularly dedicated to that topic, *Eroticism*,
is really rather staid. The book is nevertheless of great quality and achieves
what we might describe as an anthropology of eroticism. *Eroticism* is the
arena within which Bataille most explicitly, and systematically, addresses
the idea of transgression. In fact some commentators believe that given the
isolated concentration on the concept in this work alone, it is mistaken to
associate Bataille with transgression – this is not a view that the present
author shares. There are five themes to the work, being 'eroticism', 'death',
'transgression', 'taboo' and finally 'violence', which has a dynamic role in
relation to the other four.

For Bataille, being is the experience of limits and the foundational
experience and prime metaphor for this belief is the knowledge of death.
Death is the great finitude, the full stop – this insight has been shared by
others, for example Sartre in his thesis on *Being and Nothingness*. However,
the limits are intangible, socially and historically constructed and subject
to both trial and resistance. The urge to drive through the limit derives from
the life force or, to put it another way, the desire to 'complete' life – a quest
that Hegel would clearly have recognised. The constant inability to
'complete' life, however, and the recognition of that inability generates a
perpetual state of urgency and anxiety – this is part of the human condition.
Existence becomes, what Bataille has referred to as, 'an exasperated attempt
to complete being' (Bataille 1988: 89).

The sexualised human being is, to a degree unfamiliar to animals, aware
of his or her sexuality as something more than an inarticulate pressure. It
takes the form of desire, desire for another, and a desire for reciprocity. In
the act of copulation death and life meet through the 'little death', the
ending that is orgasm and the potential that is procreation. MacCabe in his
Introduction to *Eroticism* states that Bataille is:

> Concerned to place eroticism at the very centre of life but to do so
> by stressing its relationship to death as the moment at which our
> individual existence breaches the confines of the body to join the
> undifferentiated continuity of existence.
>
> (MacCabe in Bataille 2001: x)

So what Bataille seems to be putting forward is that self, being, is
locked into a self-referential void, a meaninglessness which is established
through the certain knowledge of death, the final limit. The erotic, the
desire for another, is a constant initiative through which being breaks
out into recognition by being affirmed in and through others; otherness
always being the predicate of sexual activity. So the communication of
the self with the outside is fundamentally stirred through sexuality.
Eroticism becomes, then, not a leisure pursuit of the few, not a wickedness
to be confined to evil places and bad people, not an uncomfortable aspect
of the self which should rightly be repressed or dispensed with, it becomes
the very energy of life itself.

> The whole business of eroticism is to strike to the inmost core of the
> living being, so that the heart stands still. The transition from the
> normal state to that of erotic desire presupposes a partial dissolution
> of the person as he exists in the realm of discontinuity . . . The whole
> business of eroticism is to destroy the self-contained character of the
> participators as they are in their normal lives.
>
> (Bataille 2001: 17)

Clearly this harmonises with the shock that Freud had generated by
elevating the status of sexuality to that of prime mover. Similarly, this view
ties Bataille in closer to the thinking of Lacan. Lacan's work espouses an
anti-humanism, it centralises the role of communication and language to
the life of the psyche, and he has a lasting appreciation of the fundamentally
sexualised stance taken up by the subject in the realm of the symbolic
– all elements later picked up by Kristeva. Lacan sees the polymorphous perversity expressed through the Oedipal complex not as a stage
or a plateau in arrested development, it is rather the critical moment at
which the self becomes liberated, through the family relations, into the
social world, into the arenas of culture, language and even civilisation – a
theme later addressed by Deleuze and Guattari. Lacan's writing makes no
reference to Bataille but they were very close: they were students together,
they spent time together, they shared a wife, Sylvia! Indeed, it has been

suggested that much of Lacan's *Ecrits* were an unacknowledged conversation with Bataille.

Sexuality was most important to Bataille, in life as in art. Sexuality and eroticism provided him with a whole vocabulary of metaphors which he used unsparingly throughout his work. This in itself can be quite shocking or playfully transgressive according to whether the reader wishes to turn away or to engage. Sexuality and eroticism reveal principles of disorder and this is precisely Bataille's thesis.

Bataille sees humankind's constant and passionate attempts to escape the anxiety of being as leading inevitably to recklessness and even waste. There is the ever-present danger that humans' attempts to complete life and to overcome the constraints of selfhood can threaten, and indeed, bring down life itself. So the life force is self-destructive, it can destroy what it has created. Because of our innate knowledge of this violent capacity to self-destruct, human societies restrain the damaging potential naturally and spontaneously through the constitution of taboos. Taboos, are then, not external impositions, they are a response to a self-protective inner urge. As we have already heard from Foucault in relation to what he called 'limit' (taboo), taboos and transgressions are inseparable. Hence the primitive constitution of taboo simultaneously engendered the urge to transgress and, through the affinity of this coupling, a whole range of surface structural rituals emerged concerning sexual practice. The transgression destabilises the taboo but in so doing ensures its effectiveness. As Bataille puts it: 'The transgression does not deny the taboo but transcends it and completes it' (Bataille 2001: 63). The relation between taboo and transgression is as a dynamic component in the process of cultural reproduction – it enables change while at the same time ensuring stability. So the essential relation between taboo and transgression makes sensible the utter contingency of, on the one hand, the stasis and determinacy of social structures and, on the other, the innovation and agency inherent in the practice of social action. This same relation allows us to contemplate the necessity and complementarity of continuity and change in social experience. Transgression confirms limits, it shows a consciousness of limits not their absence. As such it can also integrate with power structures and resistance, it produces places for people, expectations and a sense of dependency, which is how we often come to speak about morality.

The moral world takes shape among the dominated – the people of the earth – and looks toward the dominators just as the political world view takes shape at the level of central power and looks towards the holders of local power and the mass of the subjects. On each of the social levels that have been considered we have a pole of the norm and a pole of transgression, so that at each of these levels and as a totality, the society is continually producing an inverted image of itself. On one side, all things considered, a world of transgression, transversality, wandering; on the other, a world of the norm, of hierarchy, of immobility. On one side the possible eruption of freedom; on the other the obviousness of necessity. On one the dilution of temporality in spatiality; on the other the homogeneous and centred space of the transmutation of lived time in history, the place of emergence of a discourse of power with a claim to universal vocation. The unity divides into two, certainly, but only to close in upon itself all the more completely.

(Izard 1982: 243)

Through eroticism individuals externalise an inner experience, they meet with another, they exercise continuity and change, and they push life to the limit which is as death. It is a grand celebration of being, but none of this is intrinsically good, or rational, or God-given (remember Nietzsche). The desires we have are multiple and destabilising, the taboos we generate are multiple and stultifying. All, in a sense, is amoral and indifferent.

There is no prohibition that cannot be transgressed . . . But the taboos on which the world of reason is founded are not rational for all that. To begin with, a calm opposite to violence would not suffice to draw a clear line between the two worlds. If the opposition did not itself draw upon violence in some way, if some violent negative emotion did not make violence horrible for everyone, reason alone could not define those shifting limits authoritatively enough. Only unreasoning dread and terror could survive in the teeth of the forces let loose. This is the nature of the taboo which makes a world of calm reason possible but is itself basically a shudder appealing not to reason but to feeling, just as violence is.

(Bataille 2001: 63–4)

Now we can hear this as a critique of reason, an extension of the modernist project. Bataille certainly sets apart the world of thought and the world of eroticism but not in a contest nor even a hierarchy. It is as if they stand in a troublesome and unresolved entanglement. Thought and reason clearly are the achievements that demarcate humans from animals; and thought,

through labour, transforms nature into culture. Eroticism has been understood as a uniquely human form of sexual expression in as much as that it
is self-conscious and it constitutes taboos. Yet taboos are contra-rational,
they are a negation, and they lightly disguise the animality that powers
human sexuality. Bataille seeks to expose a version of the world which
asserts that good and normal humanity relates to the world primarily
through reason and that the sexualised part of its being is contained and
relegated to a secondary status deliberately – the history of prohibition
from primitive taboo up to modern morality testifies to this. For Bataille,
in line with Freudian and post-Freudian developments in psychoanalysis,
prefers to see the erotic, the sexual, as foremost or at least on a par with
reason in the organisation of human conduct. Bataille deconstructs the
hierarchy implicit in the older structuralist binaries of the 'sacred' and the
'profane', the pure and the impure, the majestic and the accursed. He quite
plainly celebrates and speaks on behalf of *The Accursed Share* (1991a).
Humankind's innermost ambition may then be erotic.

> Men are swayed by two simultaneous emotions: they are driven away
> by terror and drawn by an awed fascination. Taboo and transgression
> reflect these two contradictory urges. The taboo would forbid the
> transgression but the fascination compels it. Taboos and the divine are
> opposed to each other in one sense only, for the sacred aspect of the
> taboo is what draws men towards it and transfigures the original
> interdiction. The often intertwined themes of mythology spring from
> these factors.
>
> (Bataille 2001: 68)

Bataille, it would appear, also closely associates violence with the
articulation and expression of the erotic. His anthropology of erotic
practices rests serially on the exemplars of sacrifice, torture, murder,
hunting, war and cruelty. He does not employ these instances as hyperbole
but rather as metaphors, and it is clear from some of his more detailed
accounts that he equates a certain model of male, penetrative, emotionless
sexuality with a possible (but singularly one-sided) standard for eroticism.
The collision of the violent and the erotic is sustained and repetitive and,
as one comes to expect from Bataille, it renders up one's own possible
disapproval as itself a topic for suspicion and question. So, for example:

> Violence, not cruel in itself, is essentially something organised in the
> transgression of taboos. Cruelty is one of its forms; it is not necessarily

erotic but it may veer towards other forms of violence organised by transgression. Eroticism, like cruelty, is premeditated. Cruelty and eroticism are conscious intentions in a mind which has resolved to trespass into a forbidden field of behaviour. Such a determination is not a general one, but it is always possible to pass from one domain to another, for these contagious domains are both founded on the heady exhilaration of making a determined escape from the power of taboo. . . .

Cruelty may veer towards eroticism . . .

(Bataille 2001: 80)

We might do well to hold this set of assertions in mind in Chapter 5 when we analyse the extravagant and glamorous violence of the Kray Twins in 1960s London. The elision of violence and the erotic does not always claim a sympathetic audience. One might imagine that a range of feminisms would decry such a standpoint while at the same time mobilising the concept of transgression as a weapon in identity politics. In his own time Bataille, through his earlier work, was severely criticised for producing a somewhat ambiguous account of the libidinal roots of fascism. It is pretty clear where Bataille's preferences are over this issue but, as we have come to expect, his writing remains unstable on the topic. Girard catches this relative ambivalence well:

To be sure, Bataille is primarily inclined to treat violence in terms of some rare and precious condiment, the only spice still capable of stimulating the jaded appetite of modern man. Yet on occasion Bataille is able to transcend the decadent estheticism he has so fervently espoused, and explain quite simply that 'the prohibition eliminates violence, and our violent impulses (including those resulting from our sexual drives) destroy our inner calm, without which human consciousness cannot exist'.

(Girard 1998: 222)

What we cannot escape, as if it were some straightforward academic decision, is the emotional turbulence and categorical disruption that Bataille's thoughts provoke. Once we have engaged with the violent, erotic, transgressive complex we move from external representations, through interior and unconscious symbolic forms, and on to dark and private fantasies that we discover are mysteriously intruded into and perhaps even shared. It may be appropriate to conclude this sub-section of the book with a swift encounter with one of Bataille's least known works, *The Trial of Gilles de Rais* (1991b). Gilles de Rais, who was to become the model for the legendary Bluebeard, was himself a fifteenth-century multiple child-murderer, sadist, alchemist, necrophile and Satanist. He represents ultimate convergence and also the zenith of Bataille's obsessions with the extremes of human experience. Bataille calls him the 'sacred monster' and introduces him thus:

> Gilles de Rais owes his lasting glory to his crimes. But was he, as some affirm, the most abject criminal of all time? . . . Crime hides, and by far the most terrifying things are those which elude us. On the night marked out by our fear, we are bound to imagine the very worst. The worst is always possible; and also, with crime, the worst is the last thing imaginable.
>
> . . . we cannot enter upon the story of Gilles de Rais without granting him his privileged place. In the end, we cannot leave the evocative power held in everyday reality unmentioned. And faced with Gilles de Rais' crimes, we do get the sense, perhaps misleadingly, of a summit.
>
> (Bataille 1991b: 9)

And he continues:

> We must picture these sacrifices of dead children, which kept on multiplying. Let us imagine an almost silent reign of terror which does not stop growing . . . His crimes arose from the immense disorder that was unwinding him – unwinding him and unhinging him. By the criminal's confession, which the scribes of the trial took down while listening, we also know that sensual pleasure was not of the essence. Ostensibly he would sit on the belly of his victim and, in this fashion, masturbating, come on the dying body; what mattered to him was less the sexual enjoyment than to see death at work. He liked to watch. He had the body cut open, the throat cut, the members carved to pieces; he relished seeing the blood.
>
> (Bataille 1991b: 10)

This description is quite shocking (surely part of Bataille's intent), it is transgressive writing which in itself is redolent with all of the elements comprising our phenomena in Bataille's terms. We witness identity at the very margins of containment; a spiralling and an escalation out of control; the radical juxtaposition of sexuality, death and violence; the intensity of joy in line with the foreboding of anguish; the utterly wasteful;

an aristocratic excess and disregard – in short, like it or not, the quintessentially erotic.

> The characteristic feeling accompanying transgression is one of intense pleasure (at the exceeding of boundaries) and of intense anguish (at the full realization of the force of those boundaries). And nowhere is this contradictory, heterogeneous combination of pleasure and anguish more acutely present than in the inner experience of eroticism, insofar as this experience involves the practice of sexual 'perversions,' as opposed to 'normal' reproductive sexual activity. In eroticism, as in any transgressive experience, the limits of the self become unstable, 'sliding'. Rationalized exchange and productivity – or, in this case, reproductivity – become subordinated to unlimited, non-productive expenditure; purposeful action, or work, becomes subordinated to free play; and the self-preserving husbandry of everyday life becomes subordinated to the excessive, quasi-mystical state we associate with religious ecstasy and generally with the realm of the sacred.
>
> (Suleiman 1990: 75)

In the last part of the quote from Suleiman we are taken into Bataille's peculiar version of the economic life. Perhaps now we should pause and investigate other ways in which Bataille reconstructs and throws light upon the concepts of excess and eroticism, through the economy and the gift.

BATAILLE AND ECONOMY AND THE GIFT

The classical definition of economics, apart from being a dismal science, is that it concerns the distribution of scarce resources. What this has come to mean, through classical and Keynesian economics and Marxist economics also, is the study of matters relating to finance, including markets, labour and property, and the motives for action that such phenomena inspire. Clearly within Marxist economics concepts of property and profit are employed critically. Now Bataille, perverse as ever, generates a 'general economy', a theory of being in the world and relating to others which is unconstrained by money and wealth. His sense of the heterogeneous refuses the assimilation of the economic into the bourgeois consciousness and the classifications and methodologies of modern science. Taking inspiration from the Durkheimian school of sociology, particularly through the agency of Durkheim's student and son-in-law, the anthropologist Marcel Mauss, Bataille regards all phenomena as basically social phenomena. This means that they are part of a totality and therefore that they are all fundamentally related and overlapping in the way that structuralism recommends. His 'general economy' is thus a kind of homeostatic ecology of human dispositions. This is one area where Habermas (1984) has sought to criticise Bataille for his mysticism, his irrationalism and, essentially, to accuse him of starting the slippery decline into postmodernism; he may have a point! We have to understand that although Bataille had served his time as both a communist and a Marxist and clearly recognised economies within these frameworks, there was also a powerful destructive anarchistic element in his thinking, which grew stronger rather than diminished as his work progressed. This will to transgress, directly inherited from Nietzsche, but impossible ever to complete, challenged all assumptions contained within everyday life and also intellectual life. Consequently, whereas Marx (the enemy of capitalism) nevertheless sees economic life and the practice of labour as fundamental to the human species being (*homo laborens*), Bataille refuses this fateful and essentialist mode of being. Bataille sees his economy as driven by human energies in the form of urges and desires. This is what Habermas describes as 'a twist that negates the very foundations of praxis philosophy' (Habermas 1984: 89). For Bataille human sovereignty is assured not through the accumulation of profit but through the form of consumption that creates no use-value, the consumption of excess, the generation of waste and loss.

> The question of a general economy is located at the same level as that of political economy, but the science designated by the latter refers only to a restricted economy (to market values). The general economy deals with the essential problem of the use of wealth. It underlines the fact that an excess is produced that, by definition, cannot be employed in a utilitarian manner. Excess energy can be lost, without the least concern for a goal or objective, and, therefore, without any meaning.
>
> (Bataille quoted in Pefanis 1991: 17)

This is an economy of un-productivity, an expressive economy of the creative disposition of human energies (which is mostly erotic, or violent, or both). So human sovereignty cannot and must not get bogged down in the economics of necessity, such as: working to subsist; eating to survive; having sex for procreation; investing to enable continued (or increased) levels of production. Bataille is concerned with those elements of human culture which defy reduction to the classical economic binary of production and consumption. Human energy does not exist to enable the function of economies. There has to be an expressive space beyond necessity or humans revert to animals or, with the assistance of technology, become wise machines. The energy (a bit like Nietzsche's will to power) is primary, it is not a form of fuel for other systems. The origins of this energy, which must be quite critical in understanding such an economic ecology, is rarely made explicit, but he does sometimes refer to it as solar. The sun has a glorious purity for Bataille, its purpose is to dispense energy (world sustaining energy) without any return. The sun is utterly selfless, it gives but it never receives. The sun, as God, as being, as social life, but certainly as a metaphor for abundance, charges and recharges the system, but also generates a surplus of energy. This surplus, or excess, provides for interaction, sociality; it gives rise to other. It is the luxury of being.

> Bataille's argument for the necessity of luxury goes as follows: any circumscribed system receives more 'energy' from its surrounding milieu than it can profitably use up in simply maintaining its existence. Part of the excess (the 'luxury' with respect to what is strictly necessary) can be used in the growth of that system, but when that growth reaches its limit ... then the excess must be lost or destroyed or consumed without profit. The premise of this argument, and it is an empirical premise, is that there clearly is such an excess.
>
> (Bennington 1995: 48)

The general economy, that is the total system from the level of solar input to the level of sovereign individual, has a guaranteed excess which it disposes through a variety of kinds of expenditure (*depense*) and consumption. Eroticism is just such a form of expenditure, but eroticism transcends use-value (a term appropriated from Marx and recast). So eroticism uses up energy, it consumes it and destroys it. Eroticism is always an action embodying great risk, it puts all at stake because it reaches beyond the particular and attempts to capture the uncapturable, the totality – this is surely a new version of Hegel. What we also have in the general economy is a recipe for explosion. The system is a plenitude of energy, constantly recharged. There are mechanisms for the use and expenditure of the energy and some of the excess is exhausted but not all – the system has limits. This is a volatile model and suitable to Bataille's understanding of the socio-historical process. This ecology (to return to the original metaphor) is neither stable nor homeostatic, it does not balance itself, it has no stasis, it is without peace. This general economy is driven to, and by, acts of violence, it is dedicated to transgression as a way of expending its energy; thus we have war, murder, cruelty, sacrifice, torture and so on. Bennington captures this nicely when he says that:

> Bataille needs to posit limits (on this point, as on so many others, his physics and metaphysics are not essentially different from those of the Marquis de Sade). Limits as restrictions to growth (the determination of growth as finite).
>
> (Bennington 1995: 49)

Strong boundaries, a powerful symbolic world of the profane, enhances being. Human being needs to consume excess, to expend energy non-conventionally, it needs to create waste. Thus it requires a system of strong boundary maintenance that contains the contested energy and invigorates the contest. Any laxity, timidity or feebleness in the boundaries of the system inevitably generates wretchedness and degradation among its occupants. This notion is picked up by Kristeva in her writings on horror:

> The logic of prohibition, which founds the abject, has been outlined and made explicit by a number of anthropologists concerned with defilement and its sacred function in so-called primitive societies. And yet Georges Bataille remains the only one, to my knowledge, who has linked the production of the abject to the weakness of that prohibition, which, in other respects, necessarily constitutes each social order. He links abjection to 'the inability to assume with sufficient strength the imperative act of excluding'.
>
> (Kristeva 1982: 64)

So, for Bataille, consumption adopts two forms: first, the mundane routine consumption that enables both survival and also the maintenance of production (to enable such consumption); and second, that mode of consumption that is an end in itself, for example: generosity, extravagance, non-procreative sex, entertainment, conspicuous acquisition. Sovereignty lies in the recommendation and practice of the second. This might be pre-capitalist consumption or what Habermas calls 'primordial sovereignty'. If we consume for its own sake we activate a life without surplus, which is another way of thinking of a life at the limits. Through the mundane functionality that capitalism has instilled much has been lost. 'The generous, the orgiastic, the lack of measure that always characterized feudal waste has disappeared' (Habermas 1984: 90). Put another way, it is 'usefulness' that Bataille is critically addressing, as it is always action, expenditure or consumption in pursuit of something else. The paradox of utility that he presents us with is that if being useful means no more than servicing yet another purpose (like investing for the future) then utility's ultimate destiny is uselessness. It is not utility and necessity and survival that present humankind with their fundamental problems, it is excess and luxury and creativity. Life beyond utility is where sovereignty is to be found. This is a hard message to assimilate in a culture marked out by criteria of utility and quality in relation to utility, and where a person's life course is mapped by an observance of some version of what Max Weber called 'the Protestant ethic'. Bataille is flying in the face of the instrumental rationalism that is foundational to contemporary society and personal identity.

Let us, still within a concern for the economic, look now at Bataille's appropriation and reworking of Mauss's concept of the 'gift' (*le don*). We all know about gifts and all societies have gifts and gift rituals; however, since Mauss our understanding of the gift, or rather its symbolic meaning, will never be the same. Mauss begins his thesis with what looks like a methodological statement but which is, in fact, an ontological assertion of considerable significance.

> . . . in these 'early' societies, social phenomena are not discrete; each phenomenon contains all the threads of which the social fabric is composed. In these *total* social phenomena, as we propose to call them, all kinds of institutions find simultaneous expression: religious, legal, moral, and economic. In addition, the phenomena have their aesthetic aspect and they reveal morphological types. We intend in this book to isolate one important set of phenomena: namely, prestations which are in theory voluntary, disinterested, spontaneous, but are in fact obligatory and interested. The form usually taken is that of the gift generously offered; but the accompanying behaviour is formal pretence and social deception, while the transaction itself is based on obligation and economic self-interest.
>
> (Mauss 1970: 1)

Suddenly the gift has exposed the moral order. Instead of asking 'why do we give gifts?' we find ourselves anxious to know why gifts that we receive demand reciprocity. Or, to put it in Mauss's words: 'What force is there in the thing given which compels the recipient to make a return?' (Mauss 1970: 1). Mauss develops his ideas on the basis of a range of comparative material but he unifies his phenomenon under the designation *potlach*, which is a term derived from native Americans and one which has some currency among anthropologists. *Potlach* is a common practice in simple societies, across social spaces and across time. It appears as a relatively straightforward ritual but it is one that has considerable implications beyond its initiation. In essence traditional people, though more usually their leaders, award lavish gifts upon their rivals usually at specific symbolic times. That the receiver of the gift then feels an obligation to repay the generosity of the donor can be seen, on the surface, in benign terms. Quite simply the gift and its inherent obligation facilitates and ensures an integration and a reciprocity between the two groups. However, the *potlach* has a darker side, both conscious and unconscious, contained within the intentionality of the giver and the necessary response of the receiver. The constraint of obligation felt by the receiver is recognised, by all, to involve an explicit form of escalation. So to return a gift in kind, a mutual, equitable reciprocity, is both insufficient and to have misunderstood the compulsion of the *potlach*. The receiver is unquestioningly obliged to return more than was originally given. Failure so to do is to invite gross dishonour. Consequently the scale of the original gift can be such that it has the same role as a poker player in raising the stakes to 'call the bluff', ruin the game of, or simply to humiliate another player – this can be its deliberate intention. Mauss's data reveals that warring chiefs have exercised precisely this gambit in an attempt to both humiliate and impoverish their opponent. By out-doing an opponent in such a game-plan leaders gain more power and respect and prestige, so the simple gift becomes a move in a political and moral competition.

Bataille demonstrated a long-standing fascination with the *potlach*, which he sought out in the work of Mauss and regarded as serious empirical support for his notions of economy, expenditure and consumption. Bataille ignores the elements of social integration and reciprocity, which through Levi-Strauss became inspirational to the structuralist movement, and focused instead on the orgy of waste that such a ritual could ignite, even to the point of self-destruction. Pefanis supports this view when he says that:

> It is possible, however, to locate a major split in the interpretation of Mauss's gift. On the one side the structuralists have inferred a reciprocating, perhaps ultimately economic, structure in the relations of the gift exchange. Given the influence of structuralism itself, this

interpretation has become something of a paradigm. But on the other side of the split there is another, more radical and certainly more marginal, interpretation of the phenomenon identified by Mauss . . . It forms not only the basis of Bataille's anthropological vision, but his entire disposition at the level of writing.

(Pefanis 1991: 22)

For Bataille the *potlach* exemplifies purposive waste, a calculative ritual squandering of resources, a most dramatic negation of utility. This does not mean it is a thoughtless act of extravagance or a selfless act of generosity. This violation of use, which can be on a grand scale, has always power, prestige or victory as its goal. Thus there is a contradiction at work. The pragmatism of the long game (the gaining of power) is facilitated in the short term by the risk venture of waste, loss and destruction – so this can be seen as another version of use, albeit hedged around with danger and insecurity, i.e. the gambit might backfire and the gift receiver reciprocate with a larger, untoppable gift. The use-value in this sense is highly symbolic. Habermas is most instructive here:

. . . this contradiction is implanted structurally in all forms of historically embodied sovereignty, Bataille would like to use it to explain why it is that the sovereignty that expresses itself in acts of waste is used more and more for the exploitation of labor power and why it is that this source of true authority shrivels up into 'a disgraceful source of profit.'

However, the fact that sovereignty and power have been amalgamated from the very beginning and that this amalgam can be employed for the purpose of appropriating surplus value by no means already explains why the historical tendency towards the expansion and reification of the profane sphere and towards the exclusion of the sacral has actually prevailed.

(Habermas 1984: 95–6)

Bataille is not absorbing the *potlach* as a central metaphor into his general economy as a merely capricious and contrary act, he is inverting our conventional understandings of political economy and no longer privileging the capitalist mode of consciousness. This is the same manner of deconstruction that Nietzsche applied to codes of morality. It is no surprise that Bataille should find inspiration in a ritual form from a pre-capitalist economy. However, the *potlach* is not merely that, a pre-capitalist ritual and therefore primitive. Mauss was using also as a liberating force in anthropology, which until his writing had seen 'simple'/'primitive'/ 'pre-capitalist' societies as locked into a static traditional rationality (with the ritualistic means justifying the random ends). Because of the Gift thesis 'simple' societies were to be seen artfully displaying elements of instrumental rationality (with the ends justifying the means) – allegedly a characteristic of complex thought.

At the beginning of this section we defined conventional economics as the distribution of scarce resources, clearly a political act; now, through Bataille, we are looking at the selfless expenditure of excess or superfluous resources, clearly a sovereign act. Systems, ecologies, economies routinely generate surpluses, this is Bataille's belief. When systems are not growing, expanding or evolving their surpluses accumulate as profit which become embalmed in sacred symbolism – wealth/health/happiness/goodness/ morality/virtue. This surplus, this accumulated energy, must, in Bataille's view, be unloaded, expended, wasted, defecated, squandered, discharged in what can only be a profane manner. Such *dépense* may be small scale and resplendent and playful, the *jouissance* (pleasure) of eroticism or religious experience, or large scale and catastrophic like world war. If the individual does not fulfil his role in such expenditure then the accumulation of energy will inevitably lead to the large-scale solution, where all is lost. The equilibrium of the system is ensured through this worthless expenditure, and the sovereignty of the individual is ensured through not succumbing to the meaninglessness of stasis.

We may read this again as an affirmation of the very necessity of transgression for the maintenance of the system, but certainly not in functionalist terms.

BATAILLE AND THE MARQUIS DE SADE

Bataille is among a large group of French theoreticians who have claimed some intellectual lineage with the 'Divine Marquis', Donatien Alphonse François de Sade (1740–1814). Leading philosophical figures including Albert Camus, Maurice Blanchot, Philippe Sollers, Gilles Deleuze, Jean-Paul Sartre, Jacques Lacan, Guillaume Apollinaire, Michel Foucault, Roland Barthes and Pierre Klossowski have all reached for and variously articulated versions of de Sade's transgressional intent through heterologies, existentialisms, genealogies, negations and nihilisms. 'Sovereignty', a predisposition to action non-servile and unconstrained, emerges as the unifying principle. Bataille appears to have stepped further and both appropriated the concept and assumed the lifestyle.

> A reader of Sade, exposed to the atmosphere of modern French thought, cannot escape being infected by Georges Bataille. Bataille's 'sovereignty' – glorious expenditure as the possibility for a mingling of the most sacred and the unspeakably profane in their common transgression of the restricted economy of utility – is a 'natural' accompaniment to Sade's outrageous excesses. Pierre Klossowski has been accused of actually meaning Bataille when he speaks of Sade, but to have read Bataille may mean the impossibility of ever not reading Bataille when reading Sade.
>
> (Gallop 1981: 11)

The Marquis de Sade would have assumed his arrogance and transcendent vision from an aristocratic ideology of absolute power, no servant he. His experiments in pushing the extreme would then become a philosophical journey in exercising this magnificence without check and to the limit of human possibility (and beyond). Bataille derives his quest for mastery from the Hegelian Master–Slave dialectic fuelled by Nietzsche's anti-ethics. Bataille's resistance to mere utility in the function of body or mind, and thus creativity, finds its purest symbolic expression in Surrealism. Sadean sovereignty is unsustainable in its absolute relativism and its unswerving commitment to a kind of solipsism that requires to feed on the world of other yet denies its existence. There is a truculent hedonism in the execution of de Sade's appetites which betrays immortal longings and a singular prohibition on their replication. Perhaps the final Sadean irony is the essential impossibility of having others do to you as you have done unto them, the fantasy of the individual's sovereignty cannot allow such excess in others and degradation to self. Although de Sade's system is beyond good and evil, how could such judgements be made, it is nevertheless avowedly the province of the anti-Christ. Sovereign men do not do good, either by choice or by accident and the real issue here is that they do not act with other in mind. Bataille's sovereignty is that of a sociologist (albeit a peculiar one) and is thus premised on the very necessity of other and sociality.

> Sade's initial insight into sovereignty therefore needs Bataille's view to be complemented with Hegel's idea of 'recognition'. To be sovereign it is necessary to make the choice to live rather than accept the burden of

living that is placed above one . . . Like the sacred, sovereignty is something that is expelled from a society that reduces itself to homogeneity. We can still perceive sovereignty as a crucial feature of feudal society, but this society is destroyed by the bourgeois taste for accumulation . . . Medieval society was therefore a society of subjects while bourgeois society becomes a society of things.

(Richardson 1994: 121)

Whatever the accuracies, overlaps and divergencies within the works of these two doctrines of transgression, the principle of 'sovereignty' is supreme. The purpose and the significance which the concept carries for Bataille and all of the other luminaries listed above is as a replacement for and corruption of 'reason'. That sovereignty makes us look at violence, aggression and eroticism in human thought and action enables us to think outside of that all-persuasive canon of the mild-mannered but wholly calculating rationality that has forged modernity. Sovereignty begins with a self-centred responsibility to know or to learn, not a de-personalised universal quality to which we adhere, slavishly. The sovereign issue also makes its own way; it is an ontology not an epistemology orientated around binaries such as the mind/body, the ideal/material, the good/evil. Striving for sovereignty ensures a breakdown of hierarchies and a scrambling of the proper, worthy, replicable, true with the dirty, untidy, obscene and peculiar (Gallop 1981). This is another way of speaking about the 'deconstruction' that began with Nietzsche and also throws light on Bataille's perverse interest in waste, excrement and bodily orifices.

Sadian libertines violate integrity and force open closures . . . Sade alternately presents pornographic scenes and philosophical harangues. The result of this mixtures is that each undercuts the other. The brute impact of sex and violence is softened, for they can be taken seriously, can be studied and interpreted, as acting out certain philosophical questions (for example: the reality of the existence of others, the arbitrary nature of morality). Concurrently, philosophy's seriousness is tainted through the exposure of the equivocal intersubjective relations always underlying it.

The move to contaminate philosophy, whether in Sade's mode of scandal and sensationalism or in the current mode of carefully considered questioning of philosophy's a priori ideology, is an attack on . . . hierarchical distinction, underlying metaphysics since Plato . . .

(Gallop 1981: 2–3)

What this chapter has sought to achieve is, following the philosophical inspiration and burden of Hegel and Nietzsche, an intellectual gradient from modernism to postmodernism. The fulcrum in achieving this gradient has been the work of Georges Bataille, lately assembled as the missing link in a history of contemporary ideas. Our shift has been from dialectical thinking to genealogical thinking and from negation to transgression. The problematics for post-structuralism, and the 'post-' more generally, have been set and transgression has been revealed as both an intellectual implement and a life-enhancing practice. The sovereign survivor in the postmodern culture is compelled to transgress.

The following chapter contains an analysis, based in Bataille's inspirations, which itself addresses a topic brimming over with compulsion and revulsion, fascination and repulsion.

5

EXTREME SEDUCTIVENESS IS AT THE BOUNDARY OF HORROR *

Throughout history twins have always been regarded as very special . . .
(Bryan and Higgins 1995: 118)

On 8 March 1969, at the conclusion of the longest trial in the history
of British criminal justice, Mr Justice Melford Stevenson pronounced
sentences of life imprisonment for murder on both of the Kray brothers
with the added caveat ' . . . which I recommend should not be for less
than thirty years'. That thirty years has slowly reached its conclusion. And
although Ronnie Kray always seemed destined to die in Broadmoor, his
paranoid schizophrenia tempered by constant medication, and Reggie
Kray appeared equally likely to serve out every day of those predicted
three decades of incarceration, given the constant refusals to grant his
parole, the 'Twins' remain immanent in the public imagination. The Krays
have provided a constant source for media stories. They have seeded an
extensive bibliography comprising autobiographical accounts, biographical
reconstructions, commentaries, analysis, fiction and mere speculation;
and they have been the source and topic of feature films, audio tapes,
walking tours and parody. Through the agency of these and many other

cultural formations they retained, with a passive appreciation, the magnetism and public agitation that they actively sought and engendered in the heyday of their nefarious careers.

> The Krays . . . are extreme examples: they belong as spectacular textbook cases in the psychopathology of city life, living out a full arc of possibility which few of us begin to scale.
>
> (Raban 1988: 77)

Ronnie Kray's death, in Broadmoor, on 17 March 1995 set in motion a dramatic test of this enduring field of attraction. The reports of his demise made national news, occupying prime time on television and radio and front page space in the press from the *Sun* to the *Daily Telegraph*. These reports were themselves only the precursor of the real spectacle, the East End funeral. The cortege, led by a glass-sided carriage hearse drawn by six black, plumed horses and bearing the dual floral inscriptions 'Ron' and 'The Colonel' (the soubriquet from his days as a warlord), extended, when stationary, from St Matthew's Church, Bethnal Green to the Carpenter's Arms public house (their last 'official' business) and contained fifteen funereal Daimlers, even before the stretch limos began. The crowds that followed the subsequent procession to Chingford Cemetery were reported to be over a mile long – comparable in size to a major political demonstration. The wedding of Reggie Kray to Frances Shea that took place thirty years earlier, itself an outstanding example of calculated cultural representation packed with celebrity, was easily overshadowed by this latter event. Today, the whole dynasty of Kray brutalism has past; elder brother Charlie died in Belmarsh Prison, aged seventy-four, sentenced for some absurd cocaine deal, and Reggie was released from prison to die on 12 August 2000 in a Norfolk hotel.

Over the years since the trial, despite the occasional and carefully paced release of photographs from prison of those two ageing men, the public's mind returned, in Dorian Gray fashion, to the vivid images created by the fashion photographer David Bailey in the 1960s, to the tales of excessive and gratuitous violence, and to a time when London criminality appeared not only organised as never before but also integrated both with the Establishment and the vanguard of popular culture. The Bailey portraits provide windows through which to view this past; they are indelibly marked on the memoire collective of London's history. The pose, hair, ties, eyebrows and thick surly lips have become phrenological archetypes of proletarian villainy. Like modern-day police video mugshots, the elements can be rearranged to fit particular descriptions but, strangely, the end results are always vague and stereotypical, reminders of past rogues that ultimately fit popular expectations of how the criminal classes should look. This might be why the Krays are such obvious contenders for parody, such as *Monty Python's* Piranha Brothers, Hale and Pace in their 'Management' sketches and the Mitchell Brothers in BBC1's soap *EastEnders*. However, rather than ridiculing the Twins, parody often serves to celebrate and, more insidiously, to pay homage and respect their strangeness. The process by which such imitation can help to keep myth vibrant and the past alive is part of a wider tradition of cultural transmission.

Burke (1989) has argued that social and cultural historians should evaluate the mechanisms by which memory as an historical phenomenon is transmitted within different societies. Conversely, Burke argues that historical erasure or the 'uses of oblivion' are also crucial in our understanding of the competing traditions of the past. In particular the role of myth is central to our knowledge of selective memory in what he refers to as the 'social history of remembering'. And, as an act of conceptual clarification, he states:

> I am, incidentally, using that slippery term 'myth' not in the positivist sense of 'inaccurate history' but in the richer, more positive sense of a story with symbolic meaning, made up of stereotyped incidents and involving characters who are larger than life, whether they are heroes or villains.
>
> (Burke 1989: 103)

Burke raises a question that is profoundly relevant to understanding the continued fascination for the story of the Krays. He asks why myths attach themselves to some individuals (living or dead) and not to others, and why, through the existence of some media and not others, some events and individuals are more 'mythogenic' than others. The symbolic dimension of memory is important because it reminds us that all memory involves an act of 'remembrance', that is, it is transformed via the medium that is used to express it. Clearly different media organise the transmission of social memory and contribute to the formal organisation of the symbolic past. Burke posits five media that are formative in this process: beginning with oral histories; continuing through written records;

with images and the pictorial; to actions and rituals; and lastly the important social framework of space. Each of these forms also represents a methodological step away from a reliance on factual documentation towards a more hermeneutic appreciation of historical narratives. The last category, space, first arises in the classical and Renaissance practice of placing images in specific locations 'such as memory palaces and memory theatres' (Burke 1989: 101). Remembrance of the past is often linked to a series of 'striking images' that are projected on to particular geographies. There are obvious parallels here with the way in which the Krays have come to embody a particular version of East End history. Metaphorically the Twins represent a condensed version of a dark criminal past, what I (1995a) have referred to as a 'minatorial geography', which is as much to do with psychic space as social space. It is interesting to speculate at this point on the effects of the slum clearance programme that took place in the East End during the 1950s and 1960s and which eventually included the Twins' family home at 178 Vallance Road. Rather than resulting in what Burke calls a 'geographical realignment' of the past, or wiping the memory slate clean, the Kray myth has continued via a more permanent network of cultural mnemonics both in and outside of the actual social space of the East End.

When we consider the Kray myth a complex interrelation of media come into play. The most obvious, as cited above, are the written and pictorial representations that have defined the narrative of the Twins, together with the oral histories of the main protagonists. Yet it is, perhaps, the neglected aspects of action and space in the Krays' story that are integral to their mythogenic status. The Twins' tale is and always will be inextricably bound to the signs, symbols, rituals and folklore of London's East End. Symbolic acts, Burke points out, often leave little or no tangible trace. In the remarkably complex and also secretive world of the Krays the story can only be apprehended as myth and their lives understood as the violent oscillation between transgression and order (Stallybrass and White 1986). Ronnie and Reggie continue to be projected on to the living space of the East End as well as the screens of the memory palaces and theatres of our social remembering. The extraordinary scenes that accompanied Ronnie Kray's funeral illustrate, at one level, that within the East End, a culture which has been constantly associated with social disorganisation and moral decay, a dark celebration could take place that was neither a reactionary remembrance of the past nor a chauvinistic rejection of the present. At another level the funeral represented how time and history, ritual and space can converge under the auspices of myth to articulate a tradition and cultural inheritance that was moral without being moralistic. In this way the Twins frame and were framed by the East End, and that whole collective memory can be realised as a brooding presence constantly threatening to interrupt linear time.

What, then, is the compulsion that seems continually to re-image and re-present the Krays? What collective sentiments in complex with modern psychologies, across age, class and gender, established and continuously revived the magnetism of their phenomenon? Bataille, when considering the inflation and lightly repressed human disposition to excess that has grounded fascism and, indeed, all liminal behaviour, stated that: 'extreme seductiveness is at the boundary of horror' (Bataille 1985: 17). It is precisely that boundary from which we begin; a boundary that marks off the appearance from the actual form; further still, a boundary that prescribes the fragile line between the outside and the journey to the interior; and a boundary that merely gestures towards the interplay of the rational and the erotic. The boundary appears increasingly enfeebled by multiple perforations, fluid ingresses into the dark side of the self and the collectivity, yet it remains constant and to experience it is still to experience constraint. The transgression of such a line requires Nietzschean heroism, or its surrogates. Beyond this line, the chapter attempts to explain the seduction and understand the horror.

The Kray story, in its variety of tellings, is articulated through a series of disjunctions, paradoxes or, at least, irresolutions that enables its main characters, almost despite themselves, to dance at arm's length, illusive and never wholly embraced. Although in reality the manifestations of their actions were largely nasty and brutish, as objects in thought they remained delicate and even flirtatious in their resistance to singular formulation. Even the articulation of 'due process' through their downfall and legal reclassification, a ritual calculated to achieve their reduction and pronounce their mono-dimensionality, provided only a pause in their re-invention and re-emergence. As Raban stated:

> The trial did not 'seal the myth' of the Krays; rather, it broke it down into a long rehearsal of sordid facts. The dream smashed up, the daring impersonation turned to a mere lie, and society gave Ronnie only one identity in exchange for the many he had invented to exploit and puncture it.
>
> (Raban 1988: 74)

The symbolic core of the Kray enticement, and clearly central to their own sense of identity, purpose and belonging, is their very 'twinness'. They were identical or MZ twins, itself still a relatively unusual phenomenon, and a state of being subject to a higher than normal level of infant mortality. This birthright multiplied by the privations of working-class, 1930s East End life rendered their survival and maturation into adulthood if not remarkable then at least not commonplace. Many of the criminal teams that they were later to associate with and challenge for supremacy were comprised, at their kernel, of brothers like the Richardsons, the Webbs, the Lambrianous, the Nashs, the Woods, the Dixons, and the Malones, but no others were twins. Brothers provided strength through number and consanguineous allegiance but only the Krays possessed the primal bond of absolute complementarity and allure. The very rarity of twins conspires to amplify their deeds.

> Had Ronnie and Reggie been merely brothers, they would just be two hoods from a bygone day. Folk remember Jack the Hat only because he was murdered by The Kray Twins.
>
> (Donnelly 1995: 7)

The personality development and public persona(e) of twins is very different to that of non-twins. Infant twins charm and attract the attention of other mothers in the street; they create a halo through the synergy of their needs, demands and delights; they fascinate others through the verisimilitude of their hairstyle, their eyes and their matching outfits – they both mirror and contain like facing bookends. Their significance is simultaneously ancient and modern.

> From antiquity onwards, twins have had special significance and played an important role in the mythology of nearly all ancient and primitive cultures. Twins have been heroes and demi-gods, or imbued with magical powers ascribed to a double identity. In Native American legends, forces which are related and share the same space, such as the sun and the moon, are said to be twins.
>
> (Siemon 1980: 387)

These same traits in adult twins are appealing, but not in the same ways. They can arouse the vicarious appeal of a 'freak show', people sharing physical features, mannerisms, and wearing the same clothes – these are all transgressive and thus threatening images stalked by the conceptual menace of clones, cyborgs and replicants. As Bataille stated in an analysis of the deviations that nature produces:

> A 'freak' in any given fair provokes a positive impression of aggressive incongruity, a little comic, but much more a source of malaise. This malaise is, in an obscure way, tied to a profound seductiveness. And, if one can speak of a *dialectic of forms*, it is evident that it is essential to take into account deviations for which nature – even if they are most often determined to be against nature – is incontestably responsible.
>
> On a practical level this impression of incongruity is elementary and constant: it is possible to state that it manifests itself to a certain degree in the presence of any given human individual. But it is barely perceptible. That is why it is preferable to refer to monsters in order to determine it.
>
> (Bataille 1985: 55)

In adulthood the 'identicality' generates a confusion between the natural and the intentional, the compulsive with the wilful. The tension contained in this confusion both conceals and discloses a monstrous power that is experienced externally but sourced wholly within the dyad. The ultimate and particular power exercised by twins is that of exclusion, the symbolic rebuff that is generated by the 'oneness' manifested in the cryptophasia (or private language) identical twins often assume; a community of inner sanctum that defies all and any other possible membership. Testimony to this is found most poignantly in Reggie's wreath for his brother's funeral which carried the tribute 'To the other half of me'. The author Iain Sinclair notes the magnitude of this membership and the consequences of its fracture:

> Splitting the Twins, divorcing Reggie from his 'other half', was like splitting the atom – it had done something to the sky, to our perceptions of time.
>
> (Sinclair 1995: 37)

But its structural violence is more ruefully expressed by a former gang member who felt sucked into their madness and disproportionately punished for his part in their drama:

> You were never, ever, on solid ground with them . . . They played a little game all of their own. There was an unspoken language: it was what

> they didn't say as much as what they did say. There's a myth they took
> care of their own, but I never saw that. The Krays were their own.
>
> (Lambrianou, C. 1995a: 28)

A further intimidation that is presented to the collective by the
experience of twinning is the threat of loss or abandonment of identity
and purpose. The real secret of twins which holds our imaginations is
their fusion of free will and the tacit disregard for the achievement that
is our individual difference. We may struggle to constitute our own
characters through experience but the very oneness of twins is utterly
dismissive of that struggle.

The Krays, as we have already suggested, are both comic and terrifying
in their legacy. This is part of the dialectic that weaves their twinness into
the fabric of Leiris's (1988) concept of the 'sacred' in everyday life.

> What for me is the sacred? To be more exact: what does my sacred
> consist of? What objects, places or occasions awake in me that mixture
> of fear and attachment, that ambiguous attitude caused by the
> approach of something simultaneously attractive and dangerous,
> prestigious and outcast – that combination of respect and desire, and
> terror that we take as the psychological sign of the sacred.
>
> (Leiris 1988: 24)

Such sacredness constitutes phenomena that clearly undermine the
stability of commonsense categories. Even though we are familiar with
the possibility of their existence, twins challenge the uniqueness of identity
by offering a double frame of reference. In this sense twins might appear
as optical illusions, as disturbances in the visual field. They require that we
look again but ensure that we cannot divert our eyes.

There would be something arrogant and preposterous in reducing
the Kray story merely to an account of their twinness but it would be
fatuous to deny its contribution to their having been set apart, to the
creation of their sense of uniqueness and their air of strangeness that
punctured the profane everyday world surrounding them. Their status
as twins provides a forceful indicator of the source of their glamour and
charisma.

As with all binary systems, however, the creative force emerges not
so much from the complementarity of the pair but from their oppositional qualities. The Twins' oneness was shot through with active

contradictions. The older twin, Reg, was clearly overshadowed and directed by his younger brother in acts of criminality and violence as in business and publicity initiatives. Reggie appeared more easily led. Yet, as young boxers a different picture emerged that was to mark out a further contradiction: Reggie was a stylish, classical boxer whereas Ronnie was an uncontrolled streetfighting pugilist and this, perhaps superficial, observation was revealing of a deeper personality differentiation between the thinker and the intuitive. Reggie was the urbane businessman; Ronnie the psychotic thug. Reggie had a wider perspective, a more global view that would reach outside their immediate environment into the West End of London and other cities beyond; Ronnie was far more parochial both in his vision and his practice. As Pearson put it: 'In most ways Ronnie led a simple life. His life was rooted in the village life of the East End' (Pearson 1985: 85). Yet even this formulation of differences takes on the stability of a morphology or hints at a division of labour prescribed through natural disposition which is systematically eroded by what we know of their flexible and generative capacity for alterity and renewal. They were gloriously and dedicatedly unstable in their self-presentation; the very model of a post-structuralist identity. Their seeming capacity for parthenogenesis enabled an almost seamless tapestry to emerge comprised of contradictory, bathetic and incommensurable images. The 'many' Krays were irreconcilable to the Twins themselves and to their burgeoning public. They became: gentleman/thug; philanthropist/extortionist; respectable/low-life; calculating/unpredictable; kind/brutish. It is, however, important to note that the task of understanding and justifying the totality of their selfhood was not of their undertaking; it was abandoned, artfully, into the hands of the collective other. The Twins metamorphosed into image and lived through image. This is a situation not uncommon to modern celebrity but quite exceptional to men of their status and ability relative to the age in which they lived. They displayed a precocious gift for untutored self-promotion in a period when pop managers were a new phenomenon and spin doctors utterly unheard of. The contradictions interwoven with their identities and differences resounded and, indeed, continue to echo through their own attempts at autobiographical coherence (Kray and Kray 1988; Kray 1990; Kray 1993) and those of their apologists (Lambrianou, T. 1991).

In many senses the contradictions and incompatibilities within their own twinning and between their multiplicity of re-imaging produced a blurring of the immediate impact of their presence or, perhaps we might suggest, a constant lubrication of their receptibility. Nowhere is this more apparent than in relation to their sexuality. There is no disputing the powerful, if conventional, image of masculinity that they afforded, nor the part that it played in their desirability. They were tough, wealthy, authoritative, charismatic, influential, determined, handsome, well dressed, in fact 'a pair of good-looking boys who could handle themselves'. This was surely the hyperbole of machismo. Yet Ronnie was self-confessedly homosexual, actively and promiscuously so in a period when such a lifestyle was only just beginning to attain legality and, latterly, understanding, and then only in more enlightened sections of society (informed by the cinema of the period through the groundbreaking work in Deardon's *Victim* (1961) and Losey's *The Servant* (1963) as well as through Joe Orton's stage-plays). To a working-class East-Ender homosexuality was anathema and for an East End gangster unthinkable; indeed, it is widely held that Ronnie assassinated George Cornell for having called him a 'fat poof' in public. Reggie, on the other hand, had a slender heterosexual career: there were suggestions of adolescent homosexuality (Donoghue 1995); no record of any named girlfriends; he was once married and separated within the space of eight weeks; there were rumours that the marriage was unconsummated (Pearson 1985); and, subsequent to his wife's suicide, he sustained a lasting romantic attachment to her memory with no further recorded relationships with women. After his death Reggie's true lifetime orientation as a partially repressed homosexual was confirmed (Pearson 2001). Neither of these profiles lends itself to the stereotypical masculine 'hard-man' of the modern mass media, nor even the lovable 'rogue' of the English literary tradition (Williams 1993). Yet sexual the Krays were and erotic they remained in their appeal, in their violence, and in the appeal of their violent lives. The obscure, ill-defined, unspoken or unpronounced nature of the Krays' actual sexual disposition and practice became secondary to the eroticising of their short histories. It is as if an ambivalence or even an androgyny attaches to the Twins themselves; again a transgression, and in this case a primary one, which enables them a mobility across, or perhaps in spite of, existing classificatory systems. Like magical characters in fairy tales or the rootless 'germinal' figures around which literary narratives often pivot, the Krays entered into and moved freely within all and any groups. They traversed social space as if they 'didn't care who owned the place', but always with an eye to owning it themselves. Not for them the burden of conventional morality nor sexuality. They had become the mythic figures which we investigate here. As such they had no need for origins, and explanations of their behaviour leave behind what Galton (1907) originally described as 'the convenient jingle of words', nature and nurture.

To begin to understand the Kray fascination requires a rejection of the received wisdom which has become polarised as two ends of a moral continuum. It is merely to accept conventional categories to regard them as either benevolent folk heroes or malevolent psychopaths, our purpose must be neither to celebrate nor condemn but to explore the limits of their intelligibility. This is not to propound an aesthetic of moral indifference nor is it meant to imply that our understanding should not provide grounds for a moral judgement. However, to adopt such a position is, at least, to eschew the homilies and normalisations of a positivist criminology and also avoid the sentimentalising fictions the Krays' host community. As Stratton has argued in relation to serial killing, some criminal violence, ' . . . both in its generic construction and in its practice, needs to be understood in terms of its relation to the social' (Stratton 1996: 77). Stratton develops this point in relation to the axis of modernity–postmodernity, arguing that we no longer inhabit a world marked out by a shared vocabulary of moral values and that in our present environment the moral is positively supplanted by the aesthetic. It is therefore singularly inappropriate to attempt to understand certain, apparently motiveless conduct, as if it were, in Black's (1991: 93) terms 'a crime against reason itself'.

This initial rejection of the received wisdom also problematises much of the available material on the Krays, which is written, for the most part, in the form of polemics by those who were agonistically 'with them' or 'against them'; the former comprising themselves (Kray and Kray 1988; Kray 1990; Kray 1993), their family (Kray, C. 1988; Fry and Kray 1993) and those who were gaoled alongside them (Lambianou, T. 1991), and the latter is made up of those who mounted their prosecution (Read 1991), who suffered at their hands (Webb 1993; Lambrianou, C. 1995b) or who gave evidence against them (Dickson 1986; Donoghue 1995; Mrs X 1996). Each dichotomous position is recoverable as a justification both for past actions which had calamitous results and as a rationalisation for a period of time spent either engulfed in the futility of prison life or lurking in the twilight paranoia of escaping retribution. The real Kray fascination remains, however: in the public attitude; in the size and composition of the crowd that attended Ronnie's funeral; in the vast number of Londoners who continue to claim an historical association with the Twins or their family (often despite impossible biographical and temporal discrepancies); and in the strength provided by their imagery in summoning up a better age, a time of stability and safety policed by their 'brotherhood'.

> Walk anywhere in the East End with the twins, and everybody knew 'em. 'All right, Reg?' 'Lovely day, Ron.' As much as they were feared in criminal circles, they were very well liked by the local population. The twins were genuinely pleasant and polite and, towards women, charming and respectful . . . Ronnie used to come out every Sunday for a stroll, impeccably dressed as always . . . Every person he passed would call out a greeting.
>
> Much has been said and written about the so-called Robin Hood syndrome and, yes, its an accurate parallel. Although the Kray twins pursued a legitimate career in clubland they earned much of their living from crime and violence, and much of what they got they gave away.
>
> Reggie and Ronnie were fascinating people, very moral men in many ways. They had a code of ethics . . .
>
> The twins also believed in a certain honour among thieves, something that has gone out of the window today . . .
>
> (Lambrianou, T. 1991: 99–100)

This extract distils, in a short space, many of the cliches that have been and continue to be applied to their government of the community. The only fables missing from this litany of 'good deeds' concern the low crime rate, the absence of rape and attacks on old people, and the lack of a necessity for household security while they ruled the streets. So there it is in essence, 'a pair of diamond geezers', unassailably etched onto the public memory as local benefactors and moral crusaders of heroic proportions.

The Krays' iconography is itself two-sided and this reflects, at a different level, the growth and zonality of their city. London, like many large conurbations, expanded initially in relation to function and density but divided latterly in terms of largely social and cultural factors; these two sets of organising principles became increasingly disconnected. The East End was identified with poverty, disease and deprivation along with violence, criminality and political dissidence (Fishman 1975, 1988). The migrant and itinerant population of the East End through the eighteenth and nineteenth centuries became a complex proletarian mass, geographically and morally juxtaposed to the reason and order that epitomised the city centre (Stedman-Jones 1971). London rapidly emerged as a leading

European city of culture and commerce but only by ghettoising and largely repressing its increasingly ungovernable East End (Garside 1984).

> Physically, culturally, and metaphorically the East End of London stands on the very periphery of British capitalism. Informed by historical precedent, East-Enders exist on the brink of the City of London's legitimate commercial enterprise and legality. Bourgeois cultural hegemony may define, via the coercive force of the market place, the parameters of the area but it rarely impinges upon the day-to-day dynamics of East End culture.
>
> (Hobbs 1988: 140)

The urban 'great divide' that continued unchecked into the early twentieth century was both real and utterly material. This social and cultural chasm was straddled only in the pioneering literature of the period and through bourgeois philanthropy and the work of moral missionaries. This separation of worlds came to resemble and recreate Britain's colonial past, and failings, on a smaller scale and with an inward perspective. The bifurcated imagery of contemporary commentators abounded with subterranean and imperial metaphors, with 'underworlds', 'low-life deeps', 'abysses', 'the outcast', 'mean streets', 'thieve's dens', 'dark continents' 'wild races', 'jungles' and 'swamps' (Walkowitz 1992). For the West End to know the East at all was to apprehend the threat and intimidation, the exotic and even the bizarre. Outstanding and exaggerated cultural motifs have become lodged in history and folklore – the Dock Strikes of 1889, the Match-Girl Strikes (Boston 1980), the Cable Street Riots, the Siege of Sidney Street (Rumbelow 1973), racial conflicts, the Ratcliffe Highway Murders (James and Critchley 1990), the Elephant Man (Howell and Ford 1980) and most notable of all, Jack the Ripper (Rumbelow 1975). These are mostly gothic images, though all factually based, none of which make reference to the mundane, everyday experience that is East End life. The Ripper, for example, is a remarkably exaggerated and oppressive West End image. Was the unfound felon a Royal? An aristocrat? A bourgeois? A doctor? He was certainly a caped gentleman who quite literally penetrated and eviscerated the body of the East as a symbolic retribution for its seduction of the West's young manhood, who travelled across town for gambling, narcotics and prostitution on a nightly basis. Less than fifty years after the Ripper murders occurred the Kray twins were born in Hoxton and were moved, in their infancy, to Bethnal Green, the epicentre of the earlier slaughter. From here they rekindled the durability of the East

End demons and assumed the authorship of the well-established local gothic narrative tradition. As Samuel (1994) began his analysis of East End imagery:

> Gothic, literary critics argue, allows us to indulge a taste for the uncanny, to play with fantasies of impossible desire, and to explore the extremes of the human condition. It leads us into the dark passages of the unconscious. It descends to the lower depths.
>
> (Samuel 1994: 381)

The East End of London has, since the mid-nineteenth century, patiently, though always reluctantly, answered the questions of its interrogators. At the outset the East End was a territory without a map; it slowly evolved into a precise cartography but the territory disappeared. Now it stands in a twilight world between 'urban place' and 'museum space', which can only mean one thing. It is a realm where many of the living constantly pay homage to the dead. Where visitors, newcomers and the dangerously curious simulate and assimilate the memories and myths that are inscribed in the names of the streets and pubs, that are in turn the only indicators of a cultural coherence. But the search for coherence is the last imperial fantasy of the urban explorer. The East End, like its two great ritualised narratives, 'The Ripper' and 'The Krays', remains beyond the scope of formal analysis; the facts escape the fiction, the protagonists are unknowable, yet they are identified as monuments to a past that cannot be erased, forgotten or displaced. And like all great monuments they are invisible.

> The place of memory in any culture is defined by an extraordinary complex discursive web of ritual and mythic, historical, political and psychological factors.
>
> (Huyssen 1995: 250)

The obverse and less oppressive side of this iconography is as it appears to and works in the favour of the East-Enders themselves, that is, as a form of cultural resistance. As an area of the city that has been historically dispossessed of articulate power, other than that mobilised through collective labour and exile's attempts at insurrection, it has elected leading figures who have assumed pneumatic proportions. Some simply demonstrated the naked power of physical prowess, particularly in the form of prize-fighters and boxers; others have become fêted as emergent entertainers from the days of music halls up to modern theatre and film; and, perhaps most significantly, the East End has lionised its most ostentatious thieves and scoundrels. The criminal motif has a long tradition stretching from Mayhew's costermonger and the hooligan (Pearson 1983; Chesney 1991) to the modern-day self-made businessman and the anti-Establishment villain. Williams catches this tradition well when he states that:

> . . . violence in urban fiction can be traced back, in one dimension, to the long tradition of 'roguery'; but in its growing dominant prevalence it is better seen as a mode of experiencing urban life which catches in its isolated areas and incidents not only an understandable kind of respectable interest (fascination and horror, in a single mode of distance) but also the most explicit and isolatable form of action, when not a society but a population is being observed and described.
>
> (Williams 1993: 227)

The rogue, or the villain, epitomises the 'attitude' that Hobbs formulated *as* the East End:

> The cultural inheritance of East London has been formed by a fusion of communities; independence, internal solidarity, and pre-industrial characteristics combining to form a community that does not conform to either proletarian or bourgeois cultural stereotypes. The vital contradiction of this cultural inheritance is that it is essentially working-class, favouring an entrepreneurial style that is rooted in pre-industrial forms of bargaining and exchange.
>
> (Hobbs 1988: 101)

Hobbs's sense of an 'attitude' has both material and ideational dimensions, that is, he refers to: a cumulative ethnic mix of Huguenot, Irish, Jewish and Bangladeshi people (the Krays were supposed to have emerged from a mixture of Jewish and Romany stock); and a cumulative response to poverty and hardship which is at once protective, itinerant and entrepreneurial. This has developed into a pattern of dealing, what Hobbs calls 'doing the business', accompanied by a code of recognition relating to who it is both safe and appropriate to deal with. The interwoven subculture of criminality has, historically, made it essential that the code is both private (embedded in slang, argot and mannerism, and located in transient and 'undercover' markets) and also heavily insulated by rules of protection (like the 'wall of silence') and the punitively upheld imperative 'thou shalt not grass'. Specifically with reference to the norms and mores of the Krays' 'manor', the East End of the 1960s, Hebdige (1975) has referred to this self-referential and self-sustaining attitude as a 'system of closure'. The system is like a stage play by Racine, Sartre or Gide; the 'world' is elsewhere and to leave the stage means death or certain ontological annihilation.

Within such a system permeated by a 'roguery' that is acceptable at all levels, symbolic heroes are elected through excess. The most audacious thefts, the most sadistic violence and an almost philosophical quest for glory in infamy are topmost in people's minds. An elision of style and brutality can emerge, as it did in the form of the Krays. The resistance is wrought through ritual and the rituals are defined by criminality. In this way the police mediate between two symbolic communities but clearly represent the interests of only one. Their inevitable corruption is predictable as a consequence of their contagion.

The stage of Bethnal Green or the East End in general, though village-like in its sense of community and tribal in its regulatory allegiance, is, of course, not bound by death but rather more modestly by an unfamiliarity that stems from its marginality. As Shields stated:

> Marginal places, those towns and regions which have been 'left behind' in the modern race for progress, evoke both nostalgia and fascination ... They all carry the image, and stigma, of their marginality which becomes indistinguishable from any basic empirical identity they may once have had.
>
> (Shields 1991: 3)

A further artful trait of the Krays, enhancing their appeal as being not only 'their own men' but also 'men of the people', was their seeming capacity to overcome this marginality and thus, in a symbolic sense, to transcend their city's 'great divide'. They gained support for this artfulness and collusion in its goals from the emergent values of an epoch which now stands as a popular metaphor for social change – the 1960s. Whatever the economic, political, social and moral realities of this period of contemporary British history, it gave rise to a series of new narratives concerning social mobility, egalitarianism, tolerance, affluence, consumption, style, sexuality and opportunity, many of which were purely ideological, but many of which suited the aspirations and trajectory of the Kray Twins and served to integrate them quite effectively into the hearts and minds, and society and pockets, of the mandarins of the emergent popular culture and, through the mass media, into the reach of the populace also. A continuous montage of press photographs depicted the Twins in the company of sports personalities, actors and actresses, entertainers, pop singers, models, fashion photographers, media personalities and politicians. Sometimes these scenes, which were for the most part strategically stage-managed by the Twins themselves, occurred in nightclubs (their own and others), sometimes at charity events, and, on one occasion, in a Tory peer's drawing room. They were clearly becoming benefactors of the poor and friends of the famous – as Ronnie shouted at his trial when losing patience with the proceedings: 'If I wasn't here now, I'd probably be drinking with Judy Garland'! Hebdige has summarised this process well:

> The Krays were . . . the darlings of the media of the sixties. Feted and filmed whenever they emerged from the womb of the Underworld, they exercised their privileges as celebrities with an adroitness and a sophisticated awareness of the importance of public relations matched only in the image-conscious field of American politics. They brought a style and polish to the projection of good image (morals apart, of course) quite lacking at that time in many of the more conventional areas of public life – summoning press conferences whenever expedient, paradoxically winning by virtue of their constant visibility in the press, some measure of freedom from police interference. As we have seen certain of the Krays' projects, when closely examined, take on a bizarre aspect more appropriate to the theatre than to the rational pursuit of profit by crime.
>
> (Hebdige 1975: 26)

Just as the American gangsters of the 1920s and 1930s had provided a constant source of entertainment for the British cinema-going public (and a set of role-models for the Krays), the home-bred gangster was now becoming domesticated, at least in the popular imagination. Villains were assuming the status of pop-stars and the hyperbole of their behaviour was similarly becoming a source of wonderment to people in general. Style and appearance were paramount and the new glamour quite successfully masked the violence and extortion from which the phenomenon took birth.

Raban (1988) invokes the plasticity of the city in relation to the plurality of identities that are possible for any given inhabitant of the urban environs. The possible and potential guises that are available make up what Raban referred to as an 'Emporium of Styles' that blurs the distinction between the 'real city' and the 'city of the imagination'. Within this dichotomy Raban situates the Kray lifestyle; pathological figures driven by a highly developed interior life of fantasy. Obsessed with the filmic images of Al Capone, Ronnie constructed a tenuous reality out of the highly charged emblems of the emergent American popular culture. Double-breasted suits, diamond cufflinks, thick and heavy gold jewellery became his sartorial trademarks; Buicks and Pontiacs his preferred method of transit. It was as if a 1930s Hollywood film set was being Surrealistically constructed in the old East End. For Ronnie ambience was all important:

> When the twins took control of a local billiard hall which they used as a headquarters, Ronnie made himself responsible for the atmosphere. He turned it into a pool-room out of an American novel, with low lights and swirling cigar smoke (assiduously blown about the place by Ronnie before it opened).
>
> (Raban 1988: 72)

In the manner of Orson Welles, Ronnie was both director and leading man in a drama that was simultaneously imaginative and factual. His private fantasies and personal obsessions seeped into the public realm via the collective archive of popular image culture. A strategy that was both tragic and transgressive, yet, paradoxically, one that would eventually lead to the Twins entering the timeless sphere of embalmed icons that remains 'sixties London'.

> We must not think of time as some continuously flowing stream moving in one direction . . . There are parts of London, I believe, where time has hardened and come to an end.
>
> (Ackroyd 1993: 5)

The exploitation of the gap between appearance and actual form was, during the period of the 1960s, accelerated and enhanced by a growing media technology initially theorised by McLuhan, subsequently aestheticised and popularised by Warhol, and from its inception, one that fatefully heralded the post-modern 'simulacra' of Baudrillard. This acceptability of style and appearance, in fact, provided a new power base and a new site of justification and moral rectitude from which the Krays could operate. They were most effective in mobilising the metaphoric space for continuous redefinition that now existed between the signifier and the signified. Such is the generative force of their mythologic legacy that we continue this process of redefinition today, even in their absence – note the contents of this chapter! They had not achieved a hyper-reality but the contemporary extravagances of the popular culture ensured little discontinuity between Ronnie's paranoid interludes and the prevalent decline of truth-value and truth-function within the academy. The philosophical and moral relativism of the 1960s can now be seen instructively in relation to the postmodern invocation of 'schizophrenia' as a methodological imperative.

The idea of the gangster as pop-star is most eloquently expressed in the period film *Performance* (1970), directed by Nicolas Roeg and Donald Cammel, which is clearly based on the Krays. Savage (1996), too, makes this connection and interprets the film as a conflict between traditional English certainties and the emergent pluralities of culture and identity that the 1960s have come to represent. The emergent themes of the film are protection, corruption, violence, sadism, sexual ambivalence, and the instability of identity. The lead role of Chas, the mobster with a strong but unreconciled erotic dimension, is played by James Fox, who had previously gained fame through his depictions of aristocrats and upper middle-class 'toffs'. Fox's conversion into the part was assisted by a dialogue coach called Litvinoff, one of Ronnie Kray's 'alleged' lovers. Litvinoff was soon to disappear and Fox to suffer a psychiatric breakdown and religious conversion that would drive him into obscurity for the next two decades. The film's narrative moves with unbroken continuity through threatening and violent behaviour, murder, courtroom manners, big business, sado-masochistic pornography, narcotic hallucinations and libidinal extravagance, all Kray motifs. There is a concluding sequence involving a final identity merger and transfer between Fox, the unlikely gangster, and Mick Jagger, playing, essentially, himself, the pop-star and cultural entrepreneur revenant. This is the ultimate 'twinning' and sublimation of one being into another. The resonances with the Twins' career are powerful and imaginative, and the scenes of distorted reality contained within the film are no less bizarre or unaccountable than the often utterly unpredictable and demonic outbursts within the context of their own lives, and, of course, their own stardom. The psycho-sexual drama that unfolds in *Performance* can be seen as having homologous relations not just with the story of the Twins but also with the complex structure of folk memories that locate the Krays within the history of English culture.

During the 1960s new forms of symbolic exchange were taking place between the different social class groups, enabled through a series of contributory factors like: the accelerating post-war boom and build in the economy; the growth of the welfare state; new housing policies; the move towards full employment; and the investment in and expansion of secondary and higher education. All of these changes were, in turn, contributing to a reconfiguration of the class structure itself. In tandem with these changes, which Harold Macmillan (prime minister in the early 1960s) formulated as 'You've never had it so good!', was a discernable secularisation of the population, including a burgeoning belief in everyone 'making-out' one way or another, and a rebellion against traditional forms of authority supported by new liberal moralities.

Established forms of symbolic exchange were legitimated when in July 1960 the Betting and Gaming Bill to legalise off-course gambling passed through Parliament. This did not invent gambling as either a social phenomenon or a social problem, but it quite effectively brought it out of the darkness and provided a series of minatory spaces where the social classes could intermingle with a shared purpose. More significantly it now meant that 'spielers' and 'dens', previously hidden, and street-corner bookies, previously mobile, could establish their place in the respectable city, set up their premises from Bethnal Green to Berkeley Square and welcome their guests – the 'punters'. The channels for the relationship between the previously demarcated criminal world and the straight world became institutionalised. The Krays, among others, were quick to see that the new 'nightclub' (and they owned four) was an uncharted and unregulated territory. All who attended stepped into a new reality and put themselves at risk. It provided the ideal location not just to profit materially from well-off 'decent' citizens but also to serve them, entertain them, charm them, seduce them, and claim their power and influence (in just the way that Dirk Bogarde, the gentleman's gentleman in Losey's film *The Servant*, systematically takes over his master's house and the house of his being). A further instance of a 'twinning' and a surrender of intentionality.

Although it is conventional to see the 1960s as a time of positive change and growth it was, in another sense, a period of great decay. We can trace this from Nietzsche's Zarathustra when he announced the decline of the 'modern':

> When I came to men I found them sitting on an old conceit; the conceit that they have long known what is good and evil for man. All talk of

virtue seemed an old and weary matter to man; and whoever wanted to
sleep well still talked of good and evil before going to sleep . . .

And I bade them throw over their old academic chairs and wherever
that old conceit had sat; I bade them laugh at their great masters of
virtue and saints and poets and world redeemers, I bade them laugh at
their gloomy sages and at whoever had at any time sat on the tree of life
like a black scarecrow. I sat down by their great tomb road among
cadavers and vultures, and I laughed at their past and its rotting,
decaying glory.

(Nietzsche 1966: 310)

The Tory Party started the 1960s with a General Election victory and
a majority of 100 seats; they were not to last the decade. They began
with a front bench in tail-coats and striped trousers and ended with
a radically reshuffled front bench in disarray during 1963. Profumo had
resigned his Cabinet post in a scandal involving prostitution, drugs,
London racketeers and Russian spies, and some while later Lord Boothby,
who was understood to be having a long-standing affair with Macmillan's
wife, was 'alleged' to have had a homosexual relationship with an East
End gangster, revealed by the *Sunday Mirror* (12 July 1964) to be none
other than Ronnie Kray. In parallel with the mobility and elevation of
the new proletarian icons of pop-singers and gangsters a popular distrust
of the Establishment had gained a firm hold of the collective mind and this
was encouraged and sustained by the treasonable satire and critique of the
new intelligentsia, the newly educated 'classless' elite. The old order was
crumbling and giving way, with maximum resistance, to the tidal wave of
renewal and invention. Just as the conceptual gap between image and reality
had provided a playground for the Krays ability for self-portraiture, so also
the void left by the expulsion and demise of the deity in his various
remaining guises of legitimacy, tradition and authority, had provided a
fresh canvas for the depiction of graven images. Now we all inhabited the
'pop' culture.

Pop is directly linked to the Second World War, both as a psychic
purge and as an economic continuum. The modern music/media
industry emerged out of the technologically driven, mass production,
fast turnover nature of the post-War economy. Its speed driven nature
is epitomized by the inaugural icon James Dean. In this struggle
between life and death the enemy is within.

(Savage 1996: 8)

As the children of the 1960s went in hot pursuit of this 'enemy', they were quite remarkable in their voracious appetite for demi-gods. The fear of freedom that appeared to mark the decade meant that as they laughed Prime Minister Macmillan and President Johnson, their teachers and university lecturers, and priests and moralists off the stage, the wings were packed with negative models of celebrity, notoriety, addiction and criminality waiting to audition for the role of leader. In this sense the decay fertilised little more than a decadence of which the Krays formed a central part. Perhaps the lasting contemporary nostalgia for that period and for its icons, the Twins included, is a longing for rebelliousness and unaccountability. The creative imagination that was certainly unleashed during that time manifested itself in a spectrum of antisocial forms. The world of the fantasy, like the world of the gangster, had emerged into public territory, and what the fantastic promotes is a freedom unfettered by responsibility. Fantasy is a very private journey, unsharable even in intimacy, and a journey through a potentially sinister and limitless space.

All of the details of the Krays' criminal activities, and particularly the vicious homicides and physical assaults that were committed by them or their shadows, constituted their story as a profound psycho-drama, but one that teetered on the brink of madness and the dissolution of the two main protagonists. Their schizoid desires and mean reactive tendencies constantly play down the conventional belief that they marshalled a vast criminal empire with precision management and rational calculation. As so often within this tale, at the conjunction of the rational and the criminally insane the facts about the Krays begin to evaporate.

In a classical sense Ronnie and Reggie were men of tragedy. They inhabited a nightmare and they were directed by forces beyond their control towards a finale that is both horrific and inevitable; it was also the finale of a decade.

> The tragic man is essentially one who becomes aware of human existence. He sees the violent and contradictory forces that stir him; he knows he is prey to human absurdity, prey to the absurdity of nature, but he affirms this reality that has left him no outlet other than crime.
> (Caillois 1988: 147)

In his discussion of the nature of 'brotherhoods' Caillois (1988) argues that what distinguishes secret societies from the wider society is the creation of a mysterious space where power, prestige and specialised knowledge are articulated and initiated. Therefore a brotherhood is never simply a secret society in the sense that it is unknowable to the wider public. Rather, the brotherhood draws from an 'undisclosable' and mysterious element that binds the members of the group. Within the brotherhood of the Krays, 'the firm', this mysterious element can be seen as the exchange of equivalents: money and death. These are the most highly charged of symbolic objects which were collected and executed by the Krays with a rhythmic and ritualised technique.

> The profane world is the world of taboos. The sacred world depends on limited acts of transgression.
>
> (Bataille 1986: 68)

Within the Bataillean theory of transgression the Krays stand in a further paradoxical relationship to the sacred and the profane. On the one hand they represent the power of the sacred with its capacity to revolt and fascinate. In this sense the Krays stand for the collective social space of taboo and transgression that the East End signifies in London's cultural memory. They became a distillation of the violence, the horror and the misery that the cultural compass of the East End has always meant to the conventional moral order. Yet the singular acts of abjection that became the hallmarks of the Twins moral universe disturbed the subtle balance between taboo and transgression.

For Bataille transgression is always best understood as a collective act whereby the broken taboo can be repaired following its transcendence. For the Krays transgression was a simple end in itself from which there could be no return.

> Taboo and transgression reflect these contradictory urges. The taboo would forbid the transgression but the fascination compels it. Taboos and the divine are opposed to each other in one sense only, for the sacred aspect of the taboo is what draws men towards it and trans-figures the original interdiction. The often intertwined themes of mythology spring from these factors.
>
> (Bataille 1986: 68)

The Krays often engaged in the liminal experience of excess and transformed their transgressions into a celebration of an inverted moral order – the world turned upside down. Yet their acts were the articulated desires and fantasies of sovereign man, the man who denies all links to other beings. This is the Sadean world of moral isolation.

> If crime leads a man to the most sensual satisfactions, the fulfilment of the most powerful desires, what could be more important than to deny that solidarity which opposes crime and prevents the enjoyment of its fruits?
>
> (Bataille 1986: 169)

In opposing all moral universes the Sadean man opens up a void where the necessary taboos can never be restored. The sensual nature of the criminal act can only be comprehended in terms of the boundary that it sequentially fractures and repairs.

Perhaps the secret of the Krays is that they simultaneously paid obeisance to the profane world ('we only hurt our own') yet created a void where the endless possibility of moral dissolution became the sovereign principle of a saga that had real, tragic and lasting effects.

> They were the best years of our lives. They called them the Swinging Sixties. The Beatles and the Rolling Stones were the rulers of pop music, Carnaby Street ruled the fashion world . . . and me and my brother ruled London. We were fucking untouchable . . .
>
> But people still remember us, don't they. Probably more people remember us than remember the Beatles.
>
> (Kray 1993: 1, 2)

NOTE

*The original version of this chapter was jointly authored by myself and my friend and colleague Justin Lorentzen. I am eternally grateful to him for his imagination and energy and for exciting my fascination for this topic. The chapter first appeared in *Theory, Culture and Society*, Vol. 14, No. 3, August 1997 and it is reproduced here with the editor's permission.

6

JOURNEY TO THE END OF THE NIGHT

In many ways this is an unruly chapter and rightly so: its inhabitants defy order. Its subterranean theme is madness, but beyond the scatological fixations of de Sade and Bataille. The psychiatrist Thomas Szasz (1961) employed as his mantra the phrase 'madness is a sane response to an insane society', but this was in the arch-liberal days of anti-psychiatry when R.D. Laing enjoyed cult status and before we realised that mental illness was, in many life-ruining manifestations, an issue of chemistry rather than bad mothering. Madness has, nevertheless, been both a topic and a resource for much contemporary critical thought with notions of disrupted categories, decentred selves, moral and political incorrectness, behaviour out of place, pain and abjection, and a scrambling of conventional grammars proving forceful devices in philosophy, art and the avante-garde.

> . . . all evidence . . . supports the view that what people now call mental illnesses are, for the most part, communications expressing unacceptable ideas, often framed in an unusual idiom.
>
> (Szasz 1961: 121)

Historically, madness has proved to be the grand transgressor. Its manifestations have been met with privilege, wonder, exclusion and horror, and its reception is always socially contexted. In the contemporary world it is a recognised motive for transgression but it is also a mitigation for having transgressed. It is a zone, available to us all, where the prison-house of language glissades into incomprehension. Rules and limits still apply; obeisance becomes the problem. 'Touched by God', the holy child among the tribe transforms into the 'possessed':

> Mysticism and possession often form in the same pockets in a society whose language thickens, loses its spiritual porosity, and becomes impermeable to the divine. In such a case, the relation to a 'beyond' vacillates between the immediacy of a diabolical seizure and the immediacy of a divine illumination . . . From this perspective there is a complicity and, to borrow a phrase from William Blake, a 'marriage of heaven and hell.
>
> (de Certeau 1990: 6)

And finally madness metamorphoses into pathology, an affront to reason that must be contained and governed. But always there is an implicit recognition of a power: a Godly power, a demonic power, a physical power, and even within the repressive tolerance of contemporary 'understanding', a power that must be 'known' because of its transgressive potential. Such power may be illusory but it is also elusive. One uncontained outlet for this nascent energy is creativity, at the margins of consciousness. Ferguson describes a primary division in lunacy 'between melancholia, a disease of under-consumption, and mania, a frenzy of excess' (Ferguson 1990: 23) – both have their muses. Many of the thinkers we have encountered so far attest to this tragic alignment of great intellect and the unquiet mind.

Foucault's (1967) groundbreaking history of derangement reveals the gradual evolution of an oppressive and excluding definition of madness. The work also displays both his Marxism and his materialism. The insane are destabilising to a society that conducts its relationships in terms of market forces. They are disobedient instances of labour-power. They are unable, unwilling or inconsistent in their labour practices. If membership and social inclusion demand productivity from citizens then a lack of productivity provides a mark of unreasonableness. The unreasonable have become gradually and systematically excluded in line with the birth of the asylum. The asylum becomes the capitalist machine to process the unproductive.

This chapter will elect some notable individuals, groups and movements that have, through modernity and beyond, explored the limits of reason, the extremities of the mind, and have, through this, broadened our recognition of transgression further. André Breton, who we shall soon encounter, declared before the parturition of Surrealism, 'Dada is a state of mind'. Artaud claimed 'I know what Surrealism is. It is the system of the world and of thought which I have always made for myself' (1956: 112). Pascal quipped 'Men are so necessarily mad, that not to be mad would amount to another form of madness' (quoted in Foucault 1967: ix). Salvador Dali ironised the issue by saying 'The only difference between me and a madman is that I am not mad'. And finally Jameson has invoked schizophrenia as a postmodern methodological imperative. Madness is redolent.

ARTAUD AND THEATRE

Drama is a root metaphor in the explanation of human conduct, from the Shakespearean 'world as stage' to the rather more technical dramaturgical sociology of Erving Goffman and his followers. Drama, in its spectrum of meanings, is also a wholly appropriate setting to consider the work and dreadful life of Antonin Artaud.

Antonin Artaud (1896–1948) is perhaps most closely associated with avante-garde theatre; however, his versatility and dexterity (and provocation) projects much further than this. His list of activities as author, director and actor extend to the following range of artistic practices (the adjective 'experimental' is assumed in each case): radio broadcasting; sound recording; film; essays; theatre; poetry; dance and visual art (some of his drawings are on display at the UK Royal Academy as I write). He is sited as an inspiration in the critical theory of Kristeva, Derrida, Deleuze and Guattari, and Foucault. His influence is acknowledged in the 'new expressionism' of Baselitz, the Royal Shakespeare Company of Peter Brook and the film-making of Fassbinder. He knew and exchanged ideas with Breton, Bataille, Cocteau, Tzara, Picasso, Braque, Masson, Miro and Debuffet. He hated Sartre, disliked Lacan, ignored Gide, and had an affair with Queneau's future wife. He lived through two world wars and worked through what must have been the most busily creative period of French, and European, art. He was a very difficult man, cold, isolated and suspicious; beautiful in youth and degenerated by his middle years. He had an extended and unresolved addiction to laudanum, opium and heroin, and fought an almost life-long battle with schizophrenia and deep clinical depression which caused him to be incarcerated in asylums and brutally treated for nearly a decade.

Artaud never really saw himself as either part of or wholly in touch with the collective. This was not due to any enmity towards his fellow man, indeed one could argue that his life's work was dedicated to a clearer and certainly more vivid communication with others. He was at least committed to wrenching theatre out of the relative gentility and luxury provided by bourgeois entertainment. He wanted a theatre of body, and noise, and more elemental form. He was largely reflexive about his state of mind and employed his madness as both an artistic and political implement. This free form, the transcending of traditional categories and constraints, this intermingling of reverie and active creation, made him the archetypal (if not the original) Surrealist but it also set him wilfully apart and placed him in a tense relationship of violence and suppression with the status quo. Thus: 'All individual acts are anti-social. Madmen are the victims par excellence of social dictatorship' (Artaud 1956: 221).

Integration was never his balm nor his desire. Existential realisation was both his objective and the cause of his martyrdom. We might regard transgression as his watchword.

> If theatre is as bloody and as inhuman as dreams, the reason for this is that it perpetuates the metaphysical notions in some Fables in a present-day, tangible manner, whose atrocity and energy are enough to prove their origins and intentions in fundamental first principles rather than reveal and unforgettably tie down the idea of continual conflict within us, where life is continually lacerated, where everything in creation rises up and attacks our condition as created beings.
>
> This being so, we can see that by its proximity to the first principles poetically infusing it with energy, this naked theatre language, a non-virtual but real language using man's nervous magnetism, must allow us to transgress the ordinary limits of art and words, actively, that is to say magically to produce a kind of total creation in real terms, where man must reassume his position between dreams and events.
>
> (Artaud 1971: 71)

Throughout his creative life Artaud was stalked by misunderstanding, rejection and failure. All this plus the debilitating illness, the poverty and the virtual imprisonment mounts up to a bow-wave of impedimenta sufficient to break the will of a lesser figure. Yet, we learn from Barber

(1993), Artaud's will was so strong that he ignored, shrugged-off or simply overcame such temporal irritations through regeneration and re-invention. Indeed, his 'triumph of the will' was such that he aspired to a body, a theatrical body, that transcended mere corporeality.

One of Artaud's more bizarre concepts, 'the body-without-organs', was later adopted by Deleuze and Guattari in their *Anti-Oedipus* thesis. Essentially, they argue, humankind is organised through two kinds of desire: the constraint of paranoia and the freedom of schizophrenia. The psyche records such desires but it does so in a mode that is without sensuousness, a creative mode that is free from instinctive connections and types of satisfaction. This is understood through the metaphor of the body-without-organs. Such a body becomes 'dis-organ-ised', such disorganisation breaks through the conventions that life within capitalism dictates and provides the scope for change, revolutionary change. Schizoanalysis becomes political in practice and intent.

> . . . schizophrenia designates not just an objective tendency of capitalism but the preferable objective tendency, in its opposition to the paranoia of tradition and its potential for radical freedom. The primary aim of schizoanalysis is to take this preferable tendency to the limit, and indeed to push it through the limits, imposed on it by capitalist paranoia: schizophrenia as revolutionary breakthrough rather than psychological breakdown . . .
>
> (Holland 1999: 3)

The schizophrenic, for Deleuze and Guattari, is not held within the Oedipal trap. Their schizophrenic, not a mere psychiatric type but a Nietzschean heroic force,

> . . . produces himself as a free man, irresponsible, solitary, and joyous, finally able to say and do something simple in his own name, without asking permission; a desire lacking nothing, a flux that overcomes barriers and codes, a name that no longer designates any ego whatever. He has simply ceased being afraid of becoming mad.
>
> (Deleuze and Guattari 1977: 131)

This description is reminiscent of Artaud himself; a man at war with the state of his art, his culture, his society and the political economy of his time. He bore indignity and pain and spoke of triumph and pride. This triumphalism was to be acted out (literally) through hyperbole, exaggeration and what, for the sake of a resonance with Bataille, we shall call excess.

> Artaud's theatrical ideas, when put into practice, can only have the effect of galvanising an audience, making it more alive and aware, sometimes politicising it, but above all bringing an element of magic into life, with pure poetry its major component. One must never forget that Artaud is a poet first and much of his most fascinating work is written in verse or poetic prose: the memorable phrase, the turning of a familiar symbol into a radical new image, the stretching of an extreme concept into an extravagance that makes it even more extreme, is typical of the man and must lie clinically at the roots of his madness as well as his genius.
>
> (Calder in Artaud 1970: 105)

Within this extravagance and extremism lies Artaud's shocking but benevolent concept of 'cruelty'.

'PATAPHYSICS', ARTAUD AND THE MANIFESTO OF CRUELTY

Before we examine Artaud's Theatre of Cruelty, chronology demands that we should first become familiar with the ideas of one of Artaud's major, and most influential, antecedents. Alfred Jarry (1873–1907) was yet another extraordinary French aesthete who made his mark on the Parisian theatre around the turn of the nineteenth century. Although chronic alcoholism, malnutrition and general self-neglect prevented him reaching middle-age he left us with two outrageous creations, *Pere Ubu* and *Dr Faustroll*, and their anarchistic new science, 'pataphysics'. Ubu emerged out of a cycle of three plays all performed to rioting audiences, and Faustroll was Jarry's literary figure. Ubu is a fat, disgusting, libidinous, flatulent, violent figure without any redeeming or restrainable feature. He continually curses, makes vile oaths, cites bodily parts, dwells in innuendo and entertains with an eloquent schoolboy filth shockingly juxtaposed with a disposition to injure or kill other characters within the play. His foul mouth is aimed at cast and audience in equal measure and he punctuates every soliloquy and exchange liberally with the expletive 'shit', or rather the original and more phonetically satisfying 'merde'! So for example Act 1 Scene 1:

Pere Ubu: Merde!
Mere Ubu: Ooh! what a nasty word. Pere Ubu, you're a dirty old man.
Pere Ubu: Watch out I don't bash yer nut in, Mere Ubu!

and later Act 1 Scene 4:

> *Pere Ubu*: Well Captain did you enjoy your dinner?
> *Captain Macnure*: Very much, Sir, except for the merde.
> *Pere Ubu*: Oh, I didn't think the merde was too bad.
> *Mere Ubu*: A little of what you fancy, they say.
> *Pere Ubu*: Captain M'Nure, I've decided to create you Duke of Lithuania.
> *Captain Macnure*: But I thought you were completely broke, Mister Ubu?
> *Pere Ubu*: In a day or two, with your help, I shall be King of Poland.
> *Captain Macnure*: You will assassinate Wenceslas?
> *Pere Ubu*: The bugger's no fool. He's guessed it.
> *Captain Macnure*: If its a question of killing Wenceslas, I'm with you. I am his deadly enemy, and I can answer for my men.
> *Pere Ubu*: (*throwing himself upon him to embrace him*). Oh, M'Nure, I love you dearly for that.
> *Captain Macnure*: Pooh, how you stink, man! Do you ever wash?
> *Pere Ubu*: Occasionally.
> *Mere Ubu*: Never!
> *Pere Ubu*: I'm going to tread on your toes.
> *Mere Ubu*: Fat lump of merde!

(Jarry 1968: 21, 25–6)

And so on. Parts of Jarry's legacy are on display in these short extracts: the disregard for the niceties of bourgeois audiences; the rudeness and abrasion; the interruption and disturbance of the audiences tranquillity; the sheer noise; a pleasure in language more than plot; a celebration of performance over representation – all paths lead to Artaud!

Now what of 'pataphysics', Jarry's new science, acclaimed by Guillaume Apollinaire the poet and polymorphous perverse pornographer? Pataphysics is the 'science of imaginary solutions' and is committed to 'examine the laws governing exceptions, and will explain the universe supplementary to this one'. Ubu saw the need for this science and leaves us with a new set of values (or a comic revaluation of values). Pataphysics apes Nietzsche and mocks Hegel but all through irony and at vast distance. The new science knows no truths, nor causality and it has no goals, it is patently unreasonable. Following so soon after Baudelaire, Jarry's absurdities can be seen as part of a mounting modernist critique regaling art, science and contemporary culture. However, even as parody, the deeply unserious and inarticulate grounds that comprise pataphysics have become a metaphor for the challenge and overthrow of conventional wisdom cited by many since, including Althusser and Baudrillard. This form of knowledge has no tradition and no authority. Pefanis, as ever, expresses this well:

> The idea of an authority is 'to go against the spirit of pataphysics' which in fact forbids the pataphysical mind, if we can refer to one as such, from organizing a social movement around an idea that has been turned into a religion. Pataphysics is an aesthetic nihilism and a will to crisis, and it is small wonder that it is taken up by the situationists. Like them, it advocated the path of active nihilism.
>
> (Pefanis 1991: 122n)

After Jarry, many were to see his work as both announcing Dada and providing the essential form for Surrealism. Artaud, in homage to Jarry and in an attempt to perpetuate and renew his innovations, established the Alfred Jarry Theatre in Paris between 1927 and 1930. The project was destined to fail but not before it had put on a number of extremely controversial performances attacking theatre's rules and conventions but through an unsystematic series of neologisms in the vocabularies of space and body. Provocative they were, but the rationale was unformulated and unreplicable. It was theatre against theatre, theatre against spectacle, illusion and representation. It was also theatre without ends, theatre without respect and, terminally, theatre without funds. The entropic tendencies inherent in the project finally erupted and left Artaud, once again, battered and depressed. However, other damage had resulted from the calculated transgressions of this œuvre. Many had seen Jarry and this legacy as part of Surrealism; Breton, the key signifier of the surreal, denied this designation. In response Artaud argued that Breton's Surrealism was becoming complacent, narrow, and insular. Breton countered with the edict that Surrealism was moving from an art disruption into the serious work of political activism whereas Artaud was continuing to work with bourgeois and profit-making art forms like commercial film and theatre. Most of all, one suspects, Breton felt challenged by the Surrealism that the Alfred Jarry Theatre actually stood for and in true Stalinist fashion he erased it. Artaud, like many others including Bataille, was expelled from the Surrealist movement for failing to follow the party (and increasingly the French Communist Party) line. Artaud was devastated and fell into the vortex of madness, poverty and absolute rejection.

Resurrection followed in the pursuit of 'cruelty'. Commentators record the origin of Artaud's Theatre of Cruelty almost as a 'road to Damascus' experience on his visiting a touring company of Balinese theatre in 1931. The experience undoubtedly provided a multi-media environment that focused his lasting desire to break out from the proscenium, stop poncing about on stage and speaking in nice voices. He says:

> The first Balinese Theatre show derived from dance, singing, mime and music – but extraordinarily little from psychological theatre such as we understand it in Europe, re-establishing theatre from a hallucinatory and fearful aspect, on a purely independent, creative level.
>
> (Artaud 1970: 36)

Unlike the Alfred Jarry Theatre, which was now exhausted, the Theatre of Cruelty was to be based on two explicit manifestos expressing the parameters of 'the new'. These manifestos are short but surprisingly explicit and provide principle in relation to details of 'the show', 'staging', 'stage language', 'musical instruments', 'lights', 'costume', 'props', 'decor' and so on. However, as we might imagine, the principles are stated in the form of challenge, negation and alternative interpretation rather than commandments. So we are told:

> Every show will contain physical, objective elements perceptible to all. Shouts, groans, apparitions, surprise, dramatic moments of all kinds, the magic beauty of the costumes modelled on certain ritualistic patterns, brilliant lighting, vocal, incantational beauty, attractive harmonies, rare musical notes, object colours, the physical rhythm of the moves whose build and fall will be wedded to the beat of moves familiar to all, the tangible appearance of new, surprising objects, masks, puppets many feet high, abrupt lighting changes, the physical action of lighting stimulating heat and cold, and so on . . . We do not intend to do away with dialogue, but to give words something of the significance they have in dreams . . . We intend to do away with stage and the auditorium . . . The actor is both a prime factor, since the show's success depends on the effectiveness of his acting, as well as a kind of neutral, pliant factor since he is rigorously denied any individual initiative. Besides, this is a field where there are no rules.
>
> (Artaud 1970: 72–6)

What emerges from the manifestos are certain fundamental critical elements that seek to alter the position of theatre in modern culture and to reconfigure the relationship between the performance and the audience. The underlying impulses of performance are what Artaud refers to as 'metaphysics' throughout his writing. And these metaphysics are, at an abstract level, about power and resistance to change. Artaud wishes to redistribute the power and instigate change. To explain, traditional theatre is organised in relation to a classical, but growing, repertoire of texts. So dramatists write plays, directors interpret those plays within a concept, actors interpret their roles within that concept, audiences receive that compound of interpretation. This process and chain of relationships constitutes a set of power relations and a movement from activity to passivity, audiences being the most passive recipients. Artaud wishes to deconstruct this edifice, to remove the grounds for authority and domination, and to generate an art form more suitable for a contemporary, educated, politically aware populace. Theatre, as we know it, is an outmoded form of communication, unsuitable for its time. The text, the play, the script, must be de-centred. Theatre must become about the performance (the metaphysics) and not about obedience to the text. As members of an audience (an idea which itself has to be reformulated) we should leave the theatrical experience engaged with and consumed by the performance, not by its proximity or faithfulness to the text. If this vast conceptual shift can be achieved, which is Artaud's goal, then what follows is another shift, this time in power, from the playwright to the director. The director becomes what Artaud has described as 'the master of sacred ceremonies', and this, in turn, accounts for the 'neutrality' and 'pliancy' of the actor referred to in the quote above. But think of the number of sacred icons that Artaud's transgressive vision seeks to desecrate, think of the demystification, the revelation of power and the democratisation – what of the deeply embedded sets of interests that this innovation would threaten?

> There can be no spectacle without an element of cruelty as the basis of every show. In our present degenerative state, metaphysics must be made to enter the mind through the body . . . First, this theatre must exist.
>
> (Artaud 1970: 77)

We begin to unravel some of the complexity that has gone into Artaud's concept of cruelty, but there is more, much more. There is a much greater emphasis on the body in this new theatre: the body shocks, risks and endangers and this is all the metaphysics of performance. On the side of the audience, as hinted at in the quote above, the body, not pure cognition, is the receptor of performance. The body is loaded with senses, largely unstimulated by conventional theatre. The invocation of body and bodily sensation by both actor and audience makes for the possibility of a unique performance and a unique communion at each and every show. The theatre of cruelty does not carry an ideal type of the perfect performance, bodies entwine and original sensation issues, there are parallels here with the act of love. This move to corporeality does not signal an anti-intellectualism, Artaud and Artaud's work are very much thought through. He is exploring novelty in experience, ideas entering 'the mind through the body'. Performances and their reception will be unique, the intended risk, danger and shock are met by chance, randomness and disruption – by both actors and audience. This provides another angle on the notion of cruelty, all parties are cruelly exposed unlike the luxuriously cocooned theatregoers of the past. This should prove a critical juncture in drama. The implicit proposition that the performance will not ape text sets drama free from various tyrannies: representation, being privileged, the preserve of the specialist, the 'cognoscenti'. Drama would cease to be a discipline.

> All I can do for the time being is to make a few remarks to justify my choice of title, the Theatre of Cruelty.
> This cruelty is not sadistic or bloody, at least not exclusively so.
> I do not systematically cultivate horror. The word cruelty must be taken in its broadest sense, not the physical, predatory sense usually ascribed to it. And in so doing, I demand the right to make a break with its usual verbal meanings . . .
> One may perfectly well envisage pure cruelty without any carnal laceration. Indeed, philosophically speaking, what is cruelty? From a mental viewpoint, cruelty means strictness, diligence, unrelenting decisiveness, irreversible and absolute determination . . .
> We are wrong to make cruelty mean merciless bloodshed, pointless pursuits unrelated to physical ills . . .
>
> (Artaud 1970: 79)

We can see here resolve and commitment, and an existential affirmation to the life (and death) of theatre as the life and death of the self. So he concludes:

> Practising cruelty involves a higher determination to which the executioner–tormentor is also subject and which he must be resolved to endure when the time comes. Above all, cruelty is very lucid, a kind

of strict control and submission to necessity. There is no cruelty without consciousness, without the application of consciousness, for the latter gives practising any act of life a blood red tinge, its cruel overtones, since it is understood that being alive always means the death of someone else.

(Artaud 1970: 80)

This passage speaks as much about Artaud's pain as it does of his alchemical theatre, but also of their intimate association. He once said of the Surrealists that they loved life as much as he despised it!

After a frenetic few years of high- and low-profile performances and a constant battle to acquire subsistence finance, the Theatre of Cruelty collapsed in 1935, but its transgressive recommendations for theatre lived on. Artaud, once again wounded by failure but driven by his creativity, now looked for further revelations of his inner self in travel. After bizarre and tortuous journeys to Mexico, Belgium and Ireland, all with distorted intent, Artaud experienced the monumental collapse that led inexorably towards his nemesis. When Artaud finally re-emerged from subjection to nine years of asylum governance in 1946 his transgressive will to power undaunted, he was to enjoy (no, perhaps rather, live through) two more years of stellar creativity before the light burnt out.

DEBORD AND THE SITUATIONIST INTERNATIONAL (SI)

There is a predominant theme, closely interwoven with that of transgression, which has preoccupied the French avante-garde from Baudelaire to Dada and Surrealism (which we will consider next). This theme attends to the unanticipated, the strange, the magical, the mad and the minatorial aspects of modernity. It is, in itself, a kind of cognitive transgression in that it resists and challenges the imposition of modernity's order. It finds beauty and creativity in chaos and juxtaposition. If the modern city classifies our lives through the organisation of streets and buildings then resistance implies an exploration of the spaces between or within them. It works with architecture, urban geography, art and political ideologies. Freedom is found not in interior decoration but in the dust it collects. The conventions of modern cities are redolent with new revelations, but we have to learn how to read the city in the in-appropriate manner. Surrealism dissipated and died after the Second World War but certain elements of it were re-kindled with a revolutionary fervour by Guy Debord (1931–94) and the Situationist

International which lasted between 1957 and 1972. The May 'Revolution' of 1968 might be regarded as its finest hour. In line with the sustained modernist critique and the emergent voice of the postmodern, SI opened up and re-explored the space between surface and depth, representation and text, simulation and reality.

> The project of the Situationist International, as Debord conceived it, was to create the Utopian society in the here and now; the Situationist International was a revolutionary micro-society whose rules and codes of conduct were in constant evolution, whose very way of life was at the heart of their programme. In the city of Paris, in his own personal kingdom, Debord was the very opposite of the harsh and dour theoretician that he was later perceived to be . . .
>
> Debord reserved particular relish for the uncommon detail of a city, which could be architectural, a strange or historically significant building, or artistic, an unusual statue or square.
>
> (Hussey 2002: 144)

The walk was a vital part of Baudelaire's method; the act of walking was subsequently recovered by the Guy Debord and the SI, suggesting strategies for a post-modern walking methodologist (Jenks 1995a: 153), these being: 'the derive', 'detournement', and, perhaps most significantly, the 'spectacle'.

The 'derive' is the practice through which 'psychogeographies' are achieved. The term, literally applied, means 'drifting'. However, that is insufficient a meaning to exhaust the concept's potential. To simply drift implies a passivity that 'blows with the wind' whereas the 'derive' demands a response to inducement, albeit unplanned and unstructured. A 'psychogeography' depends upon the walker 'seeing' and being drawn into events, situations and images by an abandonment to wholly unanticipated attraction. This is political, it is a movement that will not be planned, or organised instrumentally – it will not be mobilised. The stroll of Baudelaire's *flâneur*, or the Situationist in the 'derive', is not purposefully from A to B, not along the boulevard to *les Grands Magasins*, and not intentionally up and down the Arcades. In the 'derive' the explorer of the city follows whatever cue, or indeed clue, that the streets offer as enticement to fascination. This is no direct route, safest way, intended path; in this mode 'Keep left', 'Keep off the grass' and 'No entry' do not signify – the actual, everyday, vibrancy of street activity invites and takes individuals to other places, not previously scheduled.

> Among the various situationist methods is the *derive* [literally: 'drifting'], a technique of transient passage through varied ambiences. The derive entails playful-constructive behaviour and awareness of psycho-geographical effects; which completely distinguish it from the classical notions of the journey and the stroll. In the derive one or more persons during a certain period drop their usual motives for movement and action . . . and let themselves be drawn by the attractions of the terrain and the attractions they find there.
>
> (Debord in Knabb 1981: 50)

A psychogeography, then, derives from the subsequent 'mapping' of an unrouted route which, like primitive cartography, reveals not so much randomness and chance as spatial intentionality. It uncovers compulsive currents within the city along with unprescribed boundaries of exclusion and unconstructed gateways of opportunity. The city begins, without fantasy or exaggeration, to take on the characteristics of a map of the mind. The legend of such a mental map highlights projections and repressions in the form of 'go' and 'no-go' space. These positive and negative locational responses claim, in their turn, as deep a symbolic significance in the orientation of space as do the binary moral arbiters of 'purity' and 'danger' or the 'sacred' and the 'profane' in relation to the organisation of conduct (see our discussion in Chapter 2). Such an understanding propels Baudelaire's *flâneur* and Debord's Situationist towards an investigation of the exclusions and invitations that the city (as indeed the state of [post]modernity) seems to present. And the critical theorist of modernity experiences these binaries through other complexes of time, hierarchy, different and overlapping groups.

The concept of 'detournement' emerges from modernist avante-garde artistic practice. Simply stated it consists of the re-cycling, re-positioning, or re-employing of the existing elements of an art work, or works, into a new synthesis. The two principles of the practice are: (a) that each re-used element from a previous context must be divested of its autonomy and original signification; and (b) that the re-assembly of elements must forge an original image which generates a wholly new meaning structure for the parts, through the totality that they now comprise. 'Detournement' provides the *flâneur* and the Situationist with the perceptual tools for spatial irony. The walker in 'derive', who is therefore not oriented by convention, can playfully and artfully 'see' the juxtaposition of the elements that make up the city in new and revealing relationships.

The planned and unplanned segregations, the strategic and accidental adjacencies, and the routine but random triangulations that occur through the mobility that the city provides, and depends upon, make for a perpetual and infinite collage of imagery and a repository of fresh signification. All of this conceptual re-ordering is open to the imaginative theorising of the wandering urban cultural critic and yet mostly such techniques have come to be the province of the photo-journalist. The image of the city formed by the *flâneur* should be part of his reflexivity; it hermeneutically reveals both modernity and the projections, inhibitions, repressions and prejudices of the *flâneur*.

Finally, and formative of both of the above ideas, is the concept of 'the spectacle'.

> The world of consumption is in reality the world of the mutual spectacularization of everyone, the world of everyone's separation, estrangement and nonparticipation . . . the spectacle is the dominant mode through which people relate to each other. It is only through the spectacle that people acquire a (falsified) knowledge of certain general aspects of social life . . . It answers perfectly the needs of a reified and alienated culture: the spectacle-spectator is in itself a staunch bearer of the capitalist order.
>
> (Debord in Knabb 1981: 307–8)

The spectacle is that which constitutes the visual convention and fixity of contemporary imagery. It is a reactionary force in that it resists interpretation. It is a prior appropriation of the visual into the form of the acceptably viewable, and this 'acceptability' befits the going order. The spectacle indicates rules of what to see and how to see it, it is the 'seenness', the (re)presentational aspects of phenomena that are promoted, not the politics or aesthetics of their being 'see-worthy.' From within this critical concept the Situationist can deduce, and thus claim distance from, the necessity of objects-to-be-seen as appearing in the form of commodities. People and their places; space as an intertextuality of narratives of social life; the 'sights of the city': they are not objects at hand for the gaze of the consumer, that is, the tourist in the lives of the collective other. This takes us back to the notion that Baudelaire's *flâneur* should/ could not merely mingle with the crowd, but is an interactor and thus a constitutor of the people's crowd-like-ness. Social life is degraded rather than honoured by its transformation into the realm of 'the spectacle'. It is, ironically, the realist reduction at the core of materialist epistemologies, such as have sought to critique the *flâneur*, which is more adept at standardising and routinising the relation between signifier and signified into the form of a positive 'spectacle'. There is a possible convergence between the Situationist notion of 'spectacle' and Simmel's notion of the 'blasé' attitude characteristic of modern urban citizens, which implies indifference towards the distinctions between things (Gilloch 1997: 144). Resisting both the spectacle and the 'blasé' attitude, the *flâneur* and the Situationist exhibit a peculiar observational and political stance, well exemplified by the relations usually established with the less favoured inhabitants of the city.

Hebdige's (1979) extremely influential work on subculture and style can be seen as a series of highly sophisticated allusions to the Situationist concept of the culture of the spectacle, as a relocation and extension of the SI project and as active contribution to arguments surrounding the politicisation of culture and cultural analysis such that Debord might have approved.

The SI were a wide ranging group in both location and interest, and in the influence they exercised on other groups and traditions of thought. What remains notable about the Parisian core, and particularly Debord's work, is that it is fiercely revolutionary.

> First of all we think the world must be changed. We want the most liberating changes of the society and life in which we find ourselves confined. we know that this change is possible through appropriate actions.
>
> Our specific concern is the use of certain means of action and the discovery of new ones, means more easily recognizable in the domain of culture and mores, but applied in the perspective of all revolutionary changes.
>
> What is termed culture reflects, but also prefigures, the possibilities of organization of life of a given society. Our era is fundamentally characterized by the lagging of revolutionary political action behind the development of modern possibilities of production which call for a superior organization of the world . . .
>
> One of the contradictions of the bourgeoisie in its phase of liquidation is that while it respects the abstract principle of intellectual and artistic creation, it at first resists actual creations, then eventually exploits them.
>
> (Debord in Harrison and Wood 1992: 693–4)

At the age of sixty-three, his revolution never having quite materialised, Debord shot himself.

DADA AND SURREALISM

It is most often an impertinent and inadequate approach to creative endeavour to seek explanation by reducing it to a consequence of its material circumstances. Leonardo's line, Caravaggio's colour and Goya's figuration did not occur because of the state of their specific political economies! However, it would be hard to argue that 'the War to end all wars' that was the First World War, which described a broad quagmire corridor across Europe doubling as a cemetery for a third of its doomed youth, did not impact significantly upon the intellectual conscience of its epoch. In this period, 1914–18, Dada was born and the seeds of Surrealism scattered like shrapnel. All senses of limit and morality underwent volcanic eruption and transgression upon transgression had become sanctioned both on an individual and a collective basis. Bataille explains it thus:

> Often the transgression is permitted, often it is even prescribed.
> We feel like laughing when we consider the solemn commandment 'Thou shalt not kill' followed by a blessing on armies and the Te Deum of the apotheosis. No beating about the bush: murder is connived at immediately after being banned! The violence of war certainly betrays the God of the New Testament, but it does not oppose the God of Armies of the Old Testament in the same way. If the prohibition were a reasonable one it would mean that wars would be forbidden and we should be confronted with a choice: to ban war and to do everything possible to abolish military assassination; or else to fight and accept the law as hypocritical. But the taboos on which the world of reason is founded are not rational for all that.
>
> (Bataille 2001: 63)

We might anticipate that during a post-war period of repair and recuperation the anxious and shocked collective consciousness might begin to examine the coalition of death, the unconscious and desire with some urgency, and that this would generate the surreal. However, at the time of war and in the immediately traumatised aftermath the loss and waste and futility gave rise to the anarchistic nihilism that was Dada. Dada was a word found at random, it is French for a child's hobbyhorse,

'The child's first sound expresses the primitiveness, the beginning at zero, the new in our art' (Huelsenbeck 1936: 280). Starting in Zurich and migrating to Cologne and Paris, Dada collected an international group of proponents including Tzara, Janco, Arp, Ball, Richter, Huelsenbeck, Duchamp, Picabia and Man Ray. For these young artists the war had rung the death-knell on a particular social structure, a set of class relations, a form of capitalist economy and the art and culture that supported and entertained the rest. Dada was to read the requiem at this demise and to seek out and destroy all remaining vestiges of this decadent system. This destructive urge was also suicidal in intent, the Dadaists new that they too were artists from the old order and that they would only claim an audience because of that status. Thus they set out, with ironic zeal, to self-destruct.

So the Great War was viewed as simultaneously the awakening of the barbarism inherent in European society and the purging of these intrinsic evils. Dada was to be vigilant in its opposition to art that represented or attempted to reinstate the past; neo-Classicism would be a target. Dada was almost clear in what it was opposed to but wholly scattered as to what it was for. Dada never constituted a style, a technique, a genre. Dada was no mere -ism; the -isms, and most recently Cubism, fed the status quo. To this end Dada could be viewed as a charlatan's charter, there were no standards, no rigour, no discipline, anything would do. Dada was an action set in opposition, a process, a way of thinking, it was firmly no-thing. Art had become a *thing*! Some of this vacuous irony is contained within the following paradoxes:

> How is it that Duchamp who's phrase 'stupid as a painter' is well-known becomes if not the most influential 'painter' . . . then at least the greatest single influence on 20th Century painting, eclipsing . . . even Picasso?
>
> How can the reflexive question – What is it *to paint* modernity? So quickly degenerate into the morbid quasi-platonic essentialism of: What is *art*? Notice that the entire domain of social action is effaced in the shift from the active verbal form *to paint* to the noun (or name) *art*.
>
> How is it that the freedom essayed by Dadaist significant objects (Duchamp's *Fountain* amongst them) can without contradiction or radical doctrinal alteration make Abstract Expressionism look at first promising, then ridiculous and culminate in the ostensibly necessary end of painting? How can radical freedom and suffocating censure be identical consequences of the same programme?
>
> (Smith and Jenks 2000: 141)

Of course, Dada could not sweep away the remains of the bourgeois order, that had to be left to the Russian Revolution and the terrors of Stalinism, fortunately never quite a global movement.

Who then is Duchamp and what was his remarkable contribution? Marcel Duchamp (1887–1968) was a French painter who moved to the USA during the Great War. He orchestrated a scandal by submitting a urinal (bought from a plumbers' merchant) for exhibition in a New York academy under the pseudonym of Richard Mutt. It was refused but debates followed which ensured the gesture a place in art history. The 'found object', the 'ready made' would now come to be seen as art, because the artist 'chose' it (though Duchamp claimed that his choice was indifferent to beauty). This transgression killed the painter, ended authorial intent, changed centuries of conventions surrounding beauty, and democratised the salon. On the wall of the Tate Modern gallery in the UK today is a glass of water placed on a glass shelf (and topped up daily); this is Michael Craig-Martin's *Oak Tree*.

> The non-superiority of the artist as creator was one of the fundamental Dada pre-occupations. Linked to this is a whole complex of ideas, interpreted in a different way by each Dadaist. Poetry and painting can be produced by anybody; there is no need for a particular burst of emotion to produce anything; the umbilical cord between the object and its creator is broken; there is no fundamental difference between a man-made and a machine-made object; and the only possible intervention possible in a work is choice.
>
> (Ades 1997: 119)

Ready-mades and objects-at-hand would find a future in Surrealism, as would Dada's use of collage (which reveals the origins of Situationism's 'detournement'), and the deconstruction and mockery of language, Tzara's preference, which leads to Surrealism's 'automatic writing'.

The fractures that Dada began were to be amplified by Surrealism; perhaps Dada had simply not gone far enough. Richardson, writing of the development of Bataille's thought, states that:

> . . . he assiduously frequented bordellos whilst also making himself known in intellectual circles. Apparently finding Dadaism 'not idiotic enough', since its 'no' was too conventional, he advocated a movement that would say 'yes' to everything.
>
> (Richardson 1994: 19)

Surrealism perhaps? The transgressions that Dada's, albeit highly nihilistic, posturings achieved in relation to the limits of art and aesthetics were to lead us down a twisting path through modern art up to the contemporary mainstreaming of 'conceptual art' and the sidelining of painterly skills, but also through other routes to the politicising of art.

What are we to make of Surrealism and where shall we position it in our understanding of transgression?

> Three great systems of exclusion and division allow the human word to lay claim to purity: the play of prohibitions, the strongest of which is the prohibition of desire; the division between reason and madness; and the will to truth . . . These prohibitions certainly surround the act of speech in a very powerful way. Moreover, added to them is the obligation to say only what is reasonable, and according to the codified modes of 'non-madness' . . .
>
> From the time of its foundation in France in 1919, Surrealism responded to these games of division by revolting against them. Surrealists saw these divisions with a lucidity and a violence sharpened by the postwar despair and a sense of there being no reason to go on living.
>
> (Chenieux-Gendron 1990: 1–2)

So here, at an abstract level, we have the Surrealist urge – the denial of prohibition. Where centuries of classical philosophy, also in pursuit of the truth, had essentially recommended that we 'should not let our imaginations run away with us', the Surrealists demand that we should. Thus imagination (untrustworthy), the unconscious (inarticulate), and desire (unspoken) should now become trustworthy, articulate and find voice, they should combine as out new mode of cognition and break out from the moral constraints that contemporary classifications of experience have placed upon us. This can be in art or political action. Denial, revolution, revolt become symbolic imperatives. This notion is crystallised, through hyperbole, in Breton's famous statement from his *Second Manifesto of Surrealism*:

> . . . one can understand why Surrealism was not afraid to make for itself a tenet of total revolt, complete insubordination, of sabotage according to rule, and why it still expects nothing save from violence. The simplest Surrealist act consists of dashing down into the street, pistol in hand, and firing blindly, as fast as you can pull the trigger, into the crowd.
>
> (Breton quoted in Chenieux-Gendron 1990: 3)

This appears as a carte blanche for transgression, a moratorium on retribution, backlash or the power of limit to reassert itself – unless the reassertion is the integrative intent within the programme. Or is this the absolute sovereign revolt of Surrealism so clearly expressed by Bataille?

> We cannot reduce ourselves to utility and neither can we negate our conditions. That is why we find the *human quality* not in some definite state but in the necessarily undecided battle of the one who refuses *the given* – whatever this may be, provided it is *the given*. For man, the given was originally what the prohibition refused: the animality that no rule limited. The prohibition itself in turn became the given that man refused. But the refusal would restrict itself to the refusal to be, to suicide, if it exceeded *the limit of possibility*. The composite and contradictory forms of human life are tied to this position *in the breach*, where it was never a question of retreating, nor of going too far.
>
> (Bataille 1991b: 343)

This is the concept of sovereignty that Bataille inherited from de Sade, the primacy of self-determination over servility and obedience (and again we hear echoes of Hegel's Master–Slave dialectic). Are we then to accept Surrealism as a philosophy of absolute relativism, a belief that there are no limits?

Although perceived to be primarily about negation, the Surrealist programme as envisaged by André Breton (1896–1966) its acknowledged progenitor, was based essentially on a neo-Hegelian totality beyond the dialectics of contradiction – this was the integrative intent referred to above. So by attacking prohibitions, oppositions would be resolved: life and death, conscious and unconscious, real and imaginary, past and present. Surrealist work extols this resolution. Surrealism would clear the way by attacking, lampooning or destroying all processes and mechanisms that created or perpetuated divisions within cognition and the social. A new coming together, a new form of community was being sought.

> The community of which Surrealism was the embryo was one that sought to give form to a heterogeneous conception of community that went against the essentially homogeneous nature of the dominant capitalist reality and as such served as a complement to . . . what communism represented.
>
> (Richardson 1994: 33)

In effect, towards the later stages of the movement's development, the only unity that Surrealism experienced was that directed by and legislated for by Breton himself. Internal disobedience was met with expulsion, so Bataille and Artaud were fired.

Despite the authoritarian management of the movement by Breton, Surrealism was fundamentally a positive and constructivist development and, unlike Dada, a practice-based collective. Although bourgeois consciousness and bourgeois culture remained anathema to them, the ineffectual petulance of Dada was shed for more positive action and reflection upon that action. Surrealism made things. Although manifestly polymathic, Surrealism was primarily a literary and visual artistic movement which was concerned to find an audience for their work and to theorise about that work, thus producing an intellectual platform from which to propagate the genre. The ideas of 'platform' and genre here imply no intended stasis or invention of tradition. Intellectuals and artists began to identify with the movement and to promote its ideas and styles. Figures such as Ernst, Aragon, Crevel, Desnos, Eluard, Tanguy and Leiris formed a core (though not all adhered) together with some of the Dadaists who simply migrated into the movement, and others such as Dali, Giacometti, Buñuel, Magritte and even Picasso were later associated with the initiative.

Freud was clearly a significant influence, explicitly and implicitly, thus the bourgeois consciousness might be re-formulated as 'repression'. Art and political action was to occur without the sanction and the filter of the super-ego. Creativity untrammelled by the shackles of reason was the goal. The concept of 'automatism' was developed to imply not machine-like but rather spontaneous (automatic).

> Masson adopted the principle of automatism wholeheartedly . . . The pen moves swiftly, with no conscious idea of a subject, tracing a web of nervous but unhesitating lines from which emerge images which are sometimes picked up and elaborated, sometimes left as suggestions. The most successful of these drawings have a completeness about them which comes from the unconscious working out of textural, sensual references as well as visual ones.
>
> (Ades 1997: 129)

Painting, speaking, writing, imaging were to occur directly from dreams, the unconscious, free-association of ideas, desire, the *id* – a primal human source before the uniformity of thought style, cognition, logic, dialectics, that is *reason*, had occurred. This idea of a thought before thought was a major source of dissent among practitioners but it is also an idea to which the human intellect has often returned through the respectable form of transcendental phenomenology and the less respectable, but more accessible form of hallucinogenic drugs. The surreal was the pre-rational, pre-bourgeois, undecorated expression of the human intellect. Surrealism transgressed reason, the retribution or backlash was that it was unintelligible! Unlike Freud's psychoanalysis, for Surrealism the unconscious was not the font of pathology, it was original human quality. Freud's repair through therapy and analysis was to be seen as the reinstallation of bourgeois consciousness. Insanity for the Surrealists was not just a creative source it was also a political act.

> . . . the art of those who are classified as mentally ill constitutes a reservoir of mental health . . . Through an astonishing dialectical effect, the factors of close confinement and the renunciation of all worldly vanities, despite their pathetic aspect in terms of the individual, together provide the guarantees of a total authenticity which is sadly lacking elsewhere.
>
> (Breton quoted in Spector 1997: 159)

Surrealism, as an element of the avante-garde, experienced quite a long duration, relatively speaking. Trace elements sustained, through Situationism, up until Breton's death in 1966. The focus of attention shifted and metamorphosed as was originally envisaged – from literary beginnings into visual representations but on an increasing gradient towards radical political involvement and intervention. The abstract technicism of 'automatic writing' and 'automatism' generally receded as an attention to more symbolic forms emerged. The relative individualism espoused at the outset with private journeys into the unconscious being made public inverted into a search for the origins and attachments of the collective life, indeed an interest in sociology that has kept the French intelligentsia attached to that discipline and its moral and political potential from Durkheim and Mauss, through Levi-Strauss, Aron, Lefebvre and up to Bourdieu. Bataille saw much of his work as a sociology and he, with Leiris and Caillois, founded the College of Sociology in 1936. This saw the original Comtean positivist desire for an altruistic collective life reaffirmed in the Surrealist's desire for a new form of community, again articulated by Bataille and his colleagues through a series of essays on 'secret societies' and 'hidden associations'. Surrealism showed its collective interests further through its attention to myths and the creation of myths, myths always being deep-structural devices for maintaining the social bond in the face of change. The themes of critique, irony and death coalesced around the long present form of 'black humour', traceable to Jarry.

> It was also during the 1930s that Breton and Surrealism 'invented' black humor. Although black humor existed before Surrealism (without the name) . . .
> Breton had no difficulty in seeing both the opposition and the complementarity between behavior conducive to objective chance in the Hegelian and then the Surrealist sense of the term . . . On the one hand, a tremendous sense of hope emerges, even if what happens may turn out to be tragic instead of the marvellous things my desire expects. It is the knowledge that a magical agreement may sometimes be revealed between words formulated by a subject or train of events . . . On the other hand, humor goes in the opposite direction if its goal is to undercut the representation we give ourselves of events and their oppressive connection with the self by offering a completely subversive image of it . . . Humor undercuts the representation of the world; chance seems to attack reality itself.
>
> (Chenieux-Gendron 1990: 88)

A critical term in this quote is 'desire'. Desire was seen by the Surrealists, particularly in the later phases, as the manner in which true nature makes itself known to humanity. Desire orients action, produces priorities and imperatives and deposes the manners of any particular social structure. The exposure of desire is therefore a further implement of revolt, and such action demystifies the bourgeois consciousness. Human desires are multiple and are certainly not all sexual, but there is no doubt that the misogynistic and homophobic boys-club that Surrealism grew into certainly celebrated the release of hetero-erotic fantasy into the public domain – and treated that as political too! In sum, a lot of Surrealism's images are naughty, and purposefully so.

> Given that man was born with desires, it was in his nature, according to the Surrealists, to explore them in defiance of those forces that threaten to repress individuality and control sexuality, and this remained a guiding principle of the movement in all its phases.
> Thus the great poets of the movement . . . recorded the soaring emotions and the bodily sensations connected with love, ranging from a lyrical union with the loved one, and through the loved one, with

the physical world, to unfulfilled yearning and despair. Their use of language was shaped by desire: liberated from reason, words, they felt, should be free to 'make love' . . .

(Munday 2001: 18)

RIMBAUD

It would be impossible to exclude Arthur Rimbaud (1854–91) from this chapter of the book. His short, bizarre and shocking life carries iconic transgressional status. He was the *enfant terrible* of French literature for a brief, hyper-active period; he was certainly mad, bad and dangerous to know; and he was, in the eyes of decent folk, an absolute rotter. Even Verlaine, successful and established poet, who left his wife and child for the passion he felt for Rimbaud, was driven to shoot him later in their relationship. At the opening of his superb biography, Robb succinctly sets the character he is about to unravel at length:

> Unknown beyond the French avant-garde at the time of his death, Arthur Rimbaud (1854–1891) has been one of the most destructive and liberating influences on twentieth-century culture. He was the first poet to devise a scientifically plausible method for changing the nature of existence, the first to live a homosexual adventure as a model of social change, and the first to repudiate the myths on which his reputation still depends.
>
> Rimbaud's abandonment of poetry in his early twenties has caused more lasting, widespread consternation than the break-up of the Beatles. Even in the mid-1880s, when the French Decadents were hailing him a 'Messiah', he was already several reincarnations from his starting point. He had travelled to thirteen different countries and lived as a factory worker, a tutor, a beggar, a docker, a mercenary, a sailor, an explorer, a trader, a gun-runner, a money-changer and, in the minds of some inhabitants of southern Abyssinia, a Muslim prophet.

(Robb 2000: xiii)

In a concentrated space Rimbaud appeared to do it all, but that *is* his real story. His status in this thesis on transgression is not quite as those assembled around him. His contribution is as an archetypal exemplar of the transgressing agent, a wild but perhaps unconscious sovereign man. His poetry, largely re-discovered after his death, is of a quality and attracts a following and a critical appreciation. But his work is not a reflexive contribution to revolt, transgression, upheaval and change. His verse is gathered under French Symbolism or new Romanticism and certainly not great of its day. We could say, as Bataille did, that Rimbaud's greatness derives from the fact that he led poetry to its death, but that is not so, he only oversaw the passing of his own muse. His real greatness derives from what Wilson (2000) sees as his splendid contribution to the Bohemian myth, the tireless quest for infamy, degradation, marginality and extremes. A young Byron, without the aristocracy; a beautiful beast; the angel depraved. His psychopathy linked to an aesthetic produces the perfect ingredients for a romantic cult: 'Psychosis has been the common language of art since Rimbaud.' (Nuttall 1970: 151) Far more people refer to his axial impact on Western culture than have read his poems. Indeed his transgressive life pattern becomes the real poetic contribution to Western culture. Perhaps the really important issue here is the fascination we feel for Rimbaud, not wholly dissimilar to that generated about the Kray Twins discussed in Chapter 5. This may also take us back to why I wanted to write this book and why you ever started to read it.

> On the 'cursed, desolate shores' of this century, Rimbaud is still an ambiguous presence – warning his unknown readers of the hell to which 'derangement' inevitably leads, and showing them exactly how to get there.
>
> (Robb 2000: 445)

In this chapter we have looked at certain individuals and their theorising, certain political and artistic movements, all of which test our mechanisms of boundary maintenance. But more than this they explore the very limits of consciousness and highlight, once again, the indefatigable, inherent and infinitely variable human capacity to transgress.

7

THE WORLD TURNED UPSIDE DOWN

In this chapter we shall look at the carnival both as an historical phenomenon and, more significantly, as a lasting symbol of transgression, release and a general letting-off-of-steam among the populace. Beyond this we shall see how the actual event, now essentially defunct, has transmogrified into a concept signifying resistance, disorder and methodological irresponsibility in contemporary cultural studies.

The carnival is a pre-Lenten festival of feudal origins which carries deep symbolic significance. Deriving originally from the Latin *carnem lavare*, to remove meat, the term 'carnival' has become associated through folk etymology with the Medieval Latin *carne vale*, 'Flesh, farewell!' This expletive can be read as a direct invocation to slough off the corporeal, the actual, the prevailing material circumstances and transcend, or more specifically, transgress the going order. Through carnival the reveller becomes transported into another place. The radical adjacency to Lent, the dour period of fasting and penitence, ensures a heightened experiential opposition of excess and constraint, exuberance and limit. Indeed the pinnacle, *Mardi Gras* ('Fat Tuesday'), is the last day before Lent. There is, realised here but at a higher more philosophical level, a vivid imminence between light and dark, good and evil, and eventually life and death in a manner that enables the self to contemplate ontological relativism after Nietzsche.

> In the world of carnival the awareness of the people's immortality is combined with the realisation that established authority and truth are relative.
>
> (Bakhtin 1968 quoted in Stallybrass and White 1986: 6)

Within carnival circumstances are altered, albeit temporarily, while roles, status and hierarchies become inverted in a riot of pleasure, excess, misbehaviour and misrule. The conventional world is turned upside down. There are elaborate and evolving rituals that attach to the practice of carnival, which provide its poetics, and there are social structural forces and dynamics that ensure its politics.

> Inversion is the carnival's own special symbol, which only later shrinks to express a secular political ideal. In the feudal period its meaning is unrestrained by any practical desire for a more perfect social order or any covert appeal to a subversive concept of social justice. The carnival is complete in itself and need seek nothing 'beyond' its own sensuous fullness. A more profound reversal of conventional relations lay in its negation of the process of symbolic expression as such.
>
> (Ferguson 1990: 108)

The symbolism of carnival is rich; in reality it was much more than a period of release, or even contained anarchism. Carnival acts through strategies that ape, parody and indeed parallel the dominant social order. There is a calculated inversion of existing social forms and cultural configurations: coronations take place (Lords of Misrule are elected), laws are passed, trials are held, punishments are executed.

> Many of the traditions of carnival indulged in ritual mockery of the community's elders and betters, providing opportunity for licensed disorder. Formalised in some parts of Europe in the election of boy bishops who ridiculed their elders, in mock sermons and the ritual desecration of religious emblems, or in the absurd judgements of the Lords of Misrule, the folk imagery of pre-industrial Europe was saturated with fantasies of reprisal against the powerful and against existing moral codes.
>
> (Pearson 1983: 196)

People are no longer who they are, and the masquerade becomes the basis for interaction. Transformed identity is conveyed through mask and costume, and the revelation of true self is disallowed. The mis-rule is

contra-deductive, things are specifically *not* as we think they should be!
So, this is a finite interlude of licensed mayhem, but carnival is also an
artful and highly orchestrated tilt at sacred establishment icons. Its
unfolding is allegorical (Bristol 1985), which, in turn, reveals the deep
structural grammar of control at work within the wider society:

> The social structure is itself a kind of allegory, in that its order is also a
> sign of other, larger orders that form a chain of significance leading to
> that which does not signify – the divine Logos.
>
> (Bristol 1985: 61)

A major conduit for this swathe of transformation and misrule is
the 'grotesque'. Custom, body and self-presentation take on a fantastic
design. People and their actions become characterised by distortions
or striking incongruities in their appearance, shape or manner. Fantasy and
the bizarre become mainstream, studied liminality the order of the day.
The world and its imagery project as ludicrously eccentric, strange,
ridiculous and absurd. Think of the incommensurable details in a Bruegel
painting, the sheer cacophony of demeanours, the vortex of agitation
and the absolute commitment to inclusion – a child's playground on speed!
This is the grotesque of the carnival. The grotesque generates both a logic
and an aesthetic, it also transgresses the distinctions between humans and
animals and between classes of men and their mannerisms.

> . . . the grotesque tends to operate as a critique of a dominant ideology
> which has already set the terms designating what is high and low. It is
> indeed one of the most powerful ruses of the dominant to pretend that
> critique can only exist in the language of 'reason', 'pure knowledge' and
> 'seriousness'. Against this ruse [there is] . . . the logic of the *grotesque*,
> of excess, of the lower bodily stratum, of the fair. This logic could
> unsettle 'given' social positions and interrogate the rules of inclusion,
> exclusion and domination which structured the social ensemble. In
> the fair, the place of high and low, inside and out, was never a simple
> given: the languages of decorum and enormity 'peered into each other's
> faces'.
>
> (Stallybrass and White 1986: 43)

Now, the carnival is a fascinating substantive cultural vehicle for the
examination and analysis of transgression, but it has become much more.
Rather than remaining the province of the medieval historian, the literary

critic or the art historian, carnival has been taken up to great effect by cultural studies. With the increasing politicisation of cultural knowledge; with the increasing attention being paid to popular cultural forms, primitive, low-life, vulgar and marginalised cultural practice; and with the postmodern disassembly of traditional forms of cultural analysis, 'carnival' has come to provide a new metaphor and a new style for reading the social. As Chaney so wisely puts it:

> . . . this lies behind the 'discovery' of a Russian theorist from the early days of the Revolution. Bakhtin's ideas have been used to make important contributions to theories of cultural order, the symbolism of conflict and rethinking low forms of popular vulgarity – in particular the carnival. Bakhtin has been particularly influential in deepening concepts of culture as a form of life, so that we can go beyond patterns of lived experience to explore the structures of independence of individual and community, order and chaos, the sacred and the profane.
>
> (Chaney 1994: 39–40)

BAKHTIN, RABELAIS AND THE CARNIVALESQUE

The exposure of the work of Mikhail Bakhtin (1895–1975), the Russian literary theorist, has transported the idea of carnival into the late twentieth and early twenty-first centuries. Carnival has become a critical concept in cultural analysis, rich in resonances and possibilities, which theorists ignore at their peril. Carnival is the perfect postmodern device, it is style unrestricted, method without parameter or rigour, decentred identity and a continuously broken chain of signifiers.

> The new historian, the genealogist, will know what to make of this masquerade. He will not be too serious to enjoy it; on the contrary, he will push the masquerade to its limit and prepare the great carnival of time where masks are constantly reappearing. No longer the identification of our faint individuality with the solid identities of the past, but our 'unrealization' through the excessive choice of identities . . . Genealogy is history in the form of a concerted carnival.
>
> (Foucault 1977: 160–1)

With the effective demise of carnival as a genuine, cyclical, cultural eruption through modernity (those that appear to remain, such as Venice, Notting Hill, Rio, New Orleans, are stylised reconstructions, festivals in effect), the manner, intent or motivation of carnival practice has sunk into the academic lexicon in the form of the 'carnivalesque'. This, in large part, is the legacy of Bakhtin, who was not translated into English until 1968 when, in a post-Stalin era, it was safe for him and his ideas to emerge. Also Bakhtin's election of the carnivalesque was not separated out from his early, linguistic resistance to Russian Formalism, nor haloed as a new way of understanding until a still later date. Bennett (1986) has argued that such a development has been a misappropriation of Bakhtin's ideas which add up to a rather romanticised view of the ideological power of popular festivities, and then only in the context of Rabelais. Nevertheless, many would take the view that Bakhtin's work on *Rabelais and his World* has provided a dramatic signpost in our thinking about transgression, however, from a rather different set of traditions to the other European thinkers considered so far in this book. Largely untouched by the work of what he must have regarded as a decadent and bourgeois French avant-garde, developing through structuralisms, heterologies and post-structuralisms, Bakhtin nevertheless extolled a materialist Marxism, countered Hegelian idealism, and had a less well-documented Nietzschean view of history.

As a literary theorist and linguist Bakhtin contributes most forcefully to the school of 'dialogics'. The dialogic view of language asserts that every speech act is held, reflexively, between the preceding utterance which generated it, and the anticipated future response which will structure it. This anti-formalism is very much in tune with the idea that 'language has a life' and an aesthetic, and it certainly does not privilege any one formulation of language as 'high' or 'low', 'standard' or 'non-standard'.

> This temporary suspension, both ideal and real, of hierarchical rank created during carnival time a special type of communication impossible to everyday life. This led to the creation of special forms of marketplace speech and gesture, frank and free, permitting no distance between those who came into contact with each other and liberating from norms of etiquette and decency imposed at other times. A special carnivalesque, marketplace style of expression was formed which we find abundantly represented in Rabelais' novel.
>
> (Bakhtin 1968: 10)

And this form of speech was Bakhtin's 'heteroglossia'. Humour, common speech and vulgarity are all, therefore, proper objects of linguistic attention and not to be expelled to the margins of poetics. The carnival, as topic, can now be seen in yet a further light; it is a rich cacophony of spontaneous, generative and profane linguistic performances. Dialogics at its peak!

> At first sight, it also looks difficult to apply our intentionalist hermeneutic to collective actions, whether in words or in gestures. If we heed the admonitions of Mikhail Bakhtin, like Adorno and Gramsci, nowadays a much-cited authority in Cultural Studies long after his initial work was published in post-revolutionary Russia in the late 1920s, then utterances are almost infinite in meaning. 'Heteroglossia', the many-sidedness of the glossary or lexicon, is written into the collective but endlessly conflictual and 'dialogic' nature of linguistic exchange (especially as between social classes). This collective emphasis gives rise to Bakhtin's agreeably populist celebration of the festival as the definitive form of popular culture and best expression of the multiplicity of meaning which is the energy-house of social life.
>
> (Inglis 1993: 102–3)

The single most successful work that introduces the import of both Bakhtin and the concept of carnivalesque to cultural studies more broadly is Stallybrass and White's (1986) book on *The Politics and Poetics of Transgression*. This is a scholarly and beautiful thesis which provided considerable inspiration for this author, even though it is sustained in its critique of much post-structuralism and many of the authors already examined here. Though not a manifestly Marxist analysis, the work presents a detailed historical account of the decay and death of carnival while providing a left materialist view of the politics of popular cultural forms. In part, then, the work argues for the centrality of Bakhtin's materialism as opposed to the then fashionable psychoanalytic theories of Kristeva and Lacan, or the linguistic deconstruction of Derrida. Eagleton (1982) similarly elects Bakhtin in contrast to Derrida.

Carnival has always stood in opposition to the sacred, and in practical terms the Church has always viewed the carnival as a profane organ. It is, by and large, a result of the Church's disapproval and persecution that the practice of carnival diminished and withered in Europe, even if its symbolic significance sustained. The politics of this exorcism are perverse. The transgressions routinely perpetrated in thought, word and deed within the confines and conventions of the carnival were predictable and contained. As we have already considered, such festival both permitted and ensured 'licensed' mayhem. That carnival practices were rude, and shocking, and offensive to priestly morality is undoubtably the case, but they were entirely human practices which had not and would not be expunged by centuries of Puritanism. Beyond this they were managed within a finite time and space. To ban carnival is to release the spectre of transgression upon the full span of everyday life, to render it invisible, to pathologise it and, perhaps worst of all, to add to the piquancy of such excess now covert. Carnival threatened the going order hardly at all. The dominant ideology and the ruling group released their control for a day to regain their power in full thereafter at the cost of some slight indignity.

> It would be wrong to associate the exhilarating sense of freedom which transgression affords with any necessary or automatic political progressiveness. Often it is a powerful ritual or symbolic practice whereby the dominant squanders its symbolic capital so as to get in touch with the fields of desire which it denied itself as the price paid for its political power. Not a repressive desublimation (for just as transgression is not intrinsically progressive nor is it intrinsically conservative), it is a counter-sublimation, a delirious expenditure of the symbolic capital accrued (through the regulation of the body and the decathexis of habitus) in the successful struggle of bourgeois hegemony.
>
> (Stallybrass and White 1986: 201)

So, one of the many important points made by Stallybrass and White (1986) is that actual carnival was driven by a real social force. Or, indeed, when seen in relation to the manipulative power of calculating bourgeois reason, it was driven by a combination of social forces, albeit seeking different ends and imbalanced by their access to will to power and their relationship to the means of production. The literary carnivalesque, newly taken up by the post-structuralist reader and his inability to interact with the author (after Barthes, now dead), seems to lack that drive, that social force.

> Reading Bakhtin, it's hard not to envy Rabelais. However much one extols the virtues of *Ulysses*, or the more popular pleasures of Brighton beach or the Costa del Sol, they still lack that combination of critique and indecency typical of the carnival Rabelais could take as his source. So it appears a mostly compensatory gesture when critics enthuse about the 'carnivalesque' they find in the latest (post-) modernist novel. Surely they can't really confuse reading a good book with the experience of carnival grounded in the collective activity of the people? What seems to be lacking in textual carnival is any link with a genuine social force.
>
> (Wills 1989: 130)

The issue of authenticity here is a real and important one. Carnival was never mere decoration, but we may need to examine the notion that the contemporary might reflect a sublimation or cultural repression – the carnival underground. But first, perhaps, we should context this idea with some others. Durkheim (1971), who we met in Chapter 2, explained the symbolism of social life in terms of an timeless dichotomy: 'The sacred is par excellence that which the profane should not touch, and cannot touch with impunity' (Durkheim 1971: 40). He also counters established Kantian epistemological assumptions with the remarkable view that the categories of understanding, like time itself, are generated from social life itself. In the case of time, rather than predicting the pattern of events from an external measure it reflects the cyclical symbolic emergence of rituals, rites and feasts – like carnival: 'Carnival was the true feast of time, the feast of becoming, change and renewal. It was hostile to all that was immortalized and completed' (Bakhtin 1968: 10).

From within a timetabled modernity Durkheim's anthropological idealism is hard to grasp, yet things become more tangible when we realise that his social theory is based on an 'organismic' analogy, and this is no simple heuristic device. There is a fairly strict unitary isomorphism at work here, individual human bodies and total social bodies bear the same shape and share the same functions – is not one built out of the physical, cognitive and moral conglomeration of the other? Carnival, for example, then becomes a bodily function and the celebration of carnival a bodily movement. These are true social forces at work and working through the individual. The apparent mechanicism of this explanation is undisclosed, as real, embodied social experience is always heavily mediated through symbolism, the meaning of which is not always clear to the participants. So Jervis says:

> The body comes to be the central carnival image; it is a symbol of 'the people', i.e. of the social body. Hence the physical body is characterized as huge, ever-growing, ever-renewed, just like society itself.
>
> (Jervis 1999: 19)

He then quotes Bakhtin:

> In grotesque realism, therefore, the bodily element is deeply positive. It is presented not in a private, egotistic form, severed from the other spheres of life, but as something universal, representing the people . . . the material bodily principle is contained not in the biological

individual, not in the bourgeois ego, but in the people who are continually growing and renewed.

(Bakhtin 1968: 19)

So, the human body, the social body, the *corpus* of knowledge become interchangeable and the carnival, or the style of carnivalesque, enables us to glissade from one to another – defecation, dissociation, deconstruction. We are enabled to flatulate, to move from the centre to the periphery, to break the relation between the signifier and the signified and choose another meaning. Permission to transgress. Transgression as irony, style, intervention or even exploration but essentially as a new way of behaving, as a new basis for social relations, as a denial of conventional classificatory schema. 'Carnival releases us from the terrorism of excessive significance, multiplying and so levelling meanings' (Eagleton 1989: 185).

Shields (1991) develops an interesting thesis which resonates with our sense of modernity as a form of sublimation or cultural repression, what we referred to as 'the carnival underground'. It is Shield's view that the temporal extinction of the carnival urge has merely displaced it. The deceased carnival, through modernity, has become resurrected as the carnivalesque in new loci, what he calls 'places on the margin'. The spatial has replaced the temporal; cyclical festivities have transmogrified into places of fun and naughtiness. We no longer anticipate the joys of carnival, we go to places where its manifestations can be routinely guaranteed. Using a concept from Turner (1974), who we considered in Chapter 2, Shields speaks of the 'liminal beach', with particular reference to Brighton and its special significance within British folklore and popular culture. Brighton, a famous seaside town in the UK, epitomised youthful cavorting, people scantily clad, 'dirty weekends', silly photographs, funhouses, 'kiss-me-quick' hats, rude postcards, food that is bad for you and, for a period before the legislation changed, grounds for swift divorce. All of these, and more, constitute the ritual pleasures of the seaside resort and the static carnival now reformed. The very name 'Brighton' conjured up fighting, drinking, sex, misdemeanour – the pure pavilion of transgression.

> . . . within the carnivalesque one finds a mode of social regulation which tends to moderate the inversions and suspensions of the social order. Why isn't there a permanent, more extreme carnival? The inversion and mocking of propriety is marked by an instability wherein the normative

> order is both presented and withdrawn at the same time. While transgressions are allowed, they are restricted to minor transgressions of morbidity, voyeurism, and flirtation with the illicit. In the case of sexual modesty, the comic postcards allude to the same fertile ground of innuendo as the dirty weekend myth. But if they wink at such practices they also exert a kind of governing influence by playing so much on the breaking or bending of taboos. The subject matter is both the carnivalesque transgression of social codes and the embarrassment of being 'caught in the act'.
>
> (Shields 1991: 98)

Within a wider thesis on the postmodern tendency towards aestheti-cisation of everyday life Featherstone (1992) produces a genealogy of the carnivalesque. Developing from the popular culture of the late-Medieval period he moves up to the Parisian avant-garde of the nineteenth century, focusing throughout on Baudelaire's modernist vision of life becoming more and more like art. Whereas Shields (1991) had conceptualised the displacement of the carnival urge to the spatial margins, Featherstone charts its sublimation, through a modern civilising process, and re-emergence in the form of the bohemian lifestyle.

> . . . we see the emergence of the Bohemias which adopt the strategies of transgression in their art and lifestyle. The representation of the *boheme* existed outside the limits of bourgeois society and identified with the proletariat and the left . . . They lived cheek by jowl with the lower orders in low-rent areas of the large cities. They cultivated similar manners, valuing spontaneity, an anti-systematic work ethos, lack of attention to the sense of ordered living space and controls and conventions of the respectable middle class.
>
> (Featherstone 1992: 282–3)

Then, adopting the framework provided by Stallybrass and White (1986), Featherstone points to the structural homologies between bohemian cultural representations and more primal carnival forms: they all generate 'liminoid symbolic repertoires'. Our attention is drawn specifically to Surrealism and Expressionism and we, here, have already looked at Dadaism, pataphysics, symbolist poetry, the theatre of cruelty, and latterly Situationist performance art/politics. The transgressive inversions that are forcefully motivating and demonstrated through these various manifes-tations all embrace that which polite/bourgeois/normative society seeks to expunge. Thus, in true carnival mode, we break through the constraints of the everyday and fatefully desire the undesirable. Featherstone puts it thus: 'In effect the Other which is excluded as part of the identity-formation process becomes the object of desire' (Featherstone 1992: 283), and the resonances with Freud and taboo are apparent.

The death of carnival has not even signalled the cessation of symbolic inversion. It has gone underground, or re-emerged, or been sublimated, or re-formed or perhaps it is just what we, as human beings, do. 'Carnival' may be a concept that describes an event, 'carnivalesque' may describe a process, Bakhtin's ideas of 'hybridisation' and 'heteroglossia' may serve to describe locations, interactions or modes of communication, but, at another level, they are all ways of approaching the human disposition to transgress and mechanisms for celebrating elemental chaos despite the amnesia induced through modernity's quest for order.

However, such global claims may be unfounded. It is clear that the carnivalesque is an appealing concept but what is the nature of this appeal? It appeals to theorists who may be seeking a unifying and democratising banner under which to collect the human condition. It appeals to progressive thinkers who wish to retain a faith in the lower orders innate capacity to resist, challenge and revolt against the structural constraints and symbolic violence that the dominant culture throws at them. We have spoken here of the human disposition to transgress as if the philosophical crusade to fracture the limits and go beyond were an option for all. As Eagleton (1989) has pointed out, being human is only one way of being. Being poor, being black, being a woman may all be ontological locations that at least inhibit the human capacity for sovereign action. Nevertheless, ideas that gather the people together conceptually and celebrate their inarticulate capacity for self-liberation have great currency.

> Those liberal humanists who have now enlisted the joyous, carnivalesque Bakhtin to their cause need perhaps to explain rather more rigorously than they do why the experience represented by carnival is, historically speaking, so utterly untypical. Unless the carnivalesque body is confronted by that bitter, negative, travestying style of carnivalesque thought . . . it is difficult to see how it signifies any substantial advance on a commonplace sentimental populism, of a kind attractive to academics.
>
> (Eagleton 1989: 183)

So perhaps transgression requires privilege, status, hierarchy and social position to, itself, signify.

However, it could be argued that the discovery of the carnival as a conceptual vehicle is not the end of the problem, it is rather an illumination of the problem. What occurs at the societal level, but also at the level of the individual psyche, is that any particular order is sustained, made meaningful, lived through and yet not experienced as either totalitarian or mono-dimensional because of a conscious, and sometimes unconscious, process of radical juxtaposition. This is something that Hegel's dialectic has already shown us. Goodness attempts to expunge badness, high orders constrain and erode lower orders, the sacred is intolerant of the profane, and the centre seeks to expand to the periphery. What, however, remains is an absolute dependency and contingency between the two orders at a practical, but most significantly, at a deeply symbolic level. This point is most succinctly put by Stallybrass and White:

> A recurrent pattern emerges: the 'top' attempts to reject and eliminate the 'bottom' for reasons of prestige and status, only to discover, not only that it is in some way frequently dependent upon that low-Other (in the classic way that Hegel describes in the master–slave section of the *Phenomenology*), but also that the top includes that low symbolically, as a primary eroticized constituent of its own fantasy life. The result is a mobile, conflictual fusion of power, fear and desire in the construction of subjectivity: a psychological dependence upon precisely those Others which are being rigorously opposed and excluded at the social level. It is for this reason that what is socially peripheral is so frequently symbolically central. The low-Other is despised and denied at the level of political organization and social being whilst it is instrumentally constitutive of the shared imaginary repertoires of the dominant culture.
>
> (Stallybrass and White 1986: 5–6)

This central idea can be taken to other places in cultural analysis. Jenks, in a paper on visual urban sociology, attempts to reconstitute the *flâneur* as a conceptual device for both the desire to and the possibility of moving between the two orders.

> The *flâneur* is the metaphoric figure originally brought into being by Baudelaire, as the spectator and depictor of modern life, most especially in relation to modern art and the sights of the city. The *flâneur* moves through space and among the people with a viscosity that both enables and privileges vision.
>
> (Jenks 1995a: 145–6)

The 'sights of the city' are juxtaposed with what I call a 'minatorial geography' and the work explores the magnetic fascination of one for the other. And, interestingly, Walkowitz in an earlier work on the urban spectator of Victorian London, a city divided into an East and a West not so much by geography as by wealth, health, criminality, education, lifestyles and life chances, states:

> This bifurcated cityscape reinforced an imaginary distance between investigators and their subjects, a distance that many urban explorers felt nonetheless compelled to transgress.
>
> (Walkowitz 1992: 22)

So what is being argued is that within any social world high and low orders have an antagonistic relationship; both struggle for recognition and supremacy. However, the possibility of one depends upon the necessity of the other and they are fatefully locked in an absolute contingency. Power, fear and intimidation are clear components of this complex relation, yet this is transformed, symbolically, into a desire, a fascination (think of the Kray twins), an eroticisation (think of Mozart's eidetic composition and scatological diversions), and finally a way of letting-off-steam (and think here of the carnival's drunkenness, debauchery, overeating, defecating, belching and farting). The transition from one order to the other is transgression. Lines are stepped across. Good, decent, proper, normal, polite, nice, honest and reasonable behaviour are the province of the higher order, as is power which enables the monopolisation of these 'favourable' terms as designations for its own form of life.

> The 'poetics' of transgression reveals the disgust, fear and desire which inform the dramatic self-representation of that [bourgeois] culture . . . The poetics reveals quite clearly the contradictory political construction of bourgeois democracy. For bourgeois democracy emerged with a class which, whilst indeed progressive in its best political aspirations, had encoded in its manners, morals and imaginative writings, in its body, bearing and taste, a subliminal elitism which was constitutive of its historical being.
>
> (Stallybrass and White 1986: 202)

Yet at the moment of carnival, for Bakhtin, the line is undrawn, the differences are temporarily obliterated and transgression becomes mainstream and all are involved – a democratic idealism.

In fact, carnival does not know footlights, in the sense that it does not acknowledge actors and spectators. Footlights would destroy a carnival . . . Carnival is not a spectacle to be seen by the people; they live in it, and everyone participates because its very idea embraces all the people. While carnival lasts, there is no other life outside it. During carnival time life is subject only to its laws, that is, the laws of its own freedom. It has a universal spirit; it is a special condition of the entire world, of the world's revival and renewal, in which all take part. Such is the essence of carnival, vividly felt by all its participants.

(Bakhtin 1968: 7)

8

THEATRES OF CRUELTY

This postscript is about supreme wickedness, which, of course, we may now consider to be outside of our conceptual framework and thus invoked in a spirit of transgressive irony. It will also serve the purpose of relieving the author of the burden of some select icons and hyperbole of postmodern life which have stalked his thinking throughout this book. Transgression, as we have learned, cannot be measured, it cannot be greater or less, better or worse. It is intangible, yet the everyday world is marked out by material moments of such apparent magnitude, like the Nazi Holocaust or September 11th from which we began, as to make them assume a tangibility, a texture and a clear significance – they become criminalised.

Crime is a juridical definition of an act, it is not in the least the same thing as transgression, yet within any particular socio-historical-political order a transgressive act may become identified as such and thus processed in the form of criminality. The populace does not engage in such interpretive niceties. We, as members of a society, do not seek to understand the assault, the loss, the disarray and the violence that surrounds us through the subtleties that have engaged us here for the last seven chapters. Non-normative deeds are 'bad' deeds and the collective consciousness attempts to reconcile these irregularities through the methods of positivist criminology, or a commonplace version thereof. What are the causes of crime? Well, as a liberal society we have come to address this question, regularly, through an equation of nature and nurture. People's intrinsic nature or their upbringing have made them as they are and statistical and correlative analysis can lead to a high degree of predictability, or at least a high degree of *post hoc* explainability, in relation to their current actions.

We have learned, however grudgingly, that bad acts perpetrated today are brought about through the past. Previous dispositions and events precipitate criminality. To this extent criminals are victims of the past and our understanding of the etiology of their acts provides a mitigation for the 'abnormal' urge that could have possibly motivated such acts. However, this positivist criminological mode is not without difficulties, the first being its singular failure, as a driver of policy, to diminish let alone contain the levels of criminality within modern society, but the second is more epistemological. It can be routinely demonstrated that however compelling the data and whatever the veracity of the bio-genetic, psychological, socio-historical, political or even ecological variables concerning crime, it is clearly the case that many people who similarly occupy these causal categories appear wholly unmoved by them. That is, individuals who share similar or identical causal backgrounds to known criminals do not themselves commit crime. Beyond this many individuals who commit criminal acts do not occupy all or any of the significant causal categories. And further still, individuals who do and individuals who do not fit the causal categories may either commit or not commit the anticipated crimes for extended periods – the science cannot predict a single way of life. Such recognitions begin to divert our understandings of the criminal act away from determinism along the continuum towards free will, or at least the issue of choice.

EXISTENTIAL CRIMINOLOGY

Katz begins his stimulating thesis in the following provocative manner:

> The study of crime has been preoccupied with a search for background forces, usually defects in the offenders' psychological backgrounds or social environments, to the neglect of the positive, often wonderful attractions within the lived experience of criminality. The novelty of this book lies in its focus on the seductive qualities of crimes: those aspects in the foreground of criminality that make its various forms sensible, even sensuously compelling, ways of being.

(Katz 1988: 3)

So people may, and indeed do, commit criminal acts because they choose to, because they want to or, perhaps most difficult to grasp, because they like it! If the transgressive act and the criminal act are often compounded, which in an increasingly governed society they inevitably are, then it is essential that the element of choice is elected as a sovereign principle. We cannot, without eroding the power and import of the concept thus far established, conceive of a transgressive act where the individual was driven to it by the past, by forces out of his or her control. This would be a life of marginalisation not a life on the edge. If boundaries, prohibitions and taboos are to be tested in a transgressive manner then the relationship between the perpetrator and the act must be wilful and intended, not accidental or unconscious.

> Whatever the relevance of antecedent events and contemporaneous social conditions, something causally essential happens in the very moments in which the crime is committed. The assailant must sense, then and there, a distinctive constraint or seductive appeal that he did not sense a little while before in a substantially similar place. Although his economic status, peer group relations, Oedipal conflicts, genetic makeup, internalized machismo, history of child abuse, and the like remains the same, he must suddenly become propelled to commit the crime. Thus, the central problem is to understand the emergence of distinctive sensual dynamics.
>
> (Katz 1988: 4)

Katz, quite precisely, illuminates the wilful and the intended, he recommends the study of the foreground rather than the background of crime, and he invites us to attend to the qualities that the transgressive act may hold for its perpetrator rather than attending to legal sanction or social outrage. This is no right-wing backlash theory attempting to diminish to impact of decades of liberal tolerance, this is an action theory attempting to demonstrate how assumed categories of being become transformed into actual and particular courses of action. We conventionally explain and attempt to understand crime in a fixed relation with rationality. A classical and highly influential example of this is provided by Merton (1968) who argues, in short, that some forms of criminality may be a manifestation of people attempting to achieve an appropriate end through an inappropriate means, i.e. we all need money, not all of us have money, not all of us can earn money, so some of us have to steal to acquire money. With this kind of thinking the normative structure is retained at the highest level of generality – shared value-orientations. On the streets people rob and even kill for no significant or even discernable material gain. Surely what we are dealing with is not a rational issue but a moral and emotional issue.

> The closer one looks at crime . . . the more vividly relevant become the moral emotions. Follow vandals and amateur shoplifters as they duck into alleys and dressing rooms and you will be moved by their delights in deviance . . . Watch their strutting street display and you will be struck by the awesome fascination that symbols of evil hold for the young men who are linked in the groups we often call gangs . . . The careers of persistent robbers show us, not the increasingly precise calculations and hedged risks of 'professionals,' but men for whom gambling and other vices are a way of life, who are 'wise' in the cynical sense of the term, and who take pride in a defiant reputation as 'bad.' And if we examine the lived sensuality behind events of cold-blooded 'senseless' murder, we are compelled to acknowledge the power that may still be created in the modern world through the sensualities of defilement, spiritual chaos, and the apprehension of vengeance.
>
> (Katz 1988: 312)

What Katz is also telling us, and this is an issue critical to our thesis on transgression, is that such acts, be they defined as deviant, transgressive, criminal, wicked, non-normative, naughty or bad, are not just the province of particular groups. The desire, their sensual attraction, belongs to us all:

> Perhaps in the end, what we find so repulsive about studying the reality of crime – the reason we so insistently refuse to look closely at how street criminals destroy others and bungle their way into confinement to save their sense of purposive control over their lives – is the piercing reflection we catch when we steady our glance at those evil men.
>
> (Katz 1988: 324)

This chilling reflexive turn in Katz's conclusion, the 'know thyself' clause which steadies the hand of the social theorist but weakens the foundations of his moral highground, can be instructive in ways other than the spuriously democratic. Here let us sustain the theme of the transgressor 'saving their sense of purposive control over their lives' (Katz quoted above), which may well be an accelerative feature of the late-modern condition. Lyng (1990) develops the concept of 'edgework'. We can produce 'edgework' as on a spectrum with all excessive conduct previously considered, but as micro, interactional, and most crucially, intended. Its function to transgress I nevertheless ascribe to a condition of contemporary social life. Edgework might take the form of rock and ice climbing, bungee jumping, parachuting, hang-gliding, flying microlights, motor racing, white water rafting, downhill skiing – activities that announce sport and leisure but also carry significant and recognised threats to personal safety. That an activity should be potentially life-threatening is essential to the notion of 'edgework'. The 'edge', Lyng suggests, can be defined variously through dichotomies opposing life/death, consciousness/unconsciousness, and the ordered self/disordered self, all of which we have previously encountered in our exploration of the transgressive. There is a tendency to transfer of training in edgework so rockclimbers, for example, may also be excessive drinkers or obsessive trainers. What is central to the activity is a sense of self-realisation or determination. It is critical that the ego becomes realised in an almost histrionic context. It is not the case, either, that edgeworkers are fearless. Precisely part of the frisson of the activity is the experience of fear, its control and the perverse pleasure that this combination can provide. The capacity that such sensation has for pressing the individual beyond the experience of the normal and the everyday, on a dramatic scale, enables us to suggest that edgework has an elitist orientation; it always elevates the individual above the mundane. Apart from the obvious chemical reactions that sudden infusions of adrenalin can produce, the approach to the edge, the excessive step across the boundary, ensures that the individuals perceptions become extremely acute and concentrated. This, in turn, has an effect on the experience of time. Such temporal mastery is not without appeal – no longer do we wait but instead time stands still or is held at the convenience of completion. Another experience at the edge is that of cognitive mastery of a situation, but also a symbiosis with the environment – people become 'at one with their machines', 'part of the wave' or 'continuous with the rock'. All these symptoms and sensations, inventoried by Lyng, resonate strongly with the postmodern preoccupation with the 'hyper-real'. Quite often the experience of edgework is too overwhelming to be expressed in language (in the same way that the actions of the Krays, Brady and Hindley, the Wests and child killers just walked off the edge of language). Rock climbers fall back on mundanities like 'because it was there . . . '.

Unlike chance activities such as gambling, but just like violent crime against the person, prime instances of which we have considered, edgework demands a level of control and never simple abandonment. Random chance or caprice do not signify. Edgework becomes coherent when understood in relation to the contemporary 'risk society' that Beck (1992) and Douglas (1994) have introduced us to. If our governance, technology and social strategies seek to minimise and militate against risk, then edgework provides the individual antidote; it is the 'spontaneous, anarchic, impulsive character of experience' (Lyng 1990: 864). Lyng also tells us that, for Turner (1976), identity construction takes place between the polarities of 'institution' and 'impulse' and that we are not all evenly distributed between the expression of 'constraint' and 'spontaneity'.

Modern social theory is not wholly pessimistic concerning our inevitable compliance with late-modernities' over-socialisation and potential alienation, and many suggest that a central dynamic of today is the incessant search for self. This can become corrupted, however, into the narcissism that Lasch (1980) describes through infatuated and obsessional consumption, or what Giddens (1991) sees as the nostalgic management of ontological anxiety through psychoanalysis. People often seek spontaneity and freedom from constraint through 'edgework' which imitates the characteristics of such action. 'Edgework' focuses on the general ability to maintain control of a situation that verges on total chaos. It does so, however, through the luxury of desired choice and through the exercise of highly specific skills.

SERIAL KILLERS

> There is a tendency, in contemporary cultural studies from the margins and from far below, to understand celebrity psychos – from Schreber or Jack the Ripper to Ted Bundy or Hannibal Lecter – as condensed symbols of the social: as microcosmic histories either of social control or, conversely, of social breakdown; as maladies of sociality or pathologies of the soul; as types of the 'over-socialized' individual (the mass in person) or the 'asocial' psycho (the drive in person). Such an approach in effect constructs the subject as a reflex or cliche of his or her culture . . .
>
> (Seltzer 1998: 126)

Sadly this observation is accurate, the serial killer has become a postmodern celebrity. The paradox of their boundless excess and their utter unintelligibility elects them to the status of unique and heroic signifiers. The scale and obscurity of their transgressions (which may nevertheless reach out to any one of us) defies all moral, linguistic, epistemological and ontological narratives. The live circus of characters expands: Jack the Ripper, the Boston Strangler, John Wayne Gracy, Harold Shipman, David Berkowitz, Dennis Nilsen, Jeffrey Dahmer, Peter Sutcliffe and Ted Bundy, but the element of freak show and rogue's gallery has drifted into entertainment through film and literature. Seltzer (1998) speaks of serial killing as a 'career option' at the turn of the century but raises the question of how is such a phenomenon possible within our contemporary culture. He develops the concept of 'America's wound culture' of which the serial killer is both an instance and a key player. The American public are, in Seltzer's view, preoccupied by broken, torn and gaping bodies but even more so by the spectacle of exposed and lacerated psyches. Their cultural sensationalism through news, TV, art, film, video and artefact creates a visual environment of mental and physical trauma wholly conducive to the Foucauldian gaze and from which it is difficult to divert our eyes.

We have witnessed a persistent return to themes of death, self-destruction and even murder (remember Breton's manifesto for Surrealism) in our tour through the transgressive muse. The serial killer moves this consideration to another place. The serial killer is, at first appearance, Nietzsche's *Übermensche* in the age of mechanical reproduction. Yet despite the awesome recognition that a select few feverish individuals transgress the prohibition that most of us never even approach, but on a multiple basis, the very replication of the act renders it in some way mundane. This is not the killer in the form of the Western gunfighter accumulating victims in a quest for notoriety, nor the Second World War flying ace painting enemy logos on the side of his cockpit to signify his mounting expertise and kudos. The multiplication for the serial killer says little about an attention to other than an audience on the inside of the assailant's head. The reproduction of the act is rarely about the generation of something innovative, it is not about excitement and newness; the reproduction here is replicative, mechanical, unrequited, it is a sterile copying procedure. Many convicted serial murderers speak of a continuously cyclical pattern that never seems to complete, an endless attempt to achieve an endlessly elusive goal. Dennis Nilsen is often quoted for saying that he was always trying to kill himself but that it was always someone else who died. It is difficult to find a transgressive hero contained within such a role model, for the act of slaying another has become routinised as an inevitable outcome of a perverse obsessional pattern, almost without choice and certainly before existential sovereignty – a mimesis. The source of the serial killer's appeal to the postmodern consciousness lies rather in its modesty and unpredictability, it is the argument that comes from nowhere and devastates the truth. There is also the calculating but ultimately sly, serial disobedience. But perhaps most of all the appeal lies in the repeated manifestation of a chronically unstable personality. The merely mad are commonplace in the postmodern condition. Our modern psycho-killer paints his unconscious on reality without the intervention of interpretation or interaction.

> . . . some of the components of serial killing: the relays between murder and murder machine; the intersecting logics of seriality, prosthesis, and primary mediation that structure cases of addictive violence – and, more generally, the addiction to addiction in contemporary society; the emergence of the pathological public sphere as the scene of these crimes . . . how did the particular kind of person called the serial killer come into being and into view?
>
> (Seltzer 1998: 105)

A brilliant intermingling of contemporary cultural themes around the central motif of the serial killer occurs in Bret Easton Ellis's scandalous novel *American Psycho* (1991). Here, tedious, repetitious, compulsive and self-aggrandising consumerism slowly reveals the pornographic, insecure heart of a psychopath. The book moves off with an almost continuous litany of designer labels providing character and fashionable restaurants and bars providing a sense of space and time. The work is immensely ponderous at this stage and the hero/killer, Patrick Bateman, a Wall Street yuppie, is wholly shallow and without interest, the unremarkable every-man hidden in the crowd, the archetypal discretion of the serial killer. The violence builds as widely spaced punctuation to the text; a delivery boy and two male strangers (and their dogs) are casually and pointlessly butchered. Finally, two-thirds into the considerable narrative, Bateman has 'lunch with Bethany', an ex-girlfriend who causes him some mild humiliation for which, in the space of two pages, she is beaten, Maced in the face, nailed to the floor, has her breast slashed, her tongue cut out and her fingers bitten off. He lightly describes his simultaneous lack of satisfaction as he performs oral sex with her recently evacuated mouth. The passage is shattering in its impact and different in style. The reality principle ricochets from the utterly facile mode of Bateman's personality to the actual form of this killer: how can they be integrated? Are they incommensurable? Are we regarding a fiction within a fiction? Much later in the novel we are asked to question the veracity of Bateman's own record of events and thus we are drawn into a series of distorted realities which have never promised to be more than fiction. Bateman's deep and sickening transgressions are provided with some fascination because they are attached to the vehicle of postmodern, unconstrained amorality – the serial killer. Ellis successfully ironises this election by sustaining our excitement and interest while abandoning responsibility for his creation's actions or, indeed, his reality even within the narrative. We must beware of channelling all of our allures and anxieties into any one transgressive possibility. And yet . . .

BAD GIRLS

Time has done little to diminish the public interest in the UK the ritual slaughter that came to be known as the 'Moors Murders'. Two of this cluster of killings actually took place in a dingy house in south-east Manchester but all of the deceased were finally interred on the fearfully bleak Saddleworth Moor. The original revulsion that the British public experienced in 1966 has given way to a longing, an unhealthy and retributive fascination with the case. The amplification of Myra Hindley into the status of monster has arisen in large part through the exponential accumulation of her transgressions; her excesses both numbed the emotions and severely destabilised our categories of understanding. Originally there were three confessions to murder; then two new bodies were discovered; and still there are two outstanding missing juveniles. But these victims were all children and the deliberate harming of children strikes at the most vulnerable part of our collective affects. Hindley importuned each child sacrifice single-handedly and then assisted in the subsequent murders; but worse, the process of killing and the motive for the killings were both sadistic and sexual. These were no commonplace acts of paedophilia; the cruelty and experience of domination appeared to provide an erotic ecstasy exceeding the actual physical sexual abuse that took place. One child, Lesley Anne Downey, was tape-recorded through her passion and this record of her degradation, agony and sufferings (surely the primal 'snuff-tape') became part of the killers' library of pornography. The private magic of their shared wrong-doing stood in the place of intimacy and their sly mockery of the conventional, homespun, sentimental propriety that comprised their native Lancashire community was as foreplay. Hindley once posed smiling, provocatively, over one of the hidden graves with her body language indicating the subterranean secret. Years later this same photograph was used by police to forensically reconstruct the site of the burial. Beyond this catalogue of transgressions, what perhaps shocks our taken-for-granted typologies most is that Hindley is a woman, and was, at the time, an attractive young woman. How could this be so?

> In short, our pollution behaviour is the reaction which condemns any object or idea likely to confuse or contradict cherished classifications.
> (Douglas 1966: 48)

The conflation of these factors has a seismic impact on our taken-for-granted categories of the way things ought to be. Our responses to such dangers are sustained attempts to reintegrate Hindley's excess into our comfortable world view. Forensic psychiatry offers absolution through the concept of *folie à deux* – an alchemic acceleration of evil-doing wrought through partnership. Hindley may then have been temporarily deranged but the real responsibility for the acts rests with her psychopathic lover Ian Brady, who cited cod Nietzschean ethics in mitigation. So was this really a man's crime? Lord Longford's persistent campaign on Hindley's behalf sought to naturalise her and reconcile her past 'difference' through higher education and religious conversion. But most of the British public, most of the time, revisit her lasting profanity and conspire in her eviction from our system. 'Life means life', Home Secretaries periodically announce, the most recent being David Blunkett in May 2002. The 'monster' remains intact, caged, and the excess becomes lodged as an historical necessity. A transgressive projection for us all.

Surely Myra Hindley is unique? Philosophically we know this cannot be so. A more recent UK exemplar is to be found in Rosemary West. She had eight children of her own: she sexually and physically abused them all, regardless of gender, and assisted in the murder of one daughter. This is in addition to her active part in the sexually motivated torture and slaying of twelve other young women which concluded in 1994. She provided a transgressive roller coaster from which it is difficult for even the casual observer to re-adjust. West assisted her half-witted husband in acts of rape, and experimented consistently with prostitution, lesbianism, group sex, violent sado-masochism and pornographic videos. The compulsive ending to many of their transgressive journeys to the dark side of the moon was the extinction of their object of desire (?), a meticulous dismembering of the body, and its disposal by entombment beneath their cellar floor or in the garden. They resorted to countryside burials on two occasions, presumably due to shortage of space.

Hindley and West are not categories, they are not types, they are possibilities. However, to acknowledge that possibility, to recognise that potential, is unbearable; we cannot face 'that piercing we catch when we steady our glance at those evil [wo]men' (Katz quoted above). So, we need to expel them from our lives and our minds. We have symbolic mechanisms to enable this and the creation of 'monsters' is a powerful one. As Douglas has shown, the identification of anomalies, whether in the form of people, plants or animals, is integral to the establishment of social order:

> A polluting person is always in the wrong. He has developed some wrong condition or simply crossed some line which should not have been crossed and this displacement unleashes danger for someone.
>
> (Douglas 1966: 136)

Anomalies are, in essence, the by-products of systems of ordering. Through their remarked differences, ironically, they work to firm up the boundaries which give form and substance to the conceptual categories from which they are excluded.

> The idea of society is a powerful image. It is potent in its own right to control or to stir men to action. This image has form; it has external boundaries, margins, internal structure. Its outlines contain power to reward conformity and repulse attack. There is an energy in its margins and unstructured areas. For symbols of society any human experience of structures, margins or boundaries is ready to hand.
>
> (Douglas 1966: 137)

In this sense, by refusing women who commit acts of supreme violence acceptance within the category of woman (they become monsters), the public was reaffirming to itself the essence of what women are. Thereby also reaffirming its commitment to a 'shared' social order. That is, it was a way to restore the primary image of the innate maternal and caring dispositions of womankind through relegating some would-be women (those who commit acts of atrocity) to another category essentialised through images of evil or pathology. Thus, the stigma of anomaly works to explain how certain women may be capable of actions which other, 'normal', women are not: the system of classification stays intact by resisting the 'defilement' of the abhorrent case.

There are other ways in which the collective deals with such conduct: for example that it is a form of human evil for which the devil is primarily responsible. But such beliefs hold little influence in contemporary Western society. It is not necessary to be religious to know that humankind has always a heart of darkness (Ashley 2002) and I have not concluded with this brief inventory of 'supreme wickedness' in order either to purge our collective responsibility for what has gone before or to demonstrate the depths to which transgression can lead. No category of act takes away the sins of the world, no such expiation exists. Similarly no multiplication or magnitude of transgression in another can relieve us of either the necessity or responsibility for our own. Transgression is part of the social process, it is also part of the individual psyche. Our analytic purpose is to realise its cultural context and its socially constructed meaning. Practically this may mean that a defining feature of late-modern society is that our actions are organised through a stern paradox. Namely that people (sometimes 'monsters' but more often people like ourselves) who feel trapped, threatened or violently constrained by external forces beyond their control seek excessive and transgressive experiences which, in some cases, are even more threatening to their survival and, tragically in many cases, threatening to the survival of innocents also.

BIBLIOGRAPHY

Ackroyd, P. (1993) 'London luminaries and cockney visionaries', *LWT London Lecture*, 7 December.

Ades, D. (1997) 'Dada and Surrealism' in N. Stangos (ed.), *Concepts of Modern Art: From Fauvism to Postmodernism*, London: Thames & Hudson.

Alexander, J. (1988) *Durkheimian Sociology: Cultural Studies*, Cambridge: Cambridge University Press.

Ansell Pearson, K. (1994) *An Introduction to Nietzsche as a Political Thinker*, Cambridge: Cambridge University Press.

Apollinaire, G. (1989) *Lez Onze Mille Verges*, London: Peter Owen.

Artaud, A. (1956) *Complete Works Vol. 1*, Paris: Gallimard.

Artaud, A. (1970) *The Theatre and Its Doubles* (Postface by J.Calder), London: Calder.

Ashley, J. (2002) 'Yearning for an innocent past fails to protect children', *The Guardian*, 20 August, p. 8,

Bachelard, G. (1971) *The Poetics of Reverie*, Boston: Beacon Press.

Bakhtin, M.M. (1968) *Rabelais and his World* (trans. H. Iswolsky), Cambridge, MA: MIT Press.

Barber, S. (1993) *Antonin Artaud: Blows and Bombs*, London: Faber & Faber.

Barber, S. (1999) *Artaud: The Screaming Body*, London: Creation Books.

Bataille, G. (1982) *Story of the Eye*, Harmondsworth: Penguin.

Bataille, G. (1985) *Visions of Excess: Selected Writings 1927–1939* (trans. A. Stoekl), Manchester: Manchester University Press.

Bataille, G. (1986) *Eroticism*, London: City Lights.

Bataille, G. (1988) *The Inner Experience*, Albany: State University Press.

Bataille, G. (1991a) *The Accursed Share Vols II & III*, New York: Zone Books.

Bataille, G. (1991b) *The Trial of Gilles de Rais*, Los Angeles: Amok Books.

Bataille, G. (1997) *Literature and Evil*, London: Marion Boyars.

Bataille, G. (2001) *Eroticism* (Introduction C. MacCabe), London: Penguin.

Baudelaire, C. (1964) *The Painter of Modern Life and Other Essays*, London: Phaidon.

Beck, U. (1992) *Risk Society: Towards a New Modernity*, London: Sage.

Benjamin, J. (1996) 'Master and slave: the bonds of love' in J. O'Neill (ed.) 1996.

Benjamin, W. (1969) *Charles Baudelaire: The Lyric Poet in the Era of High Capitalism*, London: Verso.

Bennett, T. (1986) 'The politics of "the popular" and popular culture' in

T. Bennett, C. Mercer and J. Woollacott (eds), *Popular Culture and Social Relations*, Milton Keynes: Open University Press.

Bennington, G. (1995) 'Introduction to Economics I' in C.B. Gill (ed.) *Bataille: Writing the Sacred*, London: Routledge.

Berman, M. (1982) *All that is Solid Melts Into Air: The Experience of Modernity*, New York: Simon & Schuster.

Berman, M. (1985) *All That is Solid Melts into Air: The Experience of Modernity*, London: Verso.

Black, J. (1991) *The Aesthetics of Murder: A Study in Romantic Literature and Contemporary Culture*, Baltimore: Johns Hopkins University Press.

Boston, S. (1980) *Women Workers and the Trade Unions*, London: Lawrence and Wishart.

Botting, F. and Wilson, S. (2001) *Bataille*, London: Palgrave.

Bourdieu, P. (1993) *The Field of Cultural Production*, Oxford: Polity Press.

Bristol, M. (1985) *Carnival and Theatre*, London: Routledge.

Bryan, E. and Higgins, R. (1995) *Infertility: New Choices, New Dilemmas*, London: Penguin.

Burke, J. (1989) 'History as social memory' in T. Butler (ed.), *Memory*, Oxford: Blackwell.

Caillois, R. (1988) 'Brotherhoods, orders, secret societies, churches' in D. Hollier (ed.) *The College of Sociology 1937–39*, Minnesota: University of Minnesota Press.

Camus, A. (1971) *The Rebel*, Harmonsworth: Penguin.

Certeau, M. de (1990) *The Possession at Loudun*, Chicago: University of Chicago Press.

Chaney, D. (1994) *The Cultural Turn: Scene-Setting Essays on Contemporary Cultural History*, London: Routledge.

Chenieux-Gendron, J. (1990) *Surrealism*, New York: Columbia University Press.

Chesney, K. (1991) *The Victorian Underworld*, Harmondsworth: Penguin.

Coveney, P. (1957) *Poor Monkey*, London: Rockcliff.

Culler, J. (1983) *On Deconstruction: Theory and Criticism after Structuralism*, London: Routledge.

Debord, G. (1983) *Society of the Spectacle*, Detroit: Black & Red.

Deleuze, G. and Guattari, F. (1977) *Anti-Oedipus: Capitalism and Schizophrenia*, New York: Viking Press.

Derrida, J. (1976) *Of Grammatology*, Baltimore: Johns Hopkins University Press.

Derrida, J. and Thevenin, P. (1998) *The Secret Art of Antonin Artaud*, Cambridge, MA: MIT Press.

Dickson, J. (1986) *Murder without Conviction*, London: Sphere.

Donelly, J. (1995) 'The twofold grief that lies in loss of a twin', *Glasgow Herald*, 18 July.

Donoghue, A. (1995) *The Krays' Lieutenant*, London: Smith Gryphon.

Douglas, M. (1966) *Purity and Danger*, London: Routledge.

Douglas, M. (1994) *Risk and Blame: Essays in Cultural Theory*, London: Routledge.

Durkheim, E. (1964a) *The Division of Labour in Society*, New York: Free Press.

Durkheim, E. (1964b) *The Rules of Sociological Method*, New York: Free Press.

Durkheim, E. (1971) *Elementary Forms of the Religious Life*, London: George Allen & Unwin.

Eagleton, T. (1982) 'Wittgenstein's friends', *New Left Review* 135: 64–90.

Eagleton, T. (1989) 'Bakhtin, Schopenhauer, Kundera' in K. Hirschkop and D. Shepherd 1989.

Ellis, B.E. (1991) *American Psycho*, London: Picador.

Featherstone, M. (1988) 'In pursuit of the postmodern: an introduction', *Theory, Culture and Society* 5, 2–3 (June).

Featherstone, M. (1992) 'Postmodernism and the aestheticization of everyday life' in S. Lash and J. Freedman (eds), *Modernity and Identity*, Oxford: Blackwell.

Ferguson, H. (1990) *The Science of Pleasure: Cosmos and Psyche in the Bourgeois World View*, London: Routledge.

Fishman, W. (1975) *East End Jewish Radicals 1875–1914*, London: Duckworth.

Fishman, W. (1988) *East End 1888*, London: Duckworth.

Foucault, M. (1967) *Madness and Civilization*, London: Tavistock.

Foucault, M. (1971) 'Orders of discourse', *Social Science Information* 10.

Foucault, M. (1977a) *Language, Counter-Memory, Practice* (contains the 1963 essay 'Preface to Transgression'), New York: Cornell University Press.

Foucault, M. (1977b) *Discipline and Punish*, London: Penguin.

Freccero, C. (1997) 'Historical violence, censorship and the serial killer: the case of American Psycho', *Diacritics* 27, 2: 44–58.

Freud, S. (1930) *Civilization and Its Discontents*, London: Hogarth Press.

Freud, S. (1950) *Totem and Taboo*, London: Routledge & Kegan Paul.

Frisby, D. (1985) *Fragments of Modernity*, Cambridge: Polity.

Fry, C. and Kray. C. (1993) *Doing the Business: Inside the Krays' Network of Glamour and Violence*, London: Smith Gryphon.

Fukuyama, F. (1992) *The End of History and the Last Man*, London: Hamish Hamilton.

Gallop, J. (1981) *Intersections: A Reading of Sade with Bataille, Blanchot and Klossowski*, Lincoln, NE, and London: University of Nebraska Press.

Galton, F. (1907) *Inquiries into Human Faculty and its Development*, London: Dent.

Garside, P. (1984) 'West End, East End: London 1890–1940' in A. Sutcliffe (ed.), *Metropolis 1890–1940*, London: Mansell.

Giddens, A. (1991) *Modernity and Self-Identity: Self and Society in the Late Modern Age*, Oxford: Polity.

Gill, C. (ed.) (1995) *Bataille: Writing the Sacred*, London: Routledge.

Gilloch, G. (1997) *Myth and Metropolis: Walter Benjamin and the City*, Cambridge: Polity.

Girard, R. (1988) *Violence and the Sacred*, London: Athlone.

Habermas, J. (1984) 'The French path to postmodernity: Bataille between eroticism and general economics', *New German Critique* 33: 79–102.

Harrison, C. and Wood, P. (1992) *Art in Theory 1900–1990*, Oxford: Blackwell.

Hebdige, D. (1975) 'The Kray Twins – a system of closure', *Birmingham CCCS Occasional Paper* No. 21.

Hebdige, D. (1979) *Subculture: The Meaning of Style*, London: Routledge.

Hegarty, P. (2000) *Georges Bataille: Core Cultural Theorist*, London: Sage.

Hegel, G.W.F. (1947) *The Phenomenology of Mind*, London: George Allen & Unwin.

Heywood, I. (1997) *Social Theories of Art*, Basingstoke: Macmillan.

Hirschkop, K. and Shepherd, D. (1989) (eds) *Bakhtin and Cultural Theory*, Manchester: Manchester University Press.

Hirst, P. (1975) *Durkheim, Bernard and Epistemology*, London: Routledge.

Hobbes, T. ([1651] 1962) *Leviathan*, ed. M.Oakeshott, New York: Collier.

Hobbs, D. (1988) *Doing the Business*, Oxford: Oxford University Press.

Holland, E. (1999) *Deleuze and Guattari's Anti-Oedipus: Introduction to Schizoanalysis*, London: Routledge.

Houlgate, S. (1991) *Freedom, Truth and History*, London: Routledge.

Howell, M. and Ford, P. (1980) *The True History of the Elephant Man*, Harmondsworth: Penguin.

Huelsenbeck, R. ([1936] 1951) 'Dada lives', in R.J. Motherwell (ed.), *Dada Painters and Poets*, New York: Schultz Wittenborn.

Hussey, A. (2002) *The Game of War: The Life and Death of Guy Debord*, London: Random House.

Huyssen, A. (1995) *Twilight Memories: Marking Time in a Culture of Amnesia* London: Routledge.

Inglis, F. (1993) *Cultural Studies*, Oxford: Blackwell.

Izard, M. (1982) 'Transgression, transversality, wandering' in M. Izard and P. Smith (eds), *Between Belief and Transgression*, Chicago: University of Chicago Press.

James, A. and Jenks, C. (1996) 'Public perceptions of childhood criminality', *British Journal of Sociology* 47, 4: 315–31.

James, P.D. and Critchley, T.A. (1990) *The Maul and the Pear Tree*, Harmondsworth: Penguin.

Jamieson, F. (1972) *The Prison-House of Language*, Princeton, NJ: Princeton University Press.

Jarry, A. (1968) *The Ubu Plays*, London: Methuen.

Jenks, C. (1993) *Cultural Reproduction*, London: Routledge.

Jenks, C. (1993) *Culture*, London: Routledge.

Jenks, C. (1995b) 'Decoding childhood' in P. Atkinson, B. Davies and S. Delamont (eds) *Discourse and Reproduction: Essay in Honor of Basil Bernstein*, Cresskill, NJ: Hampton.

Jenks, C. (1995a) 'Watching your step: the theory and practice of the flâneur' in C. Jenks (ed.), *Visual Culture*, London: Routledge.

Jenks, C. (1996) 'Cultures of excess', Inaugural Lecture, London: Goldsmiths College, University of London.

Jenks, C. (1999) 'Durkheim's double vision' in I. Heywood and B. Sandywell (eds), *Interpreting Visual Culture*, London: Routledge.

Jenks, C. (2001) *Urban Culture*, Taipei: Academia Sinica.

Jenks, C. and Lorentzen, J. (1997) 'The Kray fascination' in *Theory, Culture and Society* 14, 3 (August): 87–107.

Jenks, C. and Neves, T. (2000) 'A walk on the wild side: urban ethnography meets the flâneur', *Cultural Values* 4, 1 (January): 1–18.

Jervis, J. (1999) *Transgressing the Modern: Explorations in the Western Experience of Otherness*, Oxford: Blackwell.

Jordanova, L. (1994) 'The hand' in L. Taylor (ed.), *Visualizing Theory*, London: Routledge.

Katz, J. (1988) *Seductions of Crime: Moral and Sensual Attractions of Doing Evil*, New York: Basic Books.

Knabb, K. (ed.) (1981) *Situationist International Anthology*, Berkeley, CA: Bureau of Public Secrets.

Kojève, A. (1969) *Introduction to the Reading of Hegel* (assembled R. Queneau; edited A. Bloom; trans. J.H. Nichols), New York: Basic Books.

Kray, C. (1988) *Me and My Brothers*, London: Grafton.

Kray, Reg (1990) *Born Fighter*, London: Arrow.

Kray, Ron (1993) *My Story*, London: Sidgwick & Jackson.

Kray, R. and Kray, R. (1988) *Our Story*, London: Sidgwick & Jackson.

Kristeva, J. (1982) *Powers of Horror: An Essay on Abjection*, New York: Columbia University Press.

Lambrianou, C. (1995b) *Escape From the Kray Madness*, London: Sidgwick & Jackson.

Lambrianou, C. (1995a) 'Married to the Mob', *Big Issue* 139 (28 July): 17–23.

Lambrianou, T. (1991) *Inside the Firm*, London: Smith Gryphon.

Land, N. (1992) *The Thirst for Annihilation: Georges Bataille and Virulent Nihilism*, London: Routledge.

Laporte, D. (1993) *A History of Shit*, Cambridge, MA: MIT Press.

Lasch, C. (1980) *The Culture of Narcissism*, London: Abacus.

Lash, S. and Friedman, J. (eds) (1992) 'Subjectivity and modernity's other' in *Modernity and Identity*, Oxford: Blackwell.

Leiris, M. (1988) 'The sacred in everyday life' in D. Hollier (ed.), *The College of Sociology 1937–39*, Minnesota: University of Minnesota Press.

Lukács, G. (1970) *Writer and Critic*, London: Merlin Press.

Lukes, S. (1985) *Emile Durkheim: His Life and Work*, Stanford, CA: Stanford University Press.

Lyng, S. (1990) 'Edgework: a social psychological analysis of voluntary risk taking', *American Journal of Sociology* 95, 4: 851–86.

McHugh, P. (1971) 'On the failure of positivism' in J. Douglas (ed.) *Understanding Everyday Life*, London: Routledge.

Matthews, E. (1996) *Twentieth-Century French Philosophy*, Oxford: Oxford University Press.

Mauss, M. (1970) *The Gift*, London: Routledge.

Merton, R. (1968) *Social Theory and Social Structure*, New York: Free Press.

Mestrovic, S. (1991) *The Coming Fin de Siècle*, London: Routledge.

Millet, C. (2002) *The Sexual Life of Catherine M.*, London: Serpent's Tail.

Mouzelis, N. (1995) *Sociological Theory: What Went Wrong?*, London: Routledge.

Mrs X. (with Morton, J.) (1996) *The Barmaid's Tale*, London: Little, Brown & Co.

Munday, J. (ed.) (2001) *Surrealism: Desire Unbound*, London: Tate Publishing.

Nietzsche, F. ([1885] 1966) *Thus Spake Zarathustra* in W. Kaufmann (ed.), *The Portable Nietzsche*, New York: Viking.

Nietzsche, F. ([1886] 1990) *Beyond Good and Evil*, London: Penguin.

Nietzsche, F. ([1887] 1994) *On the Genealogy of Morality*, Cambridge: Cambridge University Press.

Nisbet, R. (1976) *Sociology as an Art Form*, New York: Oxford University Press.

Noys, B. (2000) *Bataille*, London: Pluto.

Nuttall, J. (1970) *Bomb Culture*, London: Paladin.

O'Neill, J. (1995) *The Poverty of Postmodernism*, London: Routledge.

O'Neill, J. (1996) *Hegel's Dialectic of Desire and Recognition*, New York: Suny.

Parsons, T. (1951) *The Social System*, London: Routledge & Kegan Paul.

Parsons, T. (1968) *The Structure of Social Action*, New York: Free Press.

Patri, A. (1961) 'Dialectique du mâitre et de l'esclave' *La Contrat Social* V, 4 (July–August).

Pearson, G. (1983) *Hooligan – A History of Respectable Fears*, London: Macmillan.

Pearson, J. (1985) *The Profession of Violence*, Glasgow: Grafton Books.

Pearson, J. (2001) *The Cult of Violence*, London: Orion.

Pefanis, J. (1991) *Heterology and the Postmodern: Bataille, Baudrillard and Lyotard*, Durham and London: Duke University Press.

Popper, K. (1947) *The Open Society and Its Enemies Vol. 2: Hegel & Marx*, London: Routledge.

Poulet, G. and Kopp, R. (1969) *Who Was Baudelaire?*, Geneva: Editions d'Art Albert Sira.

Raban, J. (1988) *Soft City*, London: Harvill.

Read, L. (1991) *Nipper*, London: MacDonald.

Richardson, M. (1994) *Georges Bataille*, London: Routledge.

Robb, G. (2000) *Rimbaud*, London: Picador.

Rose, G. (1981) *Hegel Contra Sociology*, London: Athlone Press.

Rosen, S. (1969) *Nihilism: A Philosophical Essay*, New Haven: Yale University Press.

Rumbelow, D. (1973) *The Houndsditch Murders and the Seige of Sidney Street*, Harmondsworth: Penguin.

Rumbelow D. (1975) *The Complete Jack the Ripper*, Harmondsworth: Penguin.

Russell, B. (1946) *The History of Western Philosophy*, London: Allen & Unwin.

Samuel, R. (1994) *Theatres of Memory*, London: Verso.

Sartre, J-P. (1946) *Baudelaire*, Paris: Gallimard.

Savage, J. (1996) *Time Travel: From the Sex Pistols to Nirvana. Pop, Media and Sexuality 1977–96*, London: Chatto and Windus.

Seltzer, M. (1998) *Serial Killers: Death and Life in America's Wound Culture*, London: Routledge.

Shields, R. (1991) *Places on the Margin: Alternative Geographies of Modernity*, London: Routledge.

Siemon, M. (1980) 'The separation–individuation process in adult twins', *American Journal of Psychotherapy* XXXIV, 3 (July).

Sinclair, I. (1995) 'Ronnie Kray bows out', *The London Review of Books* 17, 11 (8 June).

Smart, B. (1993) *Postmodernity*, London: Routledge.

Smith, J. (1995) 'Three images of the visual: empirical, formal and normative' in C. Jenks (ed.), *Visual Culture*, London: Routledge.

Smith, J. and Jenks, C. (2000) *Images of Community: Durkheim, Social Systems and the Sociology of Art*, Aldershot: Ashgate.

Smith, S. (1989) *Hegel's Critique of Liberalism: Rights in Context*, Chicago: University of Chicago Press.

Spector, J. (1997) *Surrealist Art and Writing 1919–37: The Gold of Time*, Cambridge: Cambridge University Press.

Spengler, O. (1926) *The Decline of the West* (trans. C. Atkinson), London: Allen and Unwin.

Spivak, G. (1976) 'Translator's preface' to J. Derrida, *Of Grammatology*, Baltimore: Johns Hopkins University Press.

Stallybrass, P. and White, A. (1986) *The Politics and Poetics of Transgression*, London: Methuen.

Stedman-Jones, G. (1971) *Outcast London: A Study in the Relationship Between Classes in Victorian Society*, Oxford: Oxford University Press.

Stoekl, A. (1985) 'Introduction' to *George Bataille – Visions of Excess: Selected Writings 1927–1939*, Minneapolis: University of Minnesota Press.

Stratton, J. (1996) 'Serial killing and the transformation of the social', *Theory, Culture and Society* 13, 1: 77–98.

Suleiman, S. (1990) *Subversive Intent: Gender, Politics and the Avante-Garde*, Cambridge, MA: Harvard University Press.

Surya, M. (2002) *Georges Bataille – An Intellectual Portrait*, London: Verso.

Szasz, T. (1961) *The Myth of Mental Illness*, New York: Harper.

Tanner, M. (1990) 'Introduction' to F. Nietzsche, *Beyond Good and Evil*, London: Penguin.

Thompson, K. (1982) *Emile Durkheim*, London: Tavistock.

Turner, R. (1976) 'The real self: from institution to impulse', *American Journal of Sociology* 81, 3: 983–1016.

Turner, V. (1974) *Dreams, Fields and Metaphors*, New York: Cornell University Press.

Van Gennep, A. ([1960] 1902) *Les Rites de Passage*, London: Routledge & Kegan Paul (first pub. 1902).

Vattimo, G. (1988) *The End of Modernity*, Cambridge: Polity Press.

Walkowitz, J. (1992) *City of Dreadful Delights: Narratives of Sexual Danger in Late-Victorian London*, London: Virago Press.

Webb, B. (1993) *Running with the Krays*, Edinburgh: Mainstream.

Williams, R. (1993) *The Country and the City*, London: Hogarth Press.

Wills, C. (1989) 'Upsetting the public: carnival, hysteria and women's texts' in K. Hirschkop and D. Shepherd (eds) 1989.

Wilson, E. (2000) *Bohemians: The Glamorous Outcasts*, London: Tauris.

INDEX

Lightning Source UK Ltd.
Milton Keynes UK
UKOW06f1138100615

253238UK00011B/202/P